PAN-AFRICAN AMERICAN LITERATURE

PAN-AFRICAN AMERICAN LITERATURE

Signifyin(g) Immigrants in the Twenty-First Century

STEPHANIE LI

RUTGERS UNIVERSITY PRESS
New Brunswick, Camden, and Newark, New Jersey, and London

Library of Congress Cataloging-in-Publication Data

Names: Li, Stephanie, 1977–author.
Title: Pan-African American literature : signifyin(g) Immigrants in the Twenty-First Century / Stephanie Li.
Description: New Brunswick, New Jersey : Rutgers University Press, [2018] | Includes bibliographical references and index.
Identifiers: LCCN 2017033670 | ISBN 9780813592787 (cloth : alk. paper) | ISBN 9780813592770 (pbk. : alk. paper) | ISBN 9780813592794 (e-pub) | ISBN 9780813592817 (Web PDF)
Subjects: LCSH: American literature—African American authors—History and criticism. | African diaspora in literature. | Blacks—Race identity—America. | African Americans in literature. | Blacks in literature—21st century.
Classification: LCC PS153.N5 L472 2017 | DDC 810.9/896073—dc23 LC record available at https://lccn.loc.gov/2017033670

A British Cataloging-in-Publication record for this book is available from the British Library.

∞ The paper used in this publication meets the requirements of the American National Standard for Information Sciences—Permanence of Paper for Printed Library Materials, ANSI Z39.48-1992.

www.rutgersuniversitypress.org

Manufactured in the United States of America

To Susan D. Gubar

CONTENTS

PAN-AFRICAN AMERICAN LITERATURE

INTRODUCTION

According to Toni Morrison, the second word immigrants to the United States learn is "nigger."[1] In her 1993 essay "On the Back of Blacks," she explains that the "most enduring and efficient rite of passage into American culture" is "negative appraisals of the native-born black population. Only when the lesson of racial estrangement is learned is assimilation complete. Whatever the lived experience of immigrants with African Americans—pleasant, beneficial, or bruising—the rhetorical experience renders blacks as noncitizens, already discredited outlaws" (146). Throughout her provocative essay, Morrison refers to American identity and whiteness almost interchangeably: to be assimilated into American society is to become white.[2] While her comments provide meaningful insight into the experience of immigrants from various parts of Europe, she does not indicate what assimilation means for nonwhite immigrants, and in particular immigrants of African descent. What happens when these newcomers are themselves black or rather rendered black in America's fraught racial landscape? Must recently arrived Africans and Afro-Caribbeans also learn the "lesson of racial estrangement" that casts blacks as "noncitizens, already discredited outlaws"? If American identity depends on racial hierarchy, how are black immigrants to relate to African Americans? At what point is their "assimilation complete," and how does this process relate to both American and African American cultural life?

Morrison's comments implicitly bring the racial complexities of slavery and immigration into much-needed critical conversation. While our national narrative tends to separate these two historical experiences, the fast-changing contours of the African diaspora in the United States demand that we establish new ways of understanding black identity in the twenty-first century. As many contemporary theorists note, our increasingly globalized world requires more nuanced approaches to diasporic populations. Frieda Ekotto and Kenneth W. Harrow describe how "new conditions of globalization have generated possibilities for subject positions that cannot be simply defined by terms such as 'exile,' 'hybrid,' 'creole,' or 'diasporic'" (3). Migration is no longer a one-way journey but a fluctuating exchange of homelands, loyalties, and identifications. While the cultural and political ambitions of the past depended on conceptions of a unified self, we now live in a world that recognizes how individuals of all backgrounds are and have always been enmeshed in multiple, sometimes competing communities and identifications. Critical vocabularies that do not presume diversity and fluidity are inadequate to describe African artists for whom history is more influential than place, and the nature of creative production is more salient than attempting to pinpoint identities too often measured by Western standards. Amid such shifting conditions, we must bear in mind Michelle M. Wright's characterization of blackness as not "a fixed hierarchical identity in which the most 'authentic' enjoy top billing," but rather centered "at the intersection of multiple histories, peoples and experiences, telling us what we already knew, really: the shape of diaspora is the shape of the globe" ("Can I Call You Black?" 15).

The "shape of the globe" is an apt description of the changing face of black America. Black Africans are among the fastest growing immigrant populations in the United States, and as a recent headline in the *New York Times* affirms, this group has generated a powerful cadre of literary writers.[3] In 2010, there were one million African-born blacks living in the United States, up from a mere ten thousand in 1970. From 2000 to 2010, more black Africans came to America than were brought to all of North America during the three centuries of the slave trade; the population grew by more than 92 percent. This massive influx has drawn the attention of many scholars, who have begun to theorize and historicize the nature of what Isidore Okpewho and Nkiru Nzegwu term the "new African diaspora." Okpewho describes the older diaspora as precolonial, largely the result of enforced bondage, and associated with a nostalgic "romance of Africa" (5). By contrast, the postcolonial diaspora derives from the instabilities wrought by European intervention in Africa. Surveying the consequences of the failures of the postcolonial state, Okpewho bemoans the "abysmal lack of commitment to a unified political vision and a perennial crisis of leadership in many African nations" (7). The result has been a dramatic migration across the entire continent and the need to rethink the conditions and possibilities of diaspora. A number of twenty-first-century narratives by African-born and -identified writers offer unique insight into how this migration reverberates in the United States and what this means for American notions of blackness.

Paul Tiyambe Zeleza explains the multiple modes of analysis required to understand the new formations of migration and identity at the forefront of such narratives: "Diaspora is simultaneously a state of being and a process of becoming, a kind of voyage that encompasses the possibility of never arriving or returning, a navigation of multiple belongings, of networks of affiliation" (32). Significantly, he turns to one of the most important figures in African American intellectualism, W. E. B. Du Bois, to theorize the nature of diaspora. Zeleza proposes an expansion of Du Bois's understanding of "double consciousness" to capture the fluidity and plurality evident in contemporary diasporic experience. According to Du Bois, the African American is subject to "this sense of always looking at one's self through the eyes of others, of measuring one's soul by the tape of a world that looks on in amused contempt and pity" (3). Building on Du Bois, Zeleza suggests that only a recognition of "multiple consciousness" can address the complexity of the diasporic subject:[4]

> A diasporic identity implies a form of group consciousness constituted historically through expressive culture, politics, thought, and tradition, in which experiential and representational resources are mobilized, in varied measures, from the imaginaries of both the old and the new worlds. Diasporas are complex social and cultural communities created out of real and imagined genealogies and geographies (cultural, racial, ethnic, national, continental, transnational) of belonging, displacement, and recreation, constructed and conceived at multiple temporal and social scales, at different moments and distances from the putative homeland. (33)

Zeleza's reframing of Du Bois's groundbreaking metaphor for African American subjectivity points to the generative relationship between writings of the new African diaspora and the African American literary canon. The wave of African immigrants in the late twentieth and early twenty-first centuries has profoundly challenged what blackness means in the United States. It bears noting that the notion of multiple consciousness may be applied just as well to the experiences of native-born blacks. In fact, Black Lives Matter, the most significant African American protest movement since the civil rights era, vigorously advocates for the recognition of queer and transgender subjectivities while also affirming the rights of the undocumented and disabled. Black Lives Matter has distinguished itself through its bold rejection of narrow definitions of blackness that in the past have affirmed a patriarchal and classist approach to race. Multiplicity is not unique to the recent African immigrant but instead affirms the diversity that has always been a part of the African diaspora and in particular the experiences of African Americans. The twenty-first century is witnessing a dynamic broadening of how blackness signifies both here and abroad. Literary writers of the new African diaspora are at the forefront of exploring these exciting approaches to what black subjectivity means. This study is dedicated to charting the contours of what I term pan-African American literature—that is, literature by African-born or -identified authors centered on life in the United States. The texts I examine here deliberately signify on the African American literary canon to encompass new experiences of immigration, assimilation, and identification that challenge how blackness has been previously conceived.

Most academic work on the expanding presence and influence of recent African immigrants and their descendants in America has been sociological in nature. Texts like *The African Diaspora in North America* (2006) by Kwado Kondadu-Agyemang, Baffour K. Tayki, and John A. Arthur, *The Other African Americans* (2007) by Yoku Shaw-Taylor and Steven A. Tuch, and *Young Children of Black Immigrants* (2012) by Randy Capps and Michael Fix have been instrumental in describing patterns of education, labor, and political participation as well as shifting views on social issues. More recent texts like *Rethinking African Cultural Production* (2015) and a 2016 special issue of the *Journal of African Cultural Studies* have begun to consider the literary and artistic contributions of the new African diaspora. However, as both of these titles suggest, scholars have largely engaged authors like Chimamanda Ngozi Adichie and NoViolet Bulawayo from an African perspective. While such an approach provides a necessary foundation for understanding literature by writers born in Africa, this study offers another way to think through the start of a new literary renaissance. Rather than read these texts as African or specific to the national homelands of their authors, I consider them as part of an ever-expanding African American literary tradition. They significantly reframe our understanding of black migration by presenting diaspora as not solely defined by the traumas of the Middle Passage. Instead, migration is figured as a continuous and generative back-and-forth across the Atlantic.

As diasporic experiences revise prior conceptions of subjectivity, so do the authors examined here demand alternative approaches to understanding the range and possibilities of the African American canon. How may we understand authors like Teju Cole and Dinaw Mengestu as literary heirs to Frederick Douglass and Ralph Ellison? This is not to deny the ways in which these texts further the legacy of African novelists like Chinua Achebe and Daniachew Worku. Novels by authors who are simultaneously African and American yet not African American engage an especially broad range of texts. Just as we can no longer depend on a lexicon of hybridity and creolization to understand the changing nature of the African diaspora, the sheer breadth of intertextuality apparent in these literary works tests the limits of canons based on nation or race alone. We must take seriously Taiye Selasi's sly provocation in her essay "African Literature Doesn't Exist" to explore new ways to conceptualize literary traditions. Lines of influence and signifyin(g) discourse reverberate just as strongly between Cole and J. M. Coetzee as between Mengestu and James Baldwin. While literary categories are always evolving and exist perhaps most importantly to be transgressed, African-born or -identified writers who focus on American life raise critical questions about how race operates in literary texts. Their narratives expose the limits and possibilities of a common black identity amid a national landscape that makes race inescapable.

AFRICANS IN AMERICA

African immigrants and African Americans whose ancestors endured conditions of antebellum slavery share a racial affiliation even as their experiences are vastly different from one another. President Barack Obama, the most famous American born of a recent African migrant, claims that there are substantial continuities between these groups: "Some of the patterns of struggle and degradation that blacks here in the United States experienced aren't that different from the colonial experience in the Caribbean or the African continent."[5] Despite such commonalities, many critics have voiced concern about what the influx of Africans to the United States means for black identity as well as for efforts to improve the lives of African Americans. Uncritically grouping African immigrants and African Americans together can elide some of the significant differences that exist between these populations. Recent African immigrants are associated with higher levels of education and greater incomes than native-born blacks, and stereotypes about both groups tend to exacerbate intraracial tensions.[6] These discontinuities have led to distinct experiences of race and social difference largely centered on the unique historical conditions of migration confronted by these two populations. While African Americans suffered physical bondage and a violent schism from their homelands, African émigrés of the past few decades come to the United States with the hope that the American dream can be theirs even as they retain close ties to their countries of origin.

In a 2016 essay for the *New Yorker* published soon after the presidential election, Morrison elaborated on the particular challenge to assimilation faced by newcomers to this country: "All immigrants to the United States know (and knew) that if they want to become real, authentic Americans they must reduce their fealty to their native country and regard it as secondary, subordinate, in order to emphasize their whiteness" ("Making America White Again"). While skin color makes the "whiteness" of recent African immigrants tenuous at best, this emphasis on the cultural and social constructions wrapped up in racial difference clarifies some of the conflicts evident within the rapidly evolving black population in the United States. How have African immigrants emphasized some version of "whiteness," deliberately or not, to secure their status as "authentic Americans"? Msia Kibona Clark reminds us that such divides emerge not merely from the populations themselves: "Africans and African Americans have been pitted against each other by hundreds of years of damaging propaganda, harmful media images, and destructive school curricula" (262). One of the aims of the literature of the new African diaspora in the United States is to explore the commonalities between these groups and to chart, as Yaa Gyasi does in her recent novel *Homegoing* (2016), the unique trajectories of slavery and immigration to freedom and citizenship in this ever racially charged country.

Studies of families like Gyasi's, who arrived from Ghana in the early 1990s, demonstrate that in addition to the challenges facing any newcomers to the United States, "black immigrants must also confront the structure of racialized social systems in America, which provide rules for judging attributes of blacks and justify the practice of racism based on racial ideas" (Shaw-Taylor and Tuch 18–19). African immigrants must inevitably contend with our nation's long history of race and racism even as that history may remain invisible or, at the very least, not readily apprehended by them. Moreover, many are unfamiliar with the social and psychological consequences of white supremacy, a foundational influence on American history and social life. Kwame Anthony Appiah, who was born in London, raised in Ghana, and now teaches at New York University, observes of recent African immigrants, "Since they came from cultures where black people were in the majority and where lives continued to be largely controlled by indigenous moral and cognitive conceptions, they had no reason to believe they were inferior to white people and they had, correspondingly, less reason to resent them" (6–7).

Identifying this conclusion as a "fact . . . of crucial importance in understanding the psychology of postcolonial Africa," Appiah implies that African Americans have ultimately accepted the destructive stereotypes imposed on them. While the descendants of slaves in the Americas have certainly been treated as inferior well after emancipation, Appiah posits a startling psychological difference between Africans, who remain largely unscathed by divisions of race, and African Americans, who bear the trauma of its insidious impact and consequently struggle in their relationship to white people. While it may be impossible to determine the validity of Appiah's assumption, this conclusion highlights a more significant contrast between these populations. The stark divisions between black and white function as a specifically, if not uniquely, American phenomenon, not one inevitably derived from encounters between people of African and European descent.

Appiah notes that few "even from the 'settler' cultures of East and southern Africa, seem to have been committed to ideas of racial separation or to doctrines of racial hatred" (6). Though he begins this passage concerned with "what race meant to the new Africans affectively," Appiah shifts rather disconcertingly into a discussion of "racial separation" and "racial hatred." This conflation between race and racism is typical of African approaches to the social dynamics of the United States. In such formulations, race is treated as a mark of discrimination and struggle, rarely as a source of identity, community, and possibility. Ifemelu of

Americanah is quick to bemoan the infuriating stereotypes she confronts in the United States and perceives her African American boyfriend as too beholden to a wearisome politics of victimization. For her, blackness is a burden. It is useful only as fodder for her blog, a project she ultimately abandons because it becomes overly concerned with petty outrages. This perspective may also reflect a refusal to contend with the full complexity of race as Ifemelu opts to return to Nigeria rather than make a home in this inescapably racialized world. By contrast, President Obama's embrace of the African American community, a topic I discuss in the final chapter of this study, demonstrates how race need not be equated with racism. Instead, it can act as a powerful means of personal and political power.

Jemima Pierre strongly contests Appiah's characterization of the absence of race in Ghana as part of a larger argument about Africa as a whole: "A modern, postcolonial space is invariably a racialized one; it is a space where racial and cultural logics continue to be constituted and reconstituted in the images, institutions, and relationships of the structuring colonial moment" (xii). For Pierre, Appiah's description of race as an African American obsession is "both historically incorrect and intellectually disingenuous" (208) though typical of a broader "epistemic blindness" (4) that ties race only to the history of slavery. It is far beyond the scope of this project to argue for the centrality of race in continental African communities, and, as Jill M. Humphries explains, black transnationals are too diverse a group to have a unitary understanding of race.[7] Instead, I take seriously comments like those of Appiah or Adichie, who has stated, "In Nigeria race is not a conscious and present means of self-identification. Ethnicity is. Religion is. But not race."[8] Such disavowals of the importance of race in contemporary African societies reflect the willed blindness Pierre critiques, a blindness that fosters a troubling silence on colonialism's relationship to both race and the slave trade. This dynamic certainly warrants deep study and consideration, but my primary concern here is how recently immigrated African writers reflect on and represent race in their American encounters. The United States forces a reckoning with racial issues that may be more easily elided in certain African nations.

Regardless of the truth of Appiah's comments, his example highlights some of the changes wrought by the influx of new Africans to the United States. As the son of a prominent Ghanaian politician and a graduate of Cambridge University, Appiah exemplifies the class and educational privileges typical of much of this burgeoning population. Despite the obvious contributions these immigrants offer, such elite backgrounds can generate rifts and resentments, especially given the ongoing struggle of African Americans to attain basic educational and professional opportunities. Henry Louis Gates Jr. and Lani Guinier have both expressed concern that a majority of black undergraduates at Harvard are the children of West Indian or African immigrants.[9] This demographic shift can give the impression that institutions like Harvard are making significant advances to diversify their student body while still failing to address the paucity of African Americans at Ivy League universities.

Such changes have also caused alarm with respect to curricular and disciplinary concerns. In *White Money/Black Power* (2006), Noliwe Rooks draws attention to academia's move away from black studies and toward African Diaspora studies, noting that such a shift "embraces a Black student body that is not primarily African American and that, perhaps not surprisingly, now comprises a majority of the Black students on elite college campuses" (152).[10] Rooks further warns that "for academics and faculty, both white and Black, choosing students who are Black but disconnected from enslavement and America's history of racial injustice appears to be preferable" (155). This discomfort with discussions of slavery and racism helps explain why the alignment of Afro-Caribbeans and African Americans has drawn less critical scrutiny. Sharing an identification with North America as well as the ravages wrought by the Atlantic slave trade and its aftermath, these populations have long been considered almost coterminous.[11] By contrast, new African immigrants lack such commonalities of history and geography. Without a direct link to slavery and central events like the civil rights movement, how does this growing population change what blackness signifies in the United States? What does racial identity mean when it is shorn of much of the history so critical to how race operates in a country still beset by deep divisions of black and white?

We might include yet another question to this list of considerations: what do we call this new population? The influx of African immigrants to the United States in the final decades of the twentieth century and into the twenty-first century has precipitated a crisis in terminology.[12] How are we to separate these African Americans from the African Americans with roots tracing back to antebellum slavery? Newly arrived people from Africa are the only immigrant group faced with a settler population that is both familiar and alien to them. Those coming from Europe, Asia, and Latin America generally align with the communities of people from their home countries already living in the United States, finding support, comfort, and identity in these populations. However, African émigrés are often warned against identifying or consorting with black Americans. The narrator of Ike Oguine's *A Squatter's Tale* (2000) reflects,

> The African immigrant sometimes exhibits as much bitterness towards his African-American cousins as the worst white racist. Confronted with scenes like those we saw during that drive through West Oakland and the terrible images of inner-city violence and despair on TV, the success-obsessed immigrant wants to get as far away as possible, psychically if not physically from that horrible pit. He violently rejects any identification with what strikes him as irreversible disaster,

> the way one might disown and denounce a family member suffering from incurable alcoholism and kleptomania. (29–30)

According to Obi, Oguine's keenly observant protagonist, African Americans and African immigrants belong to the same family. However, native-born blacks must be marginalized for fear of destroying the hopes and dreams of these as yet uncorrupted strivers. This passage demonstrates the tension at the heart of the relationship between African Americans and African immigrants. They are indeed cousins, sharing a geographic origin, however temporally distant, and to some extent a common social experience, but "the terrible images of inner-city violence and despair" threaten to sever any meaningful exchange and solidarity between these populations. As Morrison suggests, the plight of many poor African Americans represents the opposite of the immigrant's hopeful dream of wealth and social advancement.

In *Americanah,* Adichie offers a possible solution to the issue of terminology, distinguishing between African Americans and American Africans, people like Ifemelu who comes to the United States from Nigeria.[13] However, this reversal of terms can be confusing and overlooks the influence of race on both groups, a concern at the forefront of John McWhorter's understanding of identity for people of African descent living in the United States. In a 2004 essay titled "Why I'm Black, Not African American," the politically conservative linguist argues that since America is now "home to millions of immigrants who were born in Africa," the descendants of slaves brought to the United States should relinquish the term "African American" and instead begin "calling ourselves Black—with a capital B." McWhorter justifies this shift in nomenclature by noting, "To term ourselves as part 'African' reinforces a sad implication: that our history is basically slave ships, plantations, lynching, fire hoses in Birmingham, and then South Central, and that we need to look back to Mother Africa to feel good about ourselves." McWhorter presents the achievements of men and women like Frederick Douglass, Ida B. Wells, and W. E. B. Du Bois as a uniquely black American legacy far removed from the land and cultures of Africa. However, in celebrating this history, McWhorter effectively draws a boundary around a native-born black experience that is not easily accessed by new African immigrants. There is even a hint of nativism in his conclusion, "A working-class black man in Cincinnati has more in common with a working-class white man in Providence than with a Ghanaian." This claim may be true in terms of culture and class, but it fails to address the experience of living with dark skin in a deeply racialized country that continues to associate black people, and in particular black men, with violence and danger. McWhorter prizes some common notion of national identity over the continuities that exist between African American and recent African immigrants. Confronted by a police officer for whatever reason, the black man from Cincinnati and the Ghanaian face a volatile encounter with potentially fatal consequences that the man from Providence neatly escapes. The men and women McWhorter newly terms "African American" inescapably bear the history of blackness on their bodies, with all its triumphs and humiliations. There is a common struggle here recognized by the narratives discussed in this study as well as by the pluralistic Black Lives Matter movement.

More than ten years since the publication of McWhorter's essay, the term "African American" is still primarily invoked to refer to the American descendants of slaves and not recent African émigrés.[14] While a definitive conclusion to this issue of nomenclature has yet to be achieved, Louis Chude-Sokei proposes the label "Newly Black Americans" to describe members of the new African diaspora.[15] Chude-Sokei's somewhat unwieldy term has the benefit of implicitly linking this group to preexisting black Americans. By emphasizing race, "Newly Black Americans" honors McWhorter's concern for a history unique to black citizens of the United States while offering the possibility of a more integrated future for these two groups. Such unity underscores Msia Kibona Clark's claim that "African Americans, as they are perceived today, are not a race, but an ethnic group within the Black/African race" (259). She thus concludes, "Black immigrants, whether from Africa or the Caribbean, constitute different ethnic groups within a Black racial identity" (260). By emphasizing such ethnic distinctions, Clark asks us to appreciate the broad diversity of the African diaspora. However, Jill M. Humphries cautions, "differences in historical meanings in the lives of African Americans and African immigrants . . . make using 'black' as a unitary identity with which to organize problematic" (276). If, as Wright reminds us, "there is no one historical moment or cultural trope to which one can link all of the African diasporic communities now living in the West" ("Can I Call You Black?" 3), what meaning does blackness even have? Where is the unity in, as Wright describes it, such "intimidating" diversity (2)?

PAN-AFRICAN AMERICAN LITERATURE

The writers of the new African diaspora are beginning to provide answers to such questions. In a recent essay for the *New York Times*, Yaa Gyasi explains that the genesis for her debut novel *Homegoing* came from a desire "to write about diaspora and reckon with the fullness of slavery, not just as it was centuries ago, but what it has left us, Ghanaians and Americans alike, today." She "started writing with a vague but important question that I put at the top of my blank screen: What does it mean to be black in America?" The answer is a novel that spans two continents as it follows two strands of the same family; one half sister bears a dynasty that survives amid the entanglements of the slave trade in what will become modern-day Ghana, while the other's descendants endure the horrors of the Middle Passage and chattel slavery in the American South. However, while Gyasi traces the historical legacy of slavery from both sides of the Atlantic and from both sides of the enslaver/slave relationship, she also answers the question that titles her essay, "Am I Black?" with a disturbing story from her childhood. Gyasi describes how as a child playing in Tennessee with two black friends, they were called "Niggers" by a pair of white boys. One of the boys then amended the attack, looking at Gyasi and saying, "Not you." Gyasi reflects, "The thing I neglected to realize that day when I was 8 was that I was a nigger well before I had a chance to prove myself otherwise, that the retraction of the word did not make up for the fact that it was uttered in the first place. It did not make up for the fact that when those boys looked at me, a nigger is what they saw." Gyasi's novel and her childhood story offer distinct but related notions of blackness. In *Homegoing*, the history of slavery and ancestral ties unite members of a single though deeply cleaved family. The story about her first encounter with the n-word would seem to make blackness a matter of interpellation. She is black because she is caught in a history that identifies dark skin with inferiority and abjection. However, prior to the appearance of the boys, Gyasi was playing with two girls she identifies simply as "both black." Is Gyasi aware of the racial identity of her friends only in retrospect? After the racial epithet is hurled on them? What unites them—the experience of racial defamation or a commonality of experience and subjectivity assumed well before the appearance of the boys?

The specific answers to these questions are less significant than the ways in which Gyasi's story gestures toward continuities and multiplicities that affirm the richness of African diasporic experience in the United States. Despite heralding from a wide variety of African nations, authors of this diaspora share a confrontation with America's unsettled racial past and a consideration of its precarious future.[16] This plurality of national representation is significant despite the fact that such distinctions tend to fall away following migration to the United States. Americans, both black and white, generally identify African immigrants not as Nigerian or Kenyan or Ghanaian but as either black or African. National or even regional differences have little significance for a nation that too often conceives of Africa as a country, not a continent. The entrenched divisions of black and white in America reduce African immigrants to a common racial identity that does not readily recognize differences of nation, tribe, or religion.

Despite this reductive approach, in the texts discussed here, African immigrants often find community and identity among émigrés from other African nations. Ifemelu notes that a Senegalese professor speaks "the same silent language as she did" (340), a language alien to her African American boyfriend. In *The Beautiful Things That Heaven Bears* (2007), the Ethiopian Sepha has two best friends, Kenneth from Kenya and Joseph from the Congo. Like Ifemelu, Sepha finds that immigrants from other African nations are easier to relate to than African Americans. This collapsing of African identity thus occurs both as a result of American ignorance of the diversity of African nations and because the racialized experiences of African immigrants share certain commonalities. These factors lead me to offer a new term for the writers explored in this study: pan-African Americans. This label reflects the diversity of their national origins while also signaling a strong association with African Americans.

As George Shepperson noted in 1962, there is an important distinction between Pan-Africanism and pan-Africanism. He explains, "'Pan-Africanism' with a capital letter is a clearly recognizable movement: the five Pan-African Congresses" while "pan-Africanism" represents "a group of movements" in which the "cultural element often predominates" (346). While Pan-Africanism emerged as a political and cultural movement devoted to the solidarity of Africans worldwide, my emphasis here is on a literary legacy that unites texts of the wide African American diaspora and therefore a small "p" notion of collective identity.[17] The African American diaspora is distinct from the African diaspora by foregrounding experiences unique to the culture, history, and geography of the United States. For this reason, the texts that I focus on here are all primarily set in America. Novels like Chris Abani's *GraceLand* (2004), Uzodinma Iweala's *Beasts of No Nation* (2005), Helon Habila's *Oil on Water* (2010), and Chinelo Okparanta's *Under the Udala Trees* (2015) are all written by African authors either educated or residing in the United States. However, the African setting of these texts complicates an explicit engagement with the African American literary canon. While Abani's *GraceLand* is certainly influenced by foundational black novels like *Invisible Man* (1952), the struggles of Elvis are rooted in Lagos and, in this way, far removed from the experiences of African Americans.

My primary focus here is to describe how recently immigrated African writers confront blackness through the history and experience of African Americans while also signifyin(g) on black letters more broadly.[18] To that end, it is important to emphasize that this study does not aim to be a comprehensive assessment of literature of the new African diaspora nor of the entirety of pan-African American literature. I purposely omit texts by African-descended authors of the Caribbean basin, Latin America, and other geographic areas. While writers like Edwidge Danticat, Junot Díaz, and Herman Carrillo, among many others, may be understood as pan-African American because of their explicit engagement with life in the United States, I limit my discussion to authors born or identified with African countries. A slew of books published in the last few years by Imbolo Mbue, Helen Oyeyemi, Okey Ndibe, and many others affirm that literature by recent African immigrants to the United States and the United Kingdom is exploding. Rather than offer a totalizing account of these diverse texts, I am most concerned with narratives that explicitly engage with the African American literary tradition and the tropes that have come to define this canon such as the talking book, invisibility, and signifyin(g). The authors selected for this study are manifestly in dialogue with African American literature and fashion themselves as, if not heirs to writers like Baldwin, Hurston, and Morrison, at least beneficiaries of those guiding talents. As I demonstrate, the intertextuality at work here affirms that this is not a matter of casual citation but instead represents a robust effort to reimagine the boundaries of the African American literary canon.

Only chapter 1, involving memoirs of war and displacement, considers texts largely set in Africa, though these stories of Lost Boys and child soldiers all conclude in the United States. These works are especially critical because they mark the beginning of twenty-first-century American interest in African stories and because they self-consciously invoke the first African American literary genre, the slave narrative. By uniting personal testimony with a political mission, these texts reflect many of the key attributes of nineteenth-century slave narratives while also responding to contemporary concerns. In later sections, I trace how Cole, Mengestu, Adichie, and Obama signify on quintessentially African American literary tropes. Although each of these writers takes on a variety of such themes, I have structured these chapters around specific engagement with a key trope, specifically rememory, invisibility, the ancestor, and fatherhood. The texts studied here offer new models of blackness that respond to the history of slavery and civil rights protest in ways that reflect the unique experiences of recent African immigrants. Pan-African Americanism represents a widening of the African American literary canon to include writers who bring issues of immigration, assimilation, diasporic identity, and African political conflict to American notions of blackness. These concerns force a reevaluation of how central African American literary concepts function. What wisdom does Morrison's ancestor have for a Nigerian woman struggling to understand American racial concepts? How can Ellisonian invisibility be a strategy of survival for immigrants haunted by traumatic pasts? These texts make the geographic and social realities of Africa as central to black experience as U.S. concerns while also establishing rich intertextual relationships with African American texts.

Pan-African American writers offer provocative challenges to how blackness has been understood as a means of organizing the African American literary canon. Does a common racial identity lead to a common literary tradition? Or do the differences that mark these two populations suggest the need for a new way of conceptualizing blackness? Chude-Sokei identifies a number of moments in texts by Mengestu, Cole, Oguine, and others that highlight important tensions between African immigrants and African Americans. From these strikingly consistent episodes of failed solidarity, he concludes, "The stress on these intraracial, cross-cultural differences is so widespread in this new literature by Africans in America that it is not too much to declare it paradigmatic of a moment and demanding of major reflection. Call it a wake-up call. To do so is to intervene on behalf of a long history of collusion, collaboration, and some degree of continuity while bringing attention to the problem of lazily assuming ideological solidarity due to race" (70). Chude-Sokei's comments refer specifically to depictions of African immigrants and African Americans that emphasize how differences in culture and national origin lead to significant political conflicts and distinctive social identities. Julius, the narrator of Cole's *Open City*, has little interest in consorting with African Americans, resorting to a conspicuous silence whenever he is invited to empathize with their racial plight. While Chude-Sokei's "wake-up call" demands that we reconsider how blackness divides as much as it unites in such texts, what does this observation mean for the African American literary canon? Julius is clearly wary of privileging color over culture, appearances over experiences, but does Cole as a literary writer also require a similar form of independence from American notions of race? Does a common racial identity produce if not ideological solidarity, then a kind of literary solidarity?

Citing the work of Khalid Koser, Chude-Sokei comments, "In the context of the new African migrations, particularly to the United States, there is no evidence whatsoever of a Pan-African movement, ideology, or even sensibility attempting to unite them" (58).[19] This observation highlights the important distinction between Pan-Africanism as a political movement and ideology and pan-African Americanism as a way of conceptualizing a wonderfully diverse and insightful literary project. In the texts studied here, relations between African Americans and African immigrants are indeed marked by discontinuity, resentment, and awkwardness. But this conclusion does not apply to literary relations as pan-African American writers consistently evoke, revise, and respond to African American authors. What does it mean to read Cole against Ellison or to compare Mengestu with Baldwin? How do the works of these young black writers share the signifyin(g) difference that has become the hallmark of the African American literary tradition?[20] This study explores how pan-African American writers signify on the African American literary tradition and offer new ways to understand the evolving experience of blackness in the United States.

PAN-AFRICAN AMERICAN WRITERS AND THE AFRICAN AMERICAN CANON

In March 2014, the third edition of *The Norton Anthology of African American Literature*, first released in 1996, was published. The current version now spans two volumes and reaches into the first decade of the twenty-first century with selections by such writers as Colson Whitehead and Tracy K. Smith. Among the new material is also Barack Obama's 2008 speech on race. The addition of "A

More Perfect Union" with its literary cadences and stirring rhetoric is both obvious and surprising. As our country's first black president and a man who comfortably cites W. E. B. Du Bois and Langston Hughes, Obama certainly deserves to be in the company of authors like Malcolm X and Gwendolyn Brooks. Yet Obama is unique among the writers included in the *Norton Anthology* in that he does not trace his roots to the North American slave trade. The son of a Kenyan father and a white Kansan mother, Obama is perhaps better grouped with writers like Cole, who was born and educated in the United States. But Cole, Mengestu, Adichie, and other pan-African American authors are notably missing from this latest edition of the anthology. What makes Obama but not these writers fit for inclusion?[21] Did he at some point become more American or, to be more specific, more African American than them? Importantly, this is a term he does not use to identify himself, instead preferring "black American," a description that would just as well apply to Cole and Mengestu.[22]

While the inclusion of Obama in the *Norton Anthology* seems natural, it does suggest that the doors to this canon might need to be opened even wider. Will fourth and fifth editions include pan-African American writers? And if not, what does their exclusion suggest about the meanings attached to blackness? In the introduction to the latest edition of the anthology, Henry Louis Gates Jr. and Valerie Smith begin the story of African American writing with slave narratives and the trope of the talking book. Bondage is the original experience given voice by African slaves and ex-slaves writing in English. Further defining the canon constituted by the anthology, Gates and Smith write, "*The Norton Anthology of African American Literature* is a celebration of more than two centuries of imaginative writing in English by persons of African descent in the United States." This definition would seem to require the inclusion of pan-African Americans; however, the editors then explain that "writers in the black tradition have repeated and revised figures, tropes, and themes in prior works, leading to formal links in a chain of tradition that connects the slave narratives to autobiographical strategies employed a full century later" (xliv).

There is a notable slippage here between an anthology of African American literature and "writers in the black tradition." Are blackness and African Americanness the same? Gates and Smith clarify in part these key terms: "Precisely because 'blackness' is a socially constructed category, it must be learned through imitation, and its literary representations must also be learned in the same way—like jazz—through repetition and revision . . . works of literature created by African Americans often extend, or signify upon, other works in the black tradition, structurally or thematically" (xliv). Gates and Smith suggest then two entryways into the *Norton Anthology*: African descent and an education in blackness. While the editors seem to elide the differences between Africanness and blackness, we must bear in mind that these are not terms that can or should be conflated. As Chude-Sokei's label suggests, the Newly Black Americans are newly black and newly American but perhaps still and ever African.

Bryan Wagner, among others, reminds us that blackness exists separately from Africa: "Blackness does not come from Africa. Rather, Africa and its diaspora become black during a particular stage in their history . . . Blackness is an adjunct to racial slavery" (1).[23] Wagner's assessment is supported by the observations of Adichie's Ifemelu in *Americanah.* Ifemelu becomes a minor celebrity in the United States through her blog, originally titled *Raceteenth or Curious Observations by a Non-American Black on the Subject of Blackness in America.*[24] Ifemelu's blog, which the novel periodically quotes at length, offers insights and advice to other African immigrants on how to understand and interact with Americans especially on topics related to race. Ifemelu explains in one of her early postings that race and blackness are foreign concepts to her: "I came from a country where race was not an issue. I did not think of myself as black and I only became black when I came to America" (292).[25] While the immigrants Morrison refers to become American by ascribing blackness to what she terms "the real aliens" (146), Ifemelu and other African immigrants become black simply by coming to the United States and being read by the color of their skin. Does their blackness prevent them from ever becoming American? Are they also forever "noncitizens" (146) due to their pigmentation? Or is the blackness that Ifemelu discovers in the United States a different kind of blackness than what Morrison describes in her essay? What does blackness mean for African immigrants?

To answer this question, we must first consider what blackness signifies to African Americans. In *Between the World and Me* (2015), Ta-Nehisi Coates, the most celebrated essayist of his generation, makes a key distinction between racial classifications and the community that has loved and sustained him throughout his life. Coates explains that race is a lie built on racism and its economic imperative: "Race is the child of racism, not the father. And the process of naming 'the people' has never been a matter of genealogy and physiognomy so much as one of hierarchy" (7). Race is the centuries-old justification of chattel slavery that posited a false notion of human difference in order to ensure the astounding profits to be reaped through mass dehumanization. But while race is an illusion used to affirm the capital of white supremacy, a community has nonetheless flourished through the signifier of blackness. What began as exploitation has transformed into the foundation of a vibrant and nurturing identity. Addressing his teenage son throughout the book, Coates explains, "They made us into a race. We made ourselves into a people. Here at The Mecca, under pain of selection, we have made a home" (149).

For Coates, the Mecca is "and shall always be Howard University" (39), but he also distinguishes that educational institution from a more amorphous and ultimately more potent force: “a machine, crafted to capture and concentrate the dark energy of all African peoples and inject it directly into the student body.” Howard does not alone represent The Mecca; instead, it generated the context for the flourishing of this dynamic home: “The history, the location, the alumni combined to create The Mecca—the crossroads of the black diaspora” (40). Though Coates attended Howard for five years, he never received a diploma. As his distinction between Howard and the Mecca implies, academic credentialing is less important than the diversity displayed daily on the campus lawn: “I saw everything I knew of my black self multiplied out into seemingly endless variations. There were the scions of Nigerian aristocrats in their business suits giving dap to bald-headed Qs in purple windbreakers and tan Timbs. There were the high-yellow progeny of AME preachers debating the clerics of Ausar-Set. There were California girls turned Muslim, born anew, in hijab and long skirt. There were Ponzi schemers and Christian cultists, Tabernacle fanatics and mathematical geniuses” (41). This range of blackness operates not only across nationality, religion, color, profession, and fashion but even across time, for as Coates tells his son, “You can no more be black like I am black than I could be black like your grandfather was” (39). In his formulation, blackness is mutable and fluid, not defined by a single essence or a series of physical features. Instead, it is constituted anew by the individual strands of its community members. And yet in Coates’s description, there is a constant tension between race as a calculated illusion designed for profit and the astounding energy of the black community in all its artistry, history, and diversity. To be black is both to bear the mark of violent exploitation and to enter into the vibrant, urgent joy of the Mecca.

The Mecca is fundamentally diasporic and in this way offers a key model for the generative possibilities of pan-African Americanism.[26] Even its name signals alliances across physical and cultural geographies. However, the Mecca’s identification with Howard University grounds it in a distinctively African American history. Howard has long been recognized as the premier historically black college in the nation, but it has also played a key role in American history, especially in terms of black cultural and political movements. Alain Locke was chair of the philosophy department when he was writing *The New Negro* (1925). Stokely Carmichael was a student at Howard, as were Ralph Bunche, Zora Neale Hurston, Thurgood Marshall, and Toni Morrison. Howard is inseparable from many of the most important moments in African American history: the ruling in *Brown v. Board of Education,* the birth of the Black Power movement, and the first Nobel Prizes awarded to African Americans. But as the Mecca, it represents a notable departure from the various cities that have been identified as “black Meccas” throughout the twentieth century and into the twenty-first.[27] Howard represents something different. It is not a city, but it is based on an institution of higher learning. While previous black Meccas have drawn black artists and entrepreneurs, Howard is organized around an educational project with wide-ranging social and political effects. Harlem continues to teem with people from Kentucky to Kenya, beckoning black professionals as well as black prophets. By contrast, the Mecca requires an explicit commitment to education and some degree of racial consciousness. This is not to suggest that all of its people identify as black, but to attend Howard or participate in the Mecca's vital energy is to take seriously the meaning and legacy of race in America.

Coates's description of the Mecca delineates two fundamental aspects of black identity: its diasporic nature and its deliberate self-fashioning. These elements have special resonance for recent African immigrants. This population is intrinsically part of the diaspora, but it is not intrinsically part of the Mecca—or, to put the matter in its starkest terms, its members are not intrinsically black. To become part of what Coates calls "this tribe that we call black" (120) requires a conscious effort to grapple with the meaning of race and racism in America. For Coates, such commitment demands an explicit engagement with history. He describes his experience as a Howard student primarily through the revelations he made studying in the university's rich library. There he aspires toward "a new story, a new history told through the lens of our struggle" (44). Even as he recognizes the dissensions of history, finding not "a coherent tradition marching lockstep but instead factions, and factions within factions" (47), he comes to a unique affirmation of the struggle endured and still enduring for black people in the United States.

Coates thus explains to his son the significance of his namesake, Samori Touré, who "struggled against French colonizers for the right to his own black body" (68). Through this struggle comes a unique form of wisdom.

> That wisdom is not unique to our people, but I think it has special meaning to those of us born out of mass rape, whose ancestors were carried off and divided up into policies and stocks. I have raised you to respect every human being as singular, and you must extend that same respect into the past. Slavery is not an indefinable mass of flesh. It is a particular, specific, enslaved woman, whose mind is as active as your own, whose range of feeling is as vast as your own. . . . For this woman, enslavement is not a parable. It is damnation. It is the never-ending night. And the length of that night is most of our history. Never forget we were enslaved in this country longer than we have been free. Never forget that for 250 years black people were born into chains—whole generations followed by more generations who knew nothing but chains. You must struggle to truly remember this past in all its nuance, error, and humanity. You must resist the common urge toward the comforting narrative of divine law, toward fairy tales that imply some irrepressible justice. The enslaved were not bricks in your road, and their lives were not chapters in your redemptive history. They were people turned to fuel for

> the American machine. Enslavement was not destined to end, and it is wrong to claim that our present circumstance—no matter how improved—as the redemption for the lives of people who never asked for the posthumous, untouchable glory of dying for their children. Our triumphs can never compensate for this. Perhaps our triumphs are not even the point. Perhaps struggle is all we have because the god of history is an atheist, and nothing about his world is meant to be. (70–71)

I have quoted this passage at length because it highlights the importance of honoring the particularity of slavery, the individual woman born into bondage whose damnation cannot be compensated by twenty-first-century victories. For Coates, to be black in America it is essential to "truly remember this past" and to understand contemporary struggles as an extension of the past, not its redemption. Slavery and its legacy are never far removed from the realities that define the lives of Coates, his son, his family, and what he calls "a tribe—on one hand, invented, and on the other, no less real" (56). This lucid description highlights the paradox at the heart of Coates's conception of race. It is at once the fiction made to justify slavery and the foundation of the community he loves. But in either formulation, the history of slavery is essential and even inescapable. How then do black Americans of all backgrounds relate or enter into such a history? As Coates explains, this is not a matter of diligent classroom study but instead requires an awareness of the immediate threat posed to black bodies in daily life.

Following his injunction to his son to "truly remember" the slave past, Coates describes learning that his college classmate, Prince Carmen Jones Jr., was killed by a police officer blocks away from the home of his fiancée and their infant daughter in September 2000. The death of Jones has both everything and nothing to do with slavery. Jones's life is not lived in "the never-ending night" of the slave woman Coates conjures only pages earlier. He was a graduate of Howard University with a bright future, a loving family, and the hope to become a radiologist like his mother. The damnation of the slave woman is not his reality, and yet his black body is not safe nearly a century and a half since emancipation. Driving to see his family, Jones was suspected of being a criminal who was being tracked by two undercover police officers. Coates reports that the suspected criminal was five foot four and 250 pounds, while Jones was six foot three and 211 pounds. Such obvious physical differences become meaningless when the suspects are black and male. Jones is trapped by a history that makes black men objects of fear and criminality and endows police officers with the authority to claim these bodies not as property of the state but as ever-present dangers to its well-being.

When Coates visits Dr. Mabel Jones, the mother of Prince Jones, she finds commonality with the experience of Solomon Northup, a free black man who in

1841 was kidnapped and sold into slavery: "'There he was,' she said, speaking of Solomon Northup. 'He had means. He had a family. He was living like a human being. And one racist act took him back. And the same is true of me. I spent years developing a career, acquiring assets, engaging responsibilities. And one racist act. It's all it takes'" (145).[28] Dr. Jones's reference to Northup highlights the continuities in black experience across centuries and the abiding vulnerability of black bodies. Dr. Jones and Northrup both believed themselves to be safe, protected by their reputations, wealth, and respectful adherence to the protocols of the country. They lived exemplary lives as upstanding citizens with beautiful happy families and fulfilling careers. But in fact, they were never safe. Northup is stolen South while Jones's son is stolen from her. More than 150 years since the publication of Northup's life story, black men remain marked. It is impossible to understand Jones's death without understanding the history of slavery and its legacy in the United States. To "truly remember this past" is to know that historical injustices shape the present contours of black life, leaving children exposed, marked, and unprotected.[29]

If history represents a gateway to black consciousness, then all of the texts explored in this study may be understood as engagements with the African American past. In her exploration of the global locations of African literature, Eileen Julien argues "that new emphases and experimentation in the creative works of African artist-intellectuals are more a matter of 'time,' which is to say history, than 'place'" (23). An encounter with African American history is the precondition of pan-African American literary production. As Julius of *Open City* walks the streets of New York, he is keenly aware of a landscape soaked with invisible trauma and violence. Beneath the office buildings and storefronts he passes lies an African burial ground from the seventeenth and eighteenth centuries. Julius recites the history of a petition by free blacks in the 1780s defending their dead against cadaver thieves who dug up the deceased for surgeons and anatomists to dissect. He concludes, "How difficult it was, from the point of view of the twenty-first century, to fully believe that these people, with the difficult lives they were forced to live, were truly people, complex in their dimensions as we are, fond of pleasures, shy of suffering, attached to their families" (221–222). It is impossible to imagine Coates expressing the kind of disbelief Julius describes here regarding the humanity of the free blacks and their dead. Even the alliterative phrase "shy of suffering" bears a writerly detachment that glosses over the brutality of such pain. While Coates demands that his son recognize the "particular, specific, enslaved woman," Julius wonders if these people "were truly people." Such doubt is an insult to the values Coates seeks to instill in his son. Although Julius credits his "twenty-first century" perspective as the key to his emotional remove, something else is clearly at work here. As I discuss in chapter 2, Cole's erudite narrator has an extremely vexed relationship to African

American history. Throughout the novel, the racialized past erupts as a series of uncanny figures that haunt Julius's perambulations and challenge his seemingly raceless intellectual identifications.

Julius exemplifies the struggle evident in many texts by writers of the new African American diaspora to come to terms with African American history. Obi of *A Squatter's Tale* discovers two narratives when he arrives in Oakland, California. On the one hand, he aspires to the immigrant's dream, fervently believing that hard work will lead to wealth and all the material trappings of American success. But running parallel to this seductive promise is the fate of African Americans, people characterized by one rich Nigerian immigrant as "venom . . . to be avoided completely. They were lazy, dishonest, dissolute, grasping" (126). African immigrants must confront the fictions and anxieties embedded in both of these narratives. Coates extols the cultural richness and excitement of the Mecca, but such belonging is predicated on an embrace of struggle, a prospect that repels both Julius and Ifemelu. There is a choice to be made here between the diasporic home Coates describes and what Morrison calls "the move into mainstream America," which "always means buying into the notion of American blacks as the real aliens" ("On the Back" 146). The texts examined here demonstrate that not all recent African immigrants want to be black and identify with Coates's Mecca. Nonetheless, their skin requires them to confront how race operates in the United States. Julius and Obi may shun African Americans, but they cannot escape the police power that kills Prince Jones. Despite these discontinuities, the very engagement with issues of race and history demonstrated by *Open City* and *Americanah* heralds them as part of an innovative pan-African American literary project.

The confrontation with history required to understand what blackness means for African immigrants elucidates why sustained introspective narratives and specifically the novel has become the central literary form for these new writers. Though poets rarely receive the attention of prose writers, it is notable that texts like *Americanah* and *Open City* have garnered so much critical and popular attention.[30] To return to Julien's observation that African artist and intellectuals are deeply concerned with time rather than place, the novel offers the best literary vehicle to capture the complexities of history. Novels require an unfolding across time that allows for an engagement with national and racial histories that emerge even against the will of narrators like Cole's Julius. With its long chronicles of New York City's fraught historical geography, *Open City* reminds us of the traumas that lie unsettled beneath our feet. Moreover, the novel has a unique position in the legacy of African American literature. Morrison reminds us that this particular literary form "is needed by African-Americans now in a way that it was not needed before" because it provides the sense of self and community necessary for any collective. She continues, "We don't live in places where we can hear those stories anymore; parents don't sit around and tell their children those classical, mythological archetypal stories that we heard years ago. But new information has got to get out, and there are several ways to do it. One is in the novel" ("Rootedness" 58). The novels I explore (as well as Obama's novelistic first book) are full of "new information" about what blackness means to recent African immigrants and the complex relationships between them and African American people and history. By using the novel form, these writers make explicit a dialogue with both literary and political consequences.

AFROPOLITANISM AND PAN-AFRICAN AMERICANISM

Obi's concern about consorting with African Americans exposes an important class divide between new African immigrants and black Americans. A number of the authors discussed in this study have been associated with Afropolitanism, a term frequently applied to artists and intellectuals with the economic means to shuttle between various international capitals. This hipster class generally shuns single identifications, instead luxuriating in a dynamic if notably exclusive hybridity. First popularized by Taiye Selasi in her essay "Bye-Bye Babar," Afropolitans are "the newest generation of African emigrants," those who in the 1960s were "young, gifted and broke" and pursued "higher education and happiness abroad." Selasi belongs to the generation born of these emigrants, children "bred on African shores then shipped to the West for higher education" and "others born in much colder climates and sent home for cultural re-indoctrination." Such wide-ranging experiences have produced significant discontinuities among a group best defined by intellectuals, writers, artists, and entrepreneurs, but Selasi finds that this diversity fosters a common perspective: "Perhaps what most typifies the Afropolitan consciousness is the refusal to oversimplify; the effort to understand what is ailing in Africa alongside the desire to honor what is wonderful, unique. Rather than essentialising the geographical entity, we seek to comprehend the cultural complexity; to honor the intellectual and spiritual legacy; and to sustain our parents' cultures." Selasi offers a definition, Afropolitan, to affirm what is ultimately a multifarious identity for this new generation. The Afropolitan writer is never reducible to a single identity but instead, as she explains, triangulates between at least three dimensions: national, racial, and cultural. These dimensions oscillate wildly according to specific regions of the world and offer a possible escape from what Emma Dabiri describes as "the depressingly limited identities widely perceived as being authentic." Might Afropolitanism be a way to end essentializing conceptions of race?

Despite the heterogeneity of the Afropolitan experience, it remains primarily elite. Selasi speaks of a class with deep economic and educational advantages. Just as the term "cosmopolitan" bears the mark of privilege if not actual luxury,

"Afropolitanism" suggests entitlement and a disregard for pressing class dynamics. While this sensibility reflects the demographic profile of recent African immigrants, it also highlights a specific experience of race. Repeatedly in the texts explored in this study, we see protagonists who leave the United States and its tiring adherence to racial protocols for other countries where blackness is not a mark of inferiority or racist projection. Such departures are possible only for the upper class and for Afropolitans who feel comfortable navigating European and African capitals.[31] Race thus remains for Afropolitans a kind of choice; it is at once the inevitable consequence of living in certain countries but a misguided form of classification in other societies. In either of such nations, the Afropolitan knows there are other worlds to be had, other ways of cataloging identity. Selasi explains, "Not all of us claim to be black. Often this relates to the way we were raised, whether proximate to other brown people (e.g. black Americans) or removed. Finally, how we conceive of race will accord with where we locate ourselves in the history that produced 'blackness' and the political processes that continue to shape it." Such an approach is impossible for African Americans whose country instantiates blackness as an irrevocable birthright. Reflecting on the escape that Paris has represented for generations of black American writers, Coates cites a friend who calls such a venture "a pointless luxury, like blowing the rent check on a pink suit" (117). The metaphor is telling as it transforms the liberating global space of the Afropolitan into an absurd luxury item, a garment impossible for the serious daily work of being black in the United States.

Many critics have inveighed against the elitism of Afropolitanism as well as its association to a materialistic lifestyle. There are dozens of websites advertising the stylish habits of Afropolitans, a fusion of hipster concerns (vegan recipes and natural beauty secrets) with calls to "know your roots" (descriptions of certain African rituals and recommendations to read up on figures like Chinua Achebe and Kwame Nkrumah). Stephanie Bosch Santana argues that it has become "a phenomenon increasingly product driven, design focused, and potentially funded by the West." The emphasis on consumerist, identitarian aspiration rather than action has led to a conspicuous gap between the seemingly postnationalist Afropolitan and the majority of Africans still struggling to survive and provide for their families. Grace A. Musila notes that while the Afropolitan vision "paints a rosy picture of connectivity, heterogeneous blends of cultures and an ethos of tolerance, the unasked question remains: what about those excluded from these circuits of consumption and access, as is the case of a majority of Johannesburg's residents?" (110). From this perspective, Afropolitans writing about life in the United States may be understood as an abandonment of the pressing problems facing many African nations. This sentiment is poignantly expressed by Brian Bwesigye, who wonders, "*Why is the Afropolitan willing to erase African realities from the literary landscape?*" Bwesigye condemns critics who claim that describing African exploitation and suffering amounts to "poverty porn," a fulfillment rather than rejection or at least reassessment of base stereotypes. He concludes, "We need a multiplicity of stories, the Afropolitan, the realist and those in between."

Bwesigye's comments are a direct response to Helon Habila, a Nigerian-born novelist and poet who teaches at George Mason University. In his damning review of NoViolet Bulawayo's *We Need New Names* (2013), Habila asks that African writers put aside the images that have come to dominate contemporary representations of Africa: "We are talking child soldiers, genocide, child prostitution, female genital mutilation, political violence, police brutality, dictatorships, predatory preachers, dead bodies on the roadside." Though Habila praises Bulawayo's "keen powers of observation and social commentary" along with "her refreshing sense of humour," he indicts her for "performing Africa," invoking fear and pity through predictable descriptions of violence, poverty, and abjection.

Bulawayo's novel is an especially important text because it is set in both Zimbabwe and the United States. Any performance of Africa is inextricable from an accompanying performance of American life. U.S. realities echo with images and patterns derived from the protagonist's memory of her hometown. Emblematic of a pan-African American sensibility, *We Need New Names* challenges readers to discover new modes of identification for texts and characters that assume transnational identifications. I conclude this introduction with a brief reading of the novel that highlights some of the key aspects of the literature of the new African American diaspora.

WE NEED NEW NAMES

Like Habila, Bulawayo may also be classified as part of the Afropolitan generation, though their American connections (Bulawayo received her MFA from Cornell University) link them to pan-African Americanism. The dynamic exchange between the United States and Zimbabwe that Bulawayo presents in *We Need New Names* demonstrates how both countries are fundamental to the emerging self-conception of Darling, the novel's adolescent narrator. It is at once a deeply Afropolitan text given its examination of Darling's hybrid identity while also clearly opposed to the elite privileges of many recent African immigrants. By bridging Afropolitan concerns with American realities, Bulawayo explores the rich depths of pan-African American writers. Its dual setting and emphasis on connections between Zimbabwe and the United States highlight the expanding contours of the black American literary landscape. It would be a mistake to identify Bulawayo as solely an Afropolitan or African American writer; instead, as the novel's title suggests, we need new names to describe texts that limn the contours of fresh encounters with blackness in America.

Although *We Need New Names* begins with Darling cavorting with her friends through a shantytown named Paradise, thoughts of America are never far from its protagonist's consciousness. In the opening chapter, Darling distinguishes herself from her friends and their future of petty thievery by imagining the better life she will lead in America: "I'm not really worried about that because when that time comes, I'll not even be here; I'll be living in America with Aunt Fostalina, eating real food and doing better things than stealing" (12). Midway through the novel, Darling moves to the United States, joining her aunt in "Destroyedmichygen," an apt name for the poverty and violence of Paradise. America proves to be an utter disappointment, less an escape from Paradise than another version of alienation and unrealized hopes. While in Zimbabwe Darling is continually preoccupied by her future in America, in the cold Midwest she longs for the familiar world she left behind. On the first page of the chapter that inaugurates her life in America, Darling reflects, "this here is not my country" as she catalogs all the beloved sights and sounds of Paradise not present in this bleak new world. She then concludes, "This place doesn't look like my America" (152), as if her America might still exist somewhere else.

Rather than representing opposite visions of wealth and poverty, joy and despair, America and Zimbabwe in *We Need New Names* figure as echoes of one another. In anticipation of an election in Paradise, the children put up posters declaring "Change, Real Change" (61), a variation on Obama's 2008 election slogan "Change we can believe in." As she watches Obama's swearing in, Darling describes him as looking "like our president's child" (158). Though Obama is hardly equivalent to Zimbabwe's president, Robert Mugabe, who has sanctioned decades of corruption, human rights violations, and disastrous economic policies, Darling's comparison reflects a valid suspicion of politicians and their promises. Bulawayo repeatedly establishes striking parallels between Darling's memories of Paradise and her current American reality. When a classmate brings a gun to school, Darling describes the chaos that ensues: "Kids and teachers were screaming and scattering all over like chickens, clogging the corridors and trying to get out all at once. It reminded me of the stampedes back home when things started to fall apart and the stores were empty, how people would pour out onto the street and run like they were dying" (219). Similarly, a scene involving Darling and her American friends watching internet porn ends as they come across a clip of the genital mutilation of an African girl. Though this episode may seem to indulge the expectations of "poverty porn" as outlined by Habila, by juxtaposing female genital mutilation with a wide array of American porn, Bulawayo demonstrates how there is no safety for these young girls either here or abroad. Her novel is less an indictment of conditions in Zimbabwe than an exploration of the dangers that exist in both countries and the contradictions that arise between them. America may vehemently condemn female genital mutilation, but a quick

Google search reveals that our nation's sexual imaginary is rife with violence against women.

Chielozona Eze identifies Darling and her friends "as true Afropolitans" ("We, Afropolitans" 117). In an attempt to reframe the contested term, Eze argues for understanding Afropolitanism as "a new ethics of being" (116). Eze defines the Afropolitan as "that human being on the African continent or of African descent who has realized that her identity can no longer be explained in purist, essentialist, and oppositional terms or by reference only to Africa" ("Rethinking African Culture" 240). Eschewing the class divides that concern Dabiri, Musila, and others, this reconceptualization echoes the claims of Amatoritsero Ede: "Afropolitanism captures the complexity of identity in a hybrid, postmodern world where centre/periphery models have become inadequate for analyzing global cultural flows, and in which African identity can no longer fit into the neat historical Pan-African uniformity" (88). My use of pan-African Americanism builds on these new formations, affirming the fluidity and diversity of diasporic experience but focalizing the African migrant at least in part through an American experience. While the Afropolitanism of Eze and Ede spans the globe from Europe to Asia and beyond, this study emphasizes the particularities of African encounters with the United States.

We Need New Names is unique among texts of the new African American diaspora because it involves a child. Among the various tropes that animate and unite pan-African American works—immigration, blackness, assimilation, American identity, community, among many others—there is one issue notably absent. None of the novels explored here focus on recent African immigrants with children. Raised by her overworked aunt and her increasingly erratic uncle, Darling suffers through sporadic phone calls with her mother, who accuses her of forgetting her family in Paradise. Darling is effectively an orphan, desperate for adult guidance and stability. Among the other novels discussed here, only Adichie's *Americanah* includes a secondary character, Aunty Uju, with a son who, though born in Nigeria, is raised entirely in the United States. At the end of the novel, Ifemelu, like Adichie, abandons Dike to focus on the more pressing and satisfying conclusion of her decades-old romance with Obinze. Cole's Julius is an erudite recluse who often seems to prefer the company of books and music to people. Mengestu's Sepha of *The Beautiful Things That Heaven Bears* develops an affecting friendship with the mixed-race daughter of his lover but remains himself childless like the protagonists of *How to Read the Air* and *All Our Names*. Other pan-African American authors also eschew the complexities of raising children in the United States. Black of Chris Abani's *The Virgin of Flames* is unmarried and primarily committed to his art and his vision of the Virgin, while Sunil of *The Secret History of Las Vegas* (2014) is caught in a grotesque murder mystery plot.

The absence of children and familial relationships in these texts is especially significant in light of the publication of *Between the World and Me*. Coates presents his meditation on black life in America as a letter to his son. His understanding of what blackness means is inextricably linked to his relationship to Samori: "Black people love their children with a kind of obsession. You are all we have, and you come to us endangered. I think we would like to kill you ourselves before seeing you killed by the streets that America made. This is a philosophy of the disembodied, of a people who control nothing, who can protect nothing, who are made to fear not just the criminals among them but the police who lord over them with all the moral authority of a protection racket" (82). The consequences of race have special resonance for parents who, like Dr. Jones, find that they can offer limited protection to their children, or protection that is more facade than reality. The trips to Europe and tuition at prestigious schools do not save Prince Jones from death, for as Coates explains, to have a black child is to be among the disembodied. Disembodiment is a trope that haunts a number of the texts I explore. Julius is more mind than matter, a fugitive of his own body like Ellison's Invisible Man, and Mengestu's protagonists continually hide from their lovers, exposing their bodies only to recede into their own secrets and lies. But for Coates, disembodiment is not a metaphor: it is a condition that defines one's relationship to the future. That future is perhaps the final part of how Coates understands his relationship to blackness. Along with the Mecca's diasporic range and its conscious embrace of history, it also depends on a future generation. By contrast, the characters described in pan-African American novels are generally loners, men and women who cherish past relationships as they struggle to forge new ones here in the United States. This does not imply a refusal to brave life in the United States as a newly black American; instead, it signals a moment of transformation as these writers contemplate the challenges and possibilities of embracing blackness.

Even as these texts depict profound anxieties about the establishment of communities, families, and relationships with African Americans, writers of the new diaspora demonstrate a remarkable intertextual relationship with the African American literary tradition. If blackness is a learned, literary practice, then they readily embrace such signifyin(g), developing and revising some of the most important African American tropes. Texts by African Lost Boys and child soldiers echo with the form and content of nineteenth-century slave narratives. Cole reinvents the talking book as an encounter with the African American uncanny, while Mengestu critiques the limits of Ellisonian invisibility. These novels also unsettle the hierarchical relationship instantiated by Morrison's conception of the ancestor as a key guardian of black identity. Cole, Mengestu, and Adichie affirm a new model of black collaboration, one that is not a vertical passing down of generational knowledge but instead mines the horizontal reaches of more egalitarian friendships and romantic relationships. Such deliberate refashioning of African American themes illustrates a widening expansion of the African American literary canon.

Pan-African American texts reinvent the meaning of blackness by placing immigration and diasporic identity at the center of their narratives and reassessing the relationship between slavery and contemporary social conditions. They demonstrate the ways in which race is an evolving and contested site of identity that is made new by the experiences of recent African immigrants. These writers refashion Morrison's opening question, how immigrants become American, by asking how Africans become African American or rather pan-African American. Blackness here becomes a bridge between people of radically different experiences. Though race often alienates and frustrates immigrants who are accustomed to living in all-black environments, it can also be a powerful form of community and political mobilization. Many of these debates will be familiar to students of African American literature as they extend discussions about the limits and possibilities of racial formations from the Harlem and Chicago Renaissances as well as the Black Arts Movement. Although their particular conditions of immigration and racialization are specific to the start of the twenty-first century, pan-African American writers engage established challenges and representations. This contemporary diaspora joins a centuries-long literary tradition. Their aesthetic strategies are familiar even as these signifyin(g) immigrants and their children tell new stories.

To highlight the unifying potential of race, the final chapter of this study offers a reading of Barack Obama's first book, *Dreams from My Father: A Story of Race and Inheritance* (1995), along with some reflections on his final years in office. Though American by birth, Obama charts in part a journey from immigrant other to black American. His example demonstrates how an ancestral connection to slavery is not required to be part of the vibrant, evolving black community. However, what we might call Obama's assimilation into African American life is not a foregone conclusion based on skin color alone. Instead, he describes his fierce commitment to public service as the initial point of connection to black life in some of Chicago's poorest neighborhoods. Obama has also had to contend with the vicissitudes of political life and the immense expectations imposed on the first black presidential candidate of a major political party and then the first black president of the United States. Throughout much of his political career, he has responded to popular opinions in ways that mitigate or seemingly ignore his racial identity. He quickly learned in his first term that there are distinct limits to how black our first black president can be. However, in his second term, Obama demonstrated a remarkable shift in his treatment of racial issues. Rather than present himself as racially transcendent, a strategy he used to great effect during the 2008 campaign, he has become increasingly comfortable identifying himself with the community he extols in *Dreams from My Father*.

Shortly before Obama's inauguration in 2008, Grant Farred identified him as "a singularly diasporic figure" (106). Obama is emblematic of a dynamic cultural, racial, and national fusion that has always been at work in American life and letters. To explore such complexity, Wai Chee Dimock offers in the introduction to *Shades of the Planet: American Literature as World Literature* (2007) a critical paradigm that "turns the United States from a discrete entity into a porous network, with no tangible edges, its circumference being continually negotiated, its criss-crossing pathways continually modified by local input, local inflections," concluding, "These dynamic exchanges suggest that the American field has never been unified, and never will be" (3). This heterogeneous conception of American literature reminds us that African American literature is also world literature, capturing not only the Afropolitan embrace of cultural complexity and the diasporic nature of Obama but also Dimock's commitment to "criss-crossing pathways." Literature of the new African American diaspora brings to light what has always been true about black literature in the United States: the transnational stakes at the heart of its very conception.

Decades of transnational studies and inquiry into our globalized world have pushed scholars in American studies to consider the nation as an inevitably malleable enterprise, bound by territorial designations that do little to reflect complex lines of influence and development. African American literature is the original transnational canon embedded in American letters. Pan-African American writers once again affirm the global reach of our national narrative and the ways in which African American literature has never been parochial or narrow but has always been an engagement with the world.

1 • SIGNIFYIN(G) ON THE SLAVE NARRATIVE

African Memoirs of War and Displacement

Before Dinaw Mengestu won a MacArthur Genius Award, before *Open City* was extolled in the pages of the *New Yorker*, and before Chimamanda Ngozi Adichie's TEDx talk was sampled in a Beyoncé song, the African literary landscape in the United States was dominated by stories of child soldiers and orphaned refugees. Pan-African American literature of the twenty-first century does not begin with novels celebrated for their incisive perspective on the struggles of contemporary black immigrants and complex intraracial dynamics. Instead, the first years of the century witnessed the publication of two best-selling books about African boys displaced by war, texts far removed from the Afropolitan aesthetic or questions about racial authenticity.

In 2006, Dave Eggers published *What Is the What: The Autobiography of Valentino Achak Deng* (2006), a genre-bending account of a Sudanese Lost Boy's resettlement in the United States. Favorably reviewed by every major national newspaper, *What Is the What* was a finalist for the National Book Critics Circle Award and received France's Prix Médicis étranger. One year after its publication, Ishmael Beah's *A Long Way Gone: Memoirs of a Boy Soldier* (2007) topped the *New York Times* best-seller list. Eggers went so far as to describe Beah as "arguably the most read African writer in contemporary literature" (179), a designation that neatly keeps his own popularity unchallenged. Many reviewers compared Beah's life story to Eggers's novel as if *A Long Way Gone* offers a sequel to Deng's experiences. Although Beah is from Sierra Leone rather than Sudan and served as a soldier in the government's army, his book offered American audiences another glimpse of the devastation caused by African civil wars.

Despite their differences, both texts present stories of black suffering relieved only through the promise of America and its nation of sympathetic readers.

It may seem incongruous, if not completely misguided, to begin this study with a discussion of a novel written by a white author. However, *What Is the What* initiated broad interest in the stories of African refugees and child soldiers among American readers of the twenty-first century. *A Long Way Gone* is one of many popular accounts of Africans escaping war and violence for the relative calm and prosperity of the West; these include Emmanuel Jal's *War Child: A Child Soldier's Story* (2010), *They Poured Fire on Us from the Sky: The True Story of Three Lost Boys from Sudan* (2006), and *Girl Soldier: A Story of Hope for Northern Uganda's Children* (2007), among others. These texts serve as crucial antecedents to the pan-African American novels explored in subsequent chapters. They not only highlight the problematic expectations of white audiences but also, more importantly, offer a model of black intertextual exchange with the most foundational African American literary genre, the slave narrative. This signifyin(g) relationship demonstrates the rich resonances between contemporary African stories and the African American canon. Like *What Is the What* and *A Long Way Gone*, antebellum slave narratives were written to inspire political action among curious if disengaged readers. Almost two centuries since Frederick Douglass's best-selling account of slave life dominated national conversations, horrifying experiences of black victims are once again offered up to Western audiences with the hope that they will bring about lasting and meaningful change.

However, while antebellum readers avidly consumed the stories of former slaves, the stark brutalities of plantation life were a few states away, not situated on a faraway continent that for contemporary Americans often remains more myth than reality. And yet the parallels between stories of African child soldiers and refugees and antebellum slave narratives demonstrate the ever-fraught politics of reading and writing about racialized suffering. This has special resonance for stories about black lives because, as Mengestu reminds us, "What attracts immediate and superficial attention to Africa's child soldiers, however, is that the brutal existence of a child soldier dovetails neatly with depictions of Africa both as a place born of hell and misery and as a continent that, like a child, can be saved."[1] Mengestu's comments reflect Cole's critique of the "White Savior Industrial Complex," which "is not about justice" but "about having a big emotional experience that validates privilege."[2] In such narratives, black victims require heroic white crusaders to bring them not just peace and prosperity but the very tools of civilization: literacy and a broad audience for their inspiring life stories. As demonstrated in later chapters, Mengestu and Cole's novels implicitly counter these racist conceptions by affirming the complexity and depth of African immigrant lives.

Both stories about African child refugees and antebellum slave narratives depend on a redemptive structure that provides readers with the satisfaction of individual triumph often coded through images of the American dream fulfilled. Douglass concludes his 1845 narrative by describing the freedoms of the North; similarly, Beah ends his memoir reveling in the support he finds among his new American friends in New York. These are stories of black lives deliberately addressed to predominantly white, middle-class American readers. Although slave narratives explicitly indicted aspects of American culture and society, texts about African refugees and soldiers showcase examples of black-on-black violence that are not directly tied to histories of Western colonialism and imperialist intervention; while the conflicts in Sudan and Sierra Leone are certainly derived from a colonial history, this background and its relationship to the United States is obscured by the immediate spectacle of internal strife within the continent. Because of this geographic and political remove, contemporary American readers encounter these stories with a greater sense of their own broad-minded magnanimity. They are not to blame for the atrocities chronicled here, and simply to purchase the book is to contribute to the worthy political mission of its author.

What Is the What, *A Long Way Gone*, and *War Child* all draw on rhetorical strategies evident in antebellum slave narratives. By attaching his name to Deng's story, Eggers echoes a literary tradition involving white authorization of black lives. Moreover, just as Douglass and Harriet Jacobs appealed to their readers through shared ideologies with deep national resonance, Beah and Eggers establish a connection to their audiences by emphasizing quintessentially American tropes of innocence and the desire for a better life. Both Douglass and Jacobs were especially attentive to the gender roles they needed to perform for their nineteenth-century readers; by contrast, Beah largely avoids issues of gender and sexuality in order to emphasize his identity as an innocent. Such a depiction may strain credibility, especially given reports of rampant rape in various African conflicts, but like slave narrators before him, Beah succeeds in offering a story palatable to his readers.[3] The middle-class Americans who look to Starbucks for book recommendations (*A Long Way Gone* was the second selection for the now defunct Starbucks reading club) may be repelled by stories of rape and sexual violence as well as by trauma that lingers far beyond the close of a two-hundred-page book. Instead the arc of redemption so common to antebellum slave narratives also structures Beah's story, which returns its sensitive, observant narrator to the childhood stolen from him by his involvement in the civil war that gripped Sierra Leone in the 1990s.

The image of latte-sipping Americans reading about Beah's harrowing experiences as a drug-addicted orphan killing and maiming his fellow countrymen exemplifies what Alexandra Schultheis identifies as the uneasy "politics of humanitarian consumption" (31). What does it mean to read stories of such violence so far removed from their geographic and political origin? How do these texts appeal to Western and specifically American readers in their account of atrocities that include child soldiering and genocide? It bears noting that *What Is the What, A Long Way Gone,* and *War Child* are not texts focused solely on self-expression and discovery; rather, they are deliberately crafted to move readers to explicit forms of action. Just as Deng hopes that his readers will help him to better the lives of his Sudanese countrymen both here and abroad, Beah describes the horrors of child soldiering in order to combat the exploitation of other young men.

Identifying a new genre of African literature, the modern slave narrative, Yogita Goyal draws a similar comparison between nineteenth-century slave narratives and a number of recent works, including *What Is the What* and Francis Bok's *Escape from Slavery* (2003). Goyal argues that these texts "reveal the refashioning of the politics of race and diaspora for a neoliberal age, where seemingly universal notions of the human once again underwrite a Western/neoimperial hegemonic agenda" (50). While Goyal carefully delineates the political dangers of mapping a modern slave discourse onto these contemporary texts, my concern here and elsewhere in this study is more literary. I read *What Is the What, A Long Way Gone,* and *War Child* as part of a signifyin(g) exchange with the slave narrative form. As the first literary texts produced by people of African descent in the Americas, slave narratives share with these African testimonies an originary place in the development of a racialized canon. The stories of Deng, Beah, and others inaugurated interest in African narratives for twenty-first-century American readers. These texts represent the first wave of African American literature of the new diaspora, setting the stage for later interest in fiction by Cole, Mengestu, Adichie, and others.

Comparing these testimonial works to antebellum slave narratives offers insight into the rhetorical strategies necessary to engage American audiences. Despite centuries of civil rights progress and literary innovations, black writers continue to rely on literary techniques that cater to middle-class ideologies and traditional gender conventions. Although the terms of black self-expression have significantly changed since the antebellum period, *What Is the What, A Long Way Gone,* and *War Child* demonstrate how stories of African suffering still contend with racialized expectations that respond to various forms of white privilege. In particular, *What Is the What* and *A Long Way Gone* depend on a discourse of innocence with profound racial undertones. Eggers presents himself through a kind of authorial erasure that claims innocence through narrative absence, while Beah draws on long-standing notions of childhood innocence that, as Robin Bernstein demonstrates, have a complex racial history. By contrast, Jal's book, set during the Second Sudanese Civil War, rejects innocence as a redemptive trope and instead refigures soldiering as a means of combating violence and exploitation through words. These texts reflect both the limitations and possibilities of black self-expression within a political and literary landscape that too often assumes African victimization and white salvation.

DAVE EGGERS'S *WHAT IS THE WHAT*

Much of the success of *What Is the What* was no doubt due to Eggers's reputation as a hip but imminently literary writer and provocateur. Reviewers consistently praised Eggers for his turn away from the self-indulgent postmodern antics of his earlier works and toward a kind of selfless exploration of the consequences of war-torn Sudan. *New York Magazine*'s David Amsden noted that Eggers was especially well suited to tell the story of one of the country's Lost Boys because he is "famously, a lost boy himself." For Amsden, "this wrenching and remarkable book" represents the culmination of all of Eggers's literary efforts from his uneven if supremely earnest fiction to the founding of the independent publishing house McSweeney's and 826 Valencia, a San Francisco nonprofit writing and tutoring center that now has chapters in eight American cities. If Eggers had at last sufficiently grown up to narrate the life of a boy orphaned and scarred by war, then America too might be ready to recognize the ongoing suffering and strife of East Africa. Although later writers like Beah and Jal published their memoirs with a greater degree of authorial control, *What Is the What* served as a necessary first step to introduce American readers to the lives of young African refugees.

One of the defining features of the slave narrative genre is the presence of authenticating documents. Published at a time when questions about black humanity and intelligence were still debated in mainstream venues, slave narratives required the testimony of noted white patrons to be considered credible. Douglass's 1845 narrative opens with a preface by William Lloyd Garrison, the most famous abolitionist of his day. Garrison's national reputation and overweening praise affirmed the veracity of Douglass's account. His preface also serves to instruct readers in how to approach a text so far removed from the daily life of middle-class white Americans. According to Garrison, Douglass is heir to Patrick Henry and endowed "with true manliness of character" (5). He must thus be understood as exemplifying the most revered American values: independence, freedom, and honor. Similarly, *Incidents in the Life of a Slave Girl* (1861) includes an introduction by noted author and activist Lydia Maria Child that testifies to the truth of Harriet Jacobs's astounding life story. Slave narratives could not have been published much less read by thousands of Americans without the imprimatur of such famous white authorities.

What Is the What similarly depended on the reputation of a white writer and champion to enter into the public sphere. Deng's story received national attention only because of Eggers's involvement in its production. However, unlike the authenticating documents of Garrison, Child, and other white patrons that guaranteed the veracity of various slave narratives, Eggers's participation in *What Is the What* confirms its fictionality. The book's title page attests to the unusual partnership between Deng and Eggers that produced its mixing of distinct literary genres. *What Is the What* is subtitled *The Autobiography of Valentino Achak Deng* but also labeled "a novel" above its ascription to Dave Eggers. The book is clearly not meant to be read like a novel such as *The Great Gatsby* (1925) or even Eggers's biographically infused *And You Shall Know Our Velocity* (2002). Rather, the peculiar amalgamation of fact and fiction liberates Eggers from the expectations of historical accuracy even as he capitalizes on the compelling details of Deng's life. While abolitionists like Garrison and Child lent credibility to the lives of slave narrators, Eggers's reputation secures interest in Deng's story and promises a literary experience that is more than just a conventional account of suffering and salvation. Factual accuracy was paramount for nineteenth-century readers, but for today's audiences, imminently comfortable with shifting notions of truth, authentication is not about the accuracy of verifying specific details. Rather, Eggers's name on the cover of *What Is the What* promises its consumers a really good story.

What Is the What along with *Zeitoun* (2009), an account of a Syrian American man's struggle through Hurricane Katrina and published three years later, signaled a radical new direction for Eggers, an author best known for his clever asides and breathless sentences. Both books adopt a direct, even spare prose style. Eggers emerges as a serious, observant narrator whose presence is felt precisely through his studied erasure; as he describes his narrative approach to Deng's story, "I knew I had to disappear completely."[4] The vibrant, at times overwhelming presence of Eggers in *A Heartbreaking Work of Staggering Genius* (*AHWOSG*) is transformed into a deliberately constructed authorial absence. These texts chart a trajectory from one form of narratorial extreme to the other. Despite such stark differences, they are united by their generic experimentation and emphasis on a community-oriented but self-reliant narrator. Eggers's unusual narrative approach highlights the fraught geopolitics of cross-racial literary reception. Although he celebrates Deng's perseverance and sensitivity, his book depends on negative depictions of African Americans. By framing Deng's story through his assault by two African Americans, *What Is the What* suggests a sharp opposition between African immigrants like Deng and heartless American blacks. This troubling dichotomy emphasizes the racial stakes of Eggers's text and the ways in which African stories are shaped, like slave narratives centuries earlier, primarily for white, middle-class readers.

In her foundational essay "Whiteness as Property," Cheryl I. Harris explains, "The right to exclude was the central principle, too, of whiteness as identity, for mainly whiteness has been characterized, not by an inherent unifying characteristic, but by the exclusion of others deemed to be 'not white'" (1736). Eggers is a writer deeply conscious of his own racial identity and the privileges that his whiteness has produced. His philanthropic work in many ways seeks to overturn racialized hierarchies by providing greater educational opportunities to disadvantaged youth. These initiatives attempt to shift the white right to exclude into an egalitarian commitment to inclusion. While programs such as 826 Valencia are certainly laudable, the translation of such efforts onto the page becomes more problematic. Both *What Is the What* and *Zeitoun* tell the story of men of color with no recognition in the text of how Eggers is connected to these narratives. Eggers effectively transforms the historically grounded white right to exclude into a new white right to include—that is, to transform the experiences of heroic racial others into universal tales of courage and endurance. Despite Eggers's stated desire to disappear in Deng's story of oppression and survival, his narrative framing exposes the insistently white underpinnings of his literary project.

The preface to *What Is the What* is the only section written by Deng, the ostensible narrator of the text that follows. Motivated by a desire to share his story with others, Deng describes how he met Eggers through a mutual associate. They developed a close relationship as Deng "told Dave what I knew and what I could remember, and from that material he created this work of art. It should be known to the readers that I was very young when some of the events in the book took place, and as a result we simply had to pronounce *What Is the What* a novel. I could not, for example, recount some conversations that took place seventeen years ago. However it should be noted that all of the major events in the book are true" (xiv). Much of what Deng states about his experiences and memory is also true of the substance that Eggers shaped into narrative form in *AHWOSG*. Nonetheless, while the latter was deemed a memoir, *What Is the What* must be called a novel. A *Washington Post* reporter described Eggers's decision to fictionalize Deng's story as a way to "solve narrative problems. By labeling the book a novel, Eggers says, he freed himself to re-create conversations, streamline complex relationships, add relevant detail and manipulate time and space in helpful ways—all while maintaining the essential truthfulness of the storytelling."[5] However, as Lee Siegel notes, all of these solutions to narrative problems were also used in *AHWOSG*.[6] Why then must the account of Deng's life be considered fiction even as the artistic license that Eggers adopted in his memoir remains within the blurry boundaries of truth?

This shift in genre designation may reflect the insistent expectations of truth assigned to memoirs generally. Only three years prior to the publication of *What Is the What*, James Frey was excoriated in the national media for fabricating parts of *A Million Little Pieces* (2003), a book initially labeled a memoir. Eggers's decision to fictionalize Deng's story may thus be read as a kind of preemptive strategy, a way to avoid endless nitpicking over the facts in order to place greater emphasis on the truth of Deng's suffering. Citing Philippe Lejeune, who argues that when reading fiction, the reader seeks resemblances to the author but looks for differences in autobiography, Michelle Peek claims that identifying *What Is the What* as fiction paradoxically "enables Eggers and Deng to elicit a more believing reader response" (120). Casting aside the expectations of factual truth, readers are able to immerse themselves in the text free of the critical gaze that has unraveled many allegedly autobiographical texts. Such an emphasis on reader response is consistent with the explicitly political goal of *What Is the What.* In the preface, Deng explains that he collaborated with Eggers because "I wanted the world to know the whole truth of my existence . . . I wanted to reach out to others to help them understand Sudan's place in our global community" (xiii–xiv). Though Deng emphasizes the importance of communicating "the whole truth of my existence," the audience he covets requires that he sacrifice this very truth for the popular artistry of Eggers.

Despite the well-intentioned rhetorical strategies of *What Is the What,* Eggers's fictionalization of Deng's story also signifies in other, more problematic ways. There is a political cost to "elicit[ing] a more believing reader response" when that belief is based on a fiction based on a fact and is further mediated through significant but repressed differences of race and class. For many readers, there was no distinction between these confused layers of meaning and invention. Writing in the *New York Times Book Review,* Francine Prose promised that after reading *What Is the What*: "You know precisely who the boys were because you have experienced their mass migration and the mass murder that occasioned it through their eyes, and in the compelling voice, of Valentino Achak Deng. By the time the members of Eggers's large and youthful fan base have repeatedly consulted the book's map of East Africa, tracing the Lost Boys' wanderings, they will be able to visualize the geographical positions of Sudan, Ethiopia and Kenya with a clarity surpassing their possibly hazy recall of anything they might have memorized for a World Civilization class." Prose presumes that the voice of the book is Deng's, while only the audience or "fan base" belongs to Eggers. As such, *What Is the What* emerges as a wonderful confluence of authorial assets: Deng has the compelling, educational story, and Eggers has the "large and youthful fan base." The result is a book that bridges an enormous divide by making what would have been a Lost Boy's lost voice into a best seller that, as Prose notes, "make[s] us painlessly absorb a hefty dose of (in several senses of the word) hard information."

The education of ignorant Americans concerning the geographical position of East African countries is certainly a worthy endeavor, but it is a mistake to assume that the voice of *What Is the What* belongs to Deng and that reading the book automatically confers the experience it recounts onto its readers. Instead, as Siegel observes, "Eggers's voice is all over the book," especially at moments of horrific violence such as the first time Valentino sees his father attacked. Siegel notes that such incidents prompt the use of multiple metaphors rather than a direct confrontation of the brutality Deng witnessed.[7] Eggers had originally planned to write a conventional biography chronicling Deng's life but later decided that he "didn't want my own voice in there." After consulting with Deng, Eggers chose to write from the first-person perspective, effectively taking Deng's voice as his own.

Elizabeth Twitchell claims that while Eggers "is perceptible and invisible in every sentence" (639), what ultimately emerges "is the voice of Valentino, a resolutely fictional construction and narrator of the novel" (638).[8] For Twitchell, *What Is the What* is a "work of determined self-erasure" (637). One might read this narrative approach as a fulfillment of Sarah Ahmed's injunction to whites "to turn away from themselves, and towards others." Eggers certainly turns away from his own story to write about Deng's life, but in so doing, he fails in what Ahmed describes as "the task for white subjects . . . to stay implicated in what they critique." Eggers turns so fully away from himself in the creation of *What Is the What* that his absence becomes the mark not of empathetic connection but of uncritical escape. His narrative approach resonates with George Lipsitz's observation that "whiteness never has to speak its name, never has to acknowledge its role as an organizing principle in social and cultural relations" (369). Self-erasure is not a neutral position but instead seeks to hide the inescapable subjectivity of that self, including its racialized investments. Or as Toni Morrison reminds us, "The world does not become raceless or will not become unracialized by assertion. The act of enforcing racelessness in literary discourse is itself a racial act" (*Playing in the Dark* 46).

Valentino's first encounter with a white man highlights this uneasy relationship between Eggers's subjectivity and the aim of self-erasure. While a young boy at the Pinyudo refugee camp, Valentino joins a group of boys to see the mysterious white man: "I followed their stares and saw what seemed to be a man who had been turned inside out. He was the absence of a man. He had been erased" (279). After nearly three hundred pages, the self-referential voice of *AHWOSG* at last emerges. The white man whom Valentino spies provides a direct correlation to the erased man Eggers wishes to become in *What Is the What*. Valentino is so taken by the sight of "the erased man" that he forgets to pull his pants up after urinating. This small, novelistic detail (which I venture to claim Deng did not himself recall) suggests that in front of the white man, Valentino can be entirely naked because he is encountering not another man but only "the absence of a man." Absence does not judge our naked, vulnerable selves because absence is just absence.

Did Deng understand Eggers to be another "erased man"—a man in whose presence, or shall we say absence, he can safely forget to pull his pants up? This is not a question answered by *What Is the What* because Deng's voice does not exist in the narrative. Instead the erased man figures as Eggers's idealized construction of himself. The erased man is the one who can channel Deng and place readers in scenes the author has never seen. But transforming this literal figure into a rhetorical device underscores the paradoxes at play throughout the text. For the erased man to be truly erased, he would no longer be a man. Eggers may want and believe that he has disappeared from the book, but the white man Valentino sees is not erased at all. Valentino only perceives him to be erased just as Eggers wants readers to understand him as similarly absent. This symbolic figure reminds us how Valentino's story exists only because of the erased man, only because of Eggers. However, just as the author of *What Is the What* cannot be fully erased, the text also depends on an audience that leaves its imprint on the narrative being told. Readers are not absent but constructed by a narrative that seeks to make whiteness invisible while, as I subsequently explain, denigrating the blackness of African Americans.

The "erased" man in *What Is the What* affirms the impossibility of Eggers's narrative ambition in the book. He cannot disappear and by meticulously constructing his own absence, he only reifies the insistent nature of his presence. This presence is made explicit in the narrative framing of the novel. The book begins with a knock on the door. Valentino, alone in his apartment, answers the door and welcomes in "a tall, sturdily built African-American woman" (3) who asks to use the phone because her car broke down. An African American man brandishing a gun then enters the apartment and orders Valentino to sit down. As Valentino lies bound and gagged, he begins to narrate his story, often directing his life experiences at the people he encounters as a result of the break-in. Many critics have praised the dual narratives of the novel. Peek and Twitchell both argue that the robbery of Valentino's Atlanta home unsettles a simplistic narrative of redemption by demonstrating how the United States is a land beset by violence and unfulfilled promises. However, the narrative frame also reflects Eggers's own racialized anxieties as well as the limits of his imagination.

The African American man who beats Valentino and ties him up is another iteration of the man Eggers describes fearing in *AHWOSG*: "a black man in an army jacket, the man I always picture when imagining being killed in such a way" (386). By his own admission, this is a man Eggers has often envisioned, though he has never actually encountered him. This, unlike the violence inflicted on Deng's father, is violence Eggers can imagine. The scenes describing the break-in have an intensity and emphasis on physical detail lacking in Valentino's description of his Sudanese experiences: "The back of my head hits the end table on the way earthward and two glasses and a clock radio fall with me. Once on the carpet, my cheek resting in its own pooling blood, I know a moment of comfort, thinking that in all likelihood he is finished" (7). Although Valentino suffers starvation, exhaustion, and accidental injury, nowhere else in the text is he presented as physically attacked by another person. Valentino reflects, "In my life I have been struck in many different ways but never with the barrel of a gun . . . I have been beaten with sticks, with rods, with brooms and stones and spears" (7). Although Valentino and presumably Deng have suffered numerous physical attacks, the incident with the two African American burglars takes on a marked singularity. Readers are never privy to the moments in Valentino's life in which he is beaten by those other objects. In a novel that describes the horrors of the Sudanese Civil War, the most intimate portrait of human cruelty involves African American assailants.

Valentino is physically tied up through the first section of the book. During this time, he provides a patient, sweeping account of his cross country journey on foot to Ethiopia. Eggers interweaves the two narratives by having Valentino address for hundreds of pages his captors, first the African American man with a gun he calls "Powder" and then a young boy, nicknamed "TV Boy," left to guard him. Eggers explains that he was inspired to use this form of address after a conversation with Deng: "We had been talking about the small indignities he'd experienced taking the bus around Atlanta, trying to get to work. He had been pushed, ignored, disrespected. And each time he would think, silently, 'If only that person knew what I'd already been through. . . .' He would direct his thoughts to whoever had treated him less than humanely, and hope for a day when his story was known far and wide, and that perhaps then his sufferings small and great would end."[9] This notion, that by telling his story to others they will value and respect him, is also expressed by Valentino in the book's first chapter. "When I first came to this country, I would tell silent stories. I would tell them to people who had wronged me. . . . I would glare at them, staring, silently hissing a story to them. *You do not understand,* I would tell them. *You would not add to my suffering if you knew what I have seen*" (29). Valentino effectively describes his ideal reader in this passage—someone who once learning his story will treat him with the care and attention he deserves. As such, the book is structured through Valentino's address to the various people he encounters in *What Is the What*. Importantly, he directs his story primarily to African American characters, first Powder and his female partner Tonya, then TV Boy and finally Julian, an emergency room attendant. Although Valentino also addresses his Christian neighbors and the clientele at the gym, only the black characters are repeatedly invoked.

Having established clear expectations for his ideal audience, Valentino finds his African American addressees clearly lacking. Looking at Powder and Tonya, Valentino concludes, "They know nothing about me, and I wonder if, knowing about my journey here, they would alter the course they've taken against me. I do not expect they would" (21–22). Valentino projects this hopelessness only on his two adult African American attackers as if they are beyond redemption; even if they hear his story, they will not be moved by it. This admission suggests that African Americans like Powder and Tonya are beyond the grasp of his story. This pessimism is conspicuously not directed toward the middle- to upper-class white gym clientele that Valentino also addresses.

Valentino is eventually rescued by his roommate who takes him to the emergency room. He is checked in by an African American man named Julian, who along with TV Boy is his primary addressee. Waiting for hours, Valentino becomes frustrated and again remembers the hardships he has had to endure. "Does this interest you, Julian? You seem to be well informed and of empathetic nature, though your compassion surely has a limit. You hear my story of being attacked in my own home, and you shake my hand and look into my eyes and promise treatment to me, but then I wait" (250). Unlike the other people Valentino has addressed, Julian knows some of his story. Although he is not aware of Valentino's experiences fleeing Sudan, he at least recognizes how Valentino has been injured by the break-in and even empathizes, having once been attacked by two teenagers. Nonetheless, Julian proves to be an inadequate audience. He does not help Valentino as the latter would like and seems to distance himself from the entire situation: "Julian leaves me on the bed, pulling the curtain, attached to a track on the ceiling, around my area of the room. I have little doubt that Julian would prefer having me here, where he does not have to see me" (316).

Despite the failures of Valentino's African American listeners, the book ends with his promise to continue telling his stories regardless of those who will not hear him: "I will tell stories to people who will listen and to people who don't want to listen, to people who seek me out and to those who run. All the while I will know that you are there. How can I pretend that you do not exist? It would be almost as impossible as you pretending that I do not exist" (535). As Twitchell notes, this final appeal acknowledges Eggers's presence as well as that of the reader (642). Although Valentino asks, "How can I pretend that you do not exist?" he has spent the entire book doing exactly that, pretending that Eggers does not exist and instead directing his story at people who cannot adequately hear him. He concludes, "It would be almost as impossible as you pretending that I do not exist" when in fact Valentino does not exist. Even if we read the "you" of this passage as the general reader, we are led to paradoxes of meaning. In this case, Valentino is simply addressing the reader, the reader whose existence shapes the genesis of the story. We are reminded that this is not a book written for Valentino or for Deng; it is written for those who do not know or understand his story. Valentino cannot pretend that his audience does not exist because he has been conjured precisely for that audience. And yet that audience pretends

Valentino is real. Reminding us of the pretenses involved in the creation of Valentino's voice, the ending is a knot of truth and meaning, of staged performance and genuine appeal.

However, one conclusion remains clear amid these paradoxes. Valentino's assertion that he will tell his stories to people who will not listen and may even run away from him establishes a clear dichotomy between those failed listeners and the "you" who gives him tremendous comfort: "It gives me strength, almost unbelievable strength, to know that you are there" (535). Ultimately, Eggers figures as both the you and the ideal audience for this story. He has heard the story and been moved to action. Because of his help, millions of dollars have been generated for the Valentino Achak Deng Foundation. However, if the redemptive value of the book is in modeling engaged reading and social practice, we cannot dismiss the fact that as an exemplary white reader, Eggers is also the social opposite of all those failed African American listeners populating the book.

ISHMAEL BEAH'S *A LONG WAY GONE*

For slave narratives to operate effectively, their authors had to align their stories with the cultural and social values of their readers. Harriet Jacobs called on women of the North to empathize with slave mothers, tapping into nineteenth-century beliefs about the sanctity of the mother-child bond. Eggers similarly enjoins white readers of *What Is the What* to sympathize with Valentino by invoking stereotypes of black American criminality. Beah's *A Long Way Gone* dispenses with the overtly racialized assumptions of *What Is the What* to find commonality with its middle-class Western readers through nostalgic overtures to a lost past.

Beah structures his memoir through an idealized notion of childhood rampant in contemporary American culture. However, as Bernstein claims, in American culture childhood is "raced white" and is "characterized by the ability to retain racial meanings but hide them under claims of holy obliviousness" (8). Beah's adamant claim to innocence despite his involvement in war crimes aligns him with a form of whiteness that involves "not merely an absence of knowledge, but an active state of repelling knowledge" (6). Beah describes how the civil war in Sierra Leone deprived him and his friends of their innocence and an idyllic youth full of American pop references. Though he admits to participating in wartime atrocities, Beah finds redemption in a return to childhood that absolves him of his crimes. However, as Jacqueline Rose reminds us, the "glorification of the child" represents "not only a refusal to acknowledge difficulties and contradictions in relation to childhood; it implies that we use the image of the child to deny those same difficulties in relation to ourselves" (8). Beah's overly romantic conception of the child obscures his responsibility in various war crimes while validating a key American mythology concerning racialized childhood innocence.

Beah begins his memoir with a short section titled "New York City, 1998" that establishes his relationship to his ideal readers:

> My high school friends have begun to suspect I haven't told them the full story of my life.
>
> "Why did you leave Sierra Leone?"
>
> "Because there is a war."
>
> "Did you witness some of the fighting?"
>
> "Everyone in the country did."
>
> "You mean you saw people running around with guns and shooting each other?"
>
> "Yes, all the time."
>
> "*Cool.*"
>
> I smile a little.
>
> "You should tell us about it sometime."
>
> "Yes, sometime." (3)

The text that follows is Beah's account of why he left Sierra Leone. Though it hardly amounts to "the full story of my life," it does provide a vivid description of "people running around with guns and shooting each other." Beah's limited response to his friends' questions suggests that he understands them to be more interested in the prurient details of his experience than in a thoughtful consideration of the trauma he endured and perpetuated. Although the story he tells is effectively a fulfillment of their request to "tell us about it sometime," his book is not for these nosy classmates easily impressed by the power of a gun. Instead Beah directs his book to readers who will not trivialize violence enacted by and on children. His evasive response to his friends further positions the reader as his true and special confidant. While his classmates prove undeserving of his story, the worldly, sensitive reader of *A Long Way Gone* is presumably far more mature and discerning. By contrast, Beah's high school friends are children themselves, quick to glorify violence and to assume that to be in a war is to act as an eager witness, not an unwilling participant. This is not a book for children, Beah reminds us, even as he rightfully belongs among such innocent classmates. This opening passage highlights the central tension of the text: how Beah is both a child and fundamentally estranged from children. The memoir depends on his ability to cultivate sympathy through the loss of his childhood, and yet the horrific nature of his experiences repudiates any simplistic claim to innocence.

The first chapter of *A Long Way Gone* positions the reader as a surrogate for Beah. He begins by stating, "There were all kinds of stories told about the war that made it sound as if it was happening in a faraway and different land" (5). This is precisely how an American reader with little understanding of the history of Sierra Leone would understand the war that gripped the nation at the end of the twentieth century. Just as Beah perceives the conflict as "happening in a faraway and different land," Americans easily distance themselves from the complexities of African politics and history. Beah places himself as far removed from such violence as his Western readers, confessing, "At times I thought that some of the stories the passersby told were exaggerated." If Beah's tales of casual violence and wanton torture are too sadistic to be believed, he suggests that he too was initially skeptical of such horrors. His only understanding of war is derived from what he "had read about in books or seen in movies such as *Rambo: First Blood*." Beah's reference to Sylvester Stallone's iconic action hero again links him to a distinctly American audience. He too has been raised on Hollywood images in which war involves a righteous rebel pitted against nefarious villains. Violence is the stuff of blockbuster images, imported from the United States, rather than native to his African homeland.

Beah describes a childhood steeped in American popular culture. As an eight-year-old boy, he started a rap and dance group with three of his friends. He learned to do "the running man" while listening to the Sugarhill Gang and Eric B. & Rakim. Like any young fan of rap music, he adopts phrases like "Peace, son" and "I'm out" (7) and takes special care of his sneakers, or what he calls *crapes*. In fact, the first time he "was touched by war" was during a journey to the neighboring town of Mattru Jong to perform with his rap group in a talent show. On the morning after their arrival, Beah and his friends learn that their hometown of Mogbwemo has been attacked by rebels. Stunned by the news, Beah notes, "The day seemed oddly normal. The sun peacefully sailed through the white clouds, birds sang from treetops, the trees danced to the quiet wind. I still couldn't believe that the war had actually reached our home" (10). Beah begins to understand what has happened only when he and his friends begin the sixteen-mile journey back to their home village. Along the way, they encounter women who "screamed the names of their children" and "children walking by themselves, shirtless, in their underwear, following the crowd. '*Nya nje oo, nya keke oo*,' my mother, my father, the children were crying." Beah's emphasis on the impact the war has on children typifies his descriptions of violence throughout his memoir. When he arrives at his grandmother's village, he encounters such gruesome sights that "people covered the eyes of their children" (12). But there is no one to shield Beah from images of dead girls and boys or of a woman carrying her bullet-riddled baby.

Beah and his friends are so overwhelmed by what they see that they return to Mattru Jong rather than continue home. While they decide what to do next, the boys "listened to rap music, trying to memorize the lyrics so that we could avoid thinking about the situation at hand. Naughty by Nature, LL Cool J, Run-D.M.C., and Heavy D & The Boyz; we had left home with only these cassettes and the clothes that we wore" (15). Beah's focus on rap music as a means of escape reminds readers that his involvement in the dance group ultimately saved him from the massacre that occurred in his village. Suddenly exiled from his home, Beah bears with him not a memento of his family or native culture but artifacts of American popular culture. The cassettes, which he carries for several years, become less a reminder of home than a promise of his future identification as an American. Moreover, on two other occasions, the cassettes save the lives of Beah and his friends by acting as proof of the boys' juvenile interests. The cassettes, items that have long been made obsolete in the United States by iPods and streaming services, invoke a certain nostalgia for Beah's adult readers. In this way, he taps into the childhood of his target audience who may align their own memories of treasured mixtapes with Beah's passion for rap music.

Beah closes his harrowing first chapter with his thoughts on an old village adage: "We must strive to be like the moon" (16). His grandmother explains that while too much rain or sun can cause problems, no one complains about the moon. Instead, people always delight in its light. Intrigued by his grandmother's comments, Beah develops a penchant for gazing at the moon and finding different shapes in its contours: "Some nights I saw the head of a man. He had a medium beard and wore a sailor's hat. Other times I saw a man with an ax chopping wood, and sometimes a woman cradling a baby at her breast. Whenever I get a chance to observe the moon now, I still see those same images I saw when I was six, and it pleases me to know that that part of my childhood is still embedded in me" (17). Beah insists that despite everything he has seen and done, a part of him remains a child. He can always return to this childhood activity and remember the boy that he was. However, it bears noting that Beah's admiration for the moon stems in part from its mutability, its ability to contain multiple images simultaneously. In the same way, throughout his memoir, Beah balances different, even contradictory selves. He is both a child and a man, a victim and a victimizer. He has indeed followed his grandmother's advice and become like the moon, though not because of its benign light; instead, by adopting its variable face, he projects a shifting sense of self.

Beah's sharpest transformation occurs when he is conscripted into the Sierra Leonean government army. This life-changing event is marked by the destruction of his beloved cassettes. Beah loses his rap tapes when he is forced to become a soldier: "As I was putting on my new army shorts, a soldier took my old pants and threw them into a blazing fire that had been set to burn our old belongings. I ran toward the fire, but the cassettes had already started to melt. Tears formed in my eyes, and my lips shook as I turned away" (110). This event inaugurates Beah's new identity as a child soldier. He is given an AK-47, which he is too afraid to even look at. While the cassettes protected Beah by linking him to the youthful activities of dancing and singing as well as to American popular culture, his gun symbolizes a frightening future.

Like his fellow soldiers, Beah relies on marijuana and *brown brown*, a mixture of cocaine and gunpowder, to numb him to the violence of his life. He also mentions that at night he watches American war movies, including *Rambo: First Blood*, *Rambo II*, and *Commando*, noting, "We all wanted to be like Rambo; we couldn't wait to implement his techniques" (121). The combination of movies and drugs completely desensitizes Beah to death as his life becomes almost inseparable from the screen images: "We were always either at the front lines, watching a war movie, or doing drugs. There was no time to be alone or to think. When we conversed with each other, we talked only about the war movies and how impressed we were with the way either the lieutenant, the corporal, or one of us had killed someone. It was as if nothing else existed outside our reality" (124). Although Rambo had previously been invoked to highlight Beah's separation from the experience of war, the movie becomes a model for him to emulate. His life is so otherworldly that only fiction can provide a meaningful corollary.

This passage also demonstrates an important rhetorical development in Beah's memoir. Rather than use the first-person pronoun, Beah adopts the collective "we" when describing his life as a soldier. This strategy defuses any individual responsibility for the lives Beah destroyed during his time as a soldier while also making him representative of an entire population. The use of the "we" is especially significant once Beah moves from the army to Benin Home, a UNICEF camp populated by other former child soldiers. Although at Benin Home Beah is free from his commanders and the mandate to kill, he continues to resort to violence: "In the morning, we beat up people from the neighborhood who were on their way to fetch water at a nearby pump. If we couldn't catch them, we threw stones at them. . . . We would fight for hours in between meals, for no reason at all" (139). Beah is unable or unwilling to separate himself from the group as if his actions are not his own but part of an overwhelming collective force that he cannot control alone. Beah becomes a victim to this "we," his individual humanity submerged by the weight of others. These senseless attacks against innocent villagers are in part fueled by Beah's drug withdrawal, but they also signal the loss of his unique voice.

Beah can return to his child self only by separating from the other boys. This transformation is consistent with the development of the self presented in antebellum slave narratives. Writers like Douglass and William Wells Brown needed to distinguish themselves as unique voices endowed with the individuality and initiative prized by their white readers. For Beah, this process begins when he goes to the hospital after punching a glass window with his fist. There he meets a nurse who tends to his hand. Beah notes that the nurse "twisted her face whenever she was removing a piece of glass that was buried deep in my skin. But when she looked at me, I was still. She searched my face to see if I was in pain. She was confused, but continued to gently remove the pieces of glass from my bleeding hand. I didn't feel a thing" (141). The nurse models the kind of affective response that Beah should have. Overwhelmed by his experiences, he has fallen into a functional numbness. The nurse tries to engage him by asking his name and wiping his forehead, but Beah resists these overtures. Recognizing their dynamic as familial, he describes her as responding to him "the way a mother would talk to a stubborn child." However, Beah again resists her care by throwing a glass of water she offers against the wall.

Esther, the nurse, finally persuades Beah to trust her in part by giving him a Walkman and a cassette of rap music. These presents return Beah to his innocent youth, but for Esther, these items are strategic since they sufficiently calm him so that she can examine his body. Esther removes Beah's headphones when she sees bullet wound scars on his legs. Esther's questions about the injury provide readers with one of the most sustained descriptions of Beah's experiences as a soldier. He explains how he was shot during an ambush and underwent surgery without anesthesia in order to remove the bullets. This disturbing incident concludes with Beah and his squad killing the men they believe responsible for the attack. "I am not sure if one of the captives was the shooter, but any captive would do at that time. So they were all lined up, six of them, with their hands tied. I shot them on their feet and watched them suffer for an entire day before finally shooting them in the head so that they would stop crying. Before I shot each man, I looked at him and saw how his eyes gave up hope and steadied before I pulled the trigger. I found their somber eyes irritating" (159). For the first time, Beah employs the first-person pronoun to describe the violence he inflicted on others. Here he is not simply obeying the commands of his superiors. Instead, he appears to be in control of the torture the captives suffer, deciding on the nature of their pain and its duration. His "irritation," a remarkably mild word that masks the rage and despair at the heart of the scene, at their "somber eyes" illustrates the extent of Beah's moral decay. He is not just a scared, submissive soldier; he is a calculated murderer.

Esther reacts by negating the very responsibility that makes this passage so notable. She tells Beah, "None of what happened was your fault. You were just a little boy." Beah is enraged by Esther's comment and immediately regrets telling her anything. Her response anticipates the failure of other Africans to listen to Beah's story and recognize his role in his wartime atrocities. The uncle who eventually welcomes Beah into his home insists that his war years never be mentioned. He tells Beah, "I told only my wife about your past life as a soldier. I kept it secret from my children. I don't think they will understand now as my wife and I do. I hope it is okay with you" (176). Beah's uncle suggests that for his children to remain children, they must remain ignorant of his nephew's experiences.

Beah is somewhat relieved by his uncle's decision but worries that his migraines, nightmares, and sadness will betray him. These physiological responses indicate that Beah suffers from posttraumatic stress disorder. Cathy Caruth explains that trauma is characterized by "the literal return of the event against the will of the one it inhabits" (5). Beah is haunted by his war memories, and hiding his pain only exacerbates his anxiety. Despite the severity of his symptoms, Beah's worries are never resolved as he describes only happy encounters with his new siblings. However, he admits to wanting to tell his uncle more: "I felt he knew that I wanted to tell him certain things but couldn't find the right words" (190). Similarly, when Beah is visited by one of the staff members from the center, he wishes he could confess his true feelings: "I wanted to tell him that I had had one severe migraine wherein the image of a burning village flashed in my mind, followed by wailings of many voices; that I had felt the back of my neck tighten and my head become heavy, as if a huge rock had been placed on it. Instead I told him only that everything was fine" (184–185).

Beah's inability to express his trauma suggests a fundamental fissure in his relationships with other Africans. Although he appears to enjoy life with his uncle's family, Beah must mask his true self before them. This dynamic validates the role of his Western audience, for as Naomi Morgenstern reminds us, "trauma sufferers need to have their testimonies witnessed" (105). Like Deng in *What Is the What*, Beah is surrounded by black witnesses who prove unable to hear his story. Only readers of *A Long Way Gone* are trusted with Beah's anguish and anxiety. In this way, the memoir becomes a testimony, uniting it to what Henry Louis Gates Jr. has identified as an important "black rhetorical trope" (52). However, this is a testimony directed specifically outside Beah's family and home culture. Beah's uncle and other family members are failed listeners who cannot bear the truth of his pain. By contrast, Western readers offer the possibility of meaningful witness to Beah's story.

Only by leaving his family and their need for his silence can Beah begin to heal from his past and recognize the experiences that shaped him. Much to the surprise of his uncle, Beah travels to New York City to take part in a conference involving children from various war-torn nations. Beah delights in hearing their stories, sharing his own, and thinking through ways to end child soldiering. At the U.N. Economic and Social Council (ECOSOC) chamber, Beah deviates from his prepared speech, deciding "to speak from my heart, instead." His candid discussion of his past can occur only in this American venue, away from his family and home country. Before the United Nations and his Western readers, Beah is free to express himself. His foreign audience offers a kind of narrative liberation for him, allowing him to share his experiences and begin the process of healing possible through storytelling. Beah affirms the importance of his Western audience at the end of his trip to America: "I was sad to leave, but I was also pleased to have met people outside of Sierra Leone. Because if I was to get killed upon my return, I knew that a memory of my existence was alive somewhere in the world" (200). Beah's comments imply that his memory exists only outside of Sierra Leone. In his home country, there is no trace of his existence because there his story has not been told. The U.N. conference and his American hosts are the sources of his legacy. This formulation further validates the role of his readers in honoring and preserving his experiences. While his family and countrymen cannot hear and accept his story, the Western readers of *A Long Way Gone* promise to keep Beah's memory alive.

EMMANUEL JAL'S *WAR CHILD*

While both *What Is the What* and *A Long Way Gone* exhibit rhetorical strategies emblematic of nineteenth-century slave narratives, Emmanuel Jal's *War Child: A Child Soldier's Story* suggests a deliberate reimagining of Douglass's 1845 narrative. *War Child* echoes many of Douglass's most famous scenes, positioning Jal as a contemporary version of America's most famous slave narrator. Jal begins his memoir by invoking the longing for literacy that structures Douglass's narrative trajectory.

> I was a child of war, born in a land without books and writing, a land where history was carried on your mother's tongue and in the songs of your village, a land swallowed up by war even as I uttered my first cry. And so, even the date of my birth was lost when my world was lost to me.... Like other Lost Boys of Sudan, I took the birth day of January 1, 1980, as an adult and have used it for the ages contained in this book. I cannot be sure exactly how old I was nor for how long I was in certain places or exactly when.

Jal's striking preface offers a troubling description of his home country. It is not clear if Sudan is inherently "a land without books and writing," steeped instead in a rich oral tradition or if war has extinguished literacy and the pleasures of reading at the time of Jal's birth. This indeterminacy plays into Western stereotypes of Africa as hopelessly primitive and ever besieged by violent conflict. Mimicking the quest for literacy that defines so many antebellum slave narratives, Jal's memoir culminates in his ascendance to international fame as a rap lyricist and performer. Just as Douglass used literacy as a symbol of his freedom and intellectual promise, Jal describes how rap music enables him to tell his story and claim his unique voice.

Jal's preface also echoes the opening of Douglass's 1845 narrative, which famously begins:

> I was born in Tuckahoe, near Hillsborough, and about twelve miles from Easton, in Talbot county, Maryland. I have no accurate knowledge of my age, never having seen any authentic record containing it. By far the larger part of the slaves know as little of their ages as horses know of theirs, and it is the wish of most masters within my knowledge to keep their slaves thus ignorant. I do not remember to have ever met a slave who could tell of his birthday. They seldom come nearer to it than planting-time, harvest-time, cherry-time, spring-time, or fall-time. A want of information concerning my own was a source of unhappiness to me even during childhood. The white children could tell their ages. I could not tell why I ought to be deprived of the same privilege. (12)

Like Douglass, Jal states that he does not know his birth date because the war destroyed his relationship to standard notions of time. For both writers, the inability to know their actual ages represents a break with basic social structures; they quite literally exist outside of time. For Douglass, this lack of knowledge marks a key difference between him and the free white children he observes. Knowledge of his age is one of the privileges of freedom, and thus his ignorance of his own indelibly marks him as a slave. Jal, however, has no point of comparison; for him, there is no corollary to the white children Douglass encounters. This absence helps to contextualize his relationship to others in his position. He explains that all of the Lost Boys of Sudan are, like him, unaware of their age, and therefore they choose January 1, 1980, as their collective birthday. This date has special resonance for those familiar with slave narratives and the history of the antebellum period in the United States. John Henry Hill explains that January 1 was "the great annual sale day" (109) in which slaves were auctioned in city squares throughout towns and cities in the South. Although the Lost Boys hardly chose January 1 to coincide with this date in American history, the coincidence is a reminder of how present experiences invoke and revise the past across the broad African diaspora.

Douglass ends the first chapter of his autobiography with his now infamous description of the whipping endured by his Aunt Hester. After being caught with a neighboring slave, his aunt is brutally flailed by her master. Though Douglass does not directly describe the nature of his master's interest in Aunt Hester, he notes that she "was a woman of noble form, and of graceful proportions, having very few equals, and fewer superiors, in personal appearance, among the colored or white women of our neighborhood" (15). Douglass's reticence to definitively assert the sexual nature of his master's attraction to Hester is typical of antebellum slave narratives. Such an overt discussion of sexual matters would have alienated his readers. However, his description of the attack that follows indulges in especially graphic detail:

> Before he commenced whipping Aunt Hester, he took her into the kitchen, and stripped her from neck to waist, leaving her neck, shoulders, and back, entirely naked. He then told her to cross her hands, calling her at the same time a d—d b—h. After crossing her hands, he tied them with a strong rope, and led her to a stool under a large hook in the joist, put in for the purpose. He made her get upon the stool, and tied her hands to the hook. She now stood fair for his infernal purpose. Her arms were stretched up at their full length, so that she stood upon the ends of her toes. He then said to her, "Now, you d—d b—h, I'll learn you how to disobey my orders!" and after rolling up his sleeves, be commenced to lay on the heavy cowskin, and soon the warm, red blood (amid heart-rending shrieks from her, and horrid oaths from him) came dripping to the floor. I was so terrified and horror-stricken at the sight, that I hid myself in a closet, and dared not venture out till long after the bloody transaction was over. I expected it would be my turn next. It was all new to me. I had never seen any thing like it before. (15)

Saidiya V. Hartman reads this gruesome passage as a "primal scene" that acts as "an inaugural moment in the formation of the enslaved" (*Scenes of Subjection* 3). Violence is foundational to slave identity, though significantly Douglass stages this violence on the body of his aunt. He remains physically unharmed, a position that likens him to his readers. Just as his audience absorbs the horror of the scene through this disturbing description, Douglass serves as a witness to his aunt's abuse. He is less a victim here than a spectator of slavery's evils.

Within the opening pages of Jal's memoir, he too describes the abuse suffered by one of his aunts, a young woman only a few years older than him. He and his Aunt Sarah are sent by their elders to buy sugar. Along the way, they are accosted by a government soldier: "Fear rippled down my back. The soldier was carrying a G3 gun and wearing combat trousers. He was a Muslim. He hated our kind." The soldier then grabs Aunt Sarah despite Jal's protests and forces her inside a hut. Jal watches the scene through a mesh-covered window:

> But now I watched without a sound as the soldier pushed Sarah to the ground and hit her before taking off his belt and one of his boots. Without a word, he pulled down one side of his army trousers as he stood above her.
>
> "Open up," he screamed as she covered herself with her hands.
>
> Sarah didn't move and the soldier raised his belt above her. I heard the sharp crack of leather against soft skin as the belt came crashing down to whip her again

> and again. It was like watching a hyena snapping at a baby antelope. Sarah looked so afraid. But she was quiet when the soldier knelt down and pulled up the skirt she was wearing before pushing the long material over her face. (15)

Jal does not understand the violation that occurs in this scene, though he senses that Aunt Sarah would not want to see him spying on her. When he finally approaches her, she says nothing and he honors this silence: "I never spoke of that day either. Somehow I knew it was a secret to be kept between us, that something very wrong had happened" (16). As in Douglass's narrative, the abuse suffered by a woman serves as an initiation, introducing Jal to the violence and hatred that will govern so much of his life.

However, while Douglass is terrified by his aunt's shrieks, Jal is left "confused," uncertain why the soldier "cuddled Sarah instead of shooting her" (17). Jal's sexual innocence reminds readers that although he may be roughly the same age as Douglass when the ex-slave witnessed Aunt Hester's abuse, Jal is operating with a different set of associations concerning the nature of childhood. As in Beah's memoir, childhood is presented in sharp contrast to the war that soon consumes his country. Jal's inability to understand his aunt's rape suggests that the episode operates as a kind of failed primal scene. It does not induce the sheer terror that Aunt Hester's beating precipitated for Douglass. This representation highlights the uncertainty of Jal's evolving world. While chattel slavery institutionalized strict categories of slave and free, black and white, the war that eventually overtakes Sudan is not so easily understood. Jal's confusion affirms his own bewilderment at the chaos and violence that soon follows. Like Beah's use of his rap cassettes as a symbol of his innocence, Jal's inability to understand his aunt's rape locates him as far removed from the atrocities of war.

In fact, Jal comes to a full recognition of what happened to his Aunt Sarah only much later in the book when he participates in his first battle. Conscripted into the SPLA (Sudanese People's Liberation Army), Jal joins a group of boys attacking an Anyuak village. Armed with an AK-47, Jal is astounded by his new power: "Excitement snapped inside me as the women did as I said. I was a soldier, not a child. They must listen to me" (101). Defining himself as a soldier through his ability to command and terrorize women, Jal becomes the kind of man who violated his aunt. The scene is full of images of frightened women: Jal "screamed at a pregnant woman who sat wailing on the ground nearby." Later he orders an elderly woman to lie down. When she resists he "started hitting the old woman. Again and again I beat her until my arm hurt." Amid the chaos of the burning huts and crying people, Jal "could see big SPLA soldiers dragging a girl toward the bush. *Kun ke bom*. Her screams cut into me as a memory flickered inside of my aunt being dragged into a hidden place by a *jallaba* troop" (102). Unlike Beah, Jal establishes a direct connection between the horrors inflicted on his family members and the destruction he wreaks: "I was in charge now. We were beating the Anyuak. What had happened to my people was happening to these. Now, it was their men who were dead, their women who were afraid, their children who were crying" (103). Jal's declaration of responsibility offers a potent echo of Douglass's primal scene. Where Douglass acts as a powerless witness to his aunt's abuse, Jal is here transformed into an agent of violence. Although he does not commit rape, his participation in the attack affirms his transformation from innocent child to terrifying soldier. Unlike Beah, Jal does not shy away from the horrors he inflicted on others. Instead, he directly implicates himself in the terror that unraveled his country. His refusal to deflect blame onto others mirrors Douglass's confession that he was not merely "a witness" but a "participant" in Aunt Hester's whipping. Although he did not directly attack his aunt, Douglass indicts himself as part of a system that terrorizes and subjugates women.

Much like Douglass's 1845 narrative, *War Child* is uniquely concerned with notions of masculinity. Jal is continually reminded by his father and other authority figures that he must eschew womanly ways and be a man. When the war arrives in Jal's village, his father explains, "I know the life you are living now is not the same as it was in the city with sweets, sugar, and biscuits. But you have to understand that this is a struggle and you are a big boy now. You must not complain or cry. You are my soldier and must show your brothers and sisters what it is like to be a man" (39). Throughout *War Child*, manhood is linked to being a soldier. By contrast, to be a woman is to be a coward or a victim. Jal describes a soldier who is punished after running away from battle: "He was called Mary and made to behave like a woman—cooking, sitting with his legs closed, and wearing a skirt—as his friends laughed that 'she' was a good wife" (138). At no point does Jal question this gendered dichotomy. When he doubts his ability to fight, he reminds himself, "You can't be weak, a woman. . . . You're a soldier" (106).

Although Douglass's 1845 narrative does not denigrate women so explicitly, the text repeatedly invokes manhood as a cognate for freedom. Recalling his fight with Mr. Covey, which he identifies as "the turning-point in my career as a slave," Douglass explains, "It rekindled the few expiring embers of freedom, and revived within me a sense of my own manhood" (50). For Douglass, it is impossible to be both a man and a slave, or, as he explains, "a happy slave is an extinct man." The strength and power associated with manhood are impossible for the abject, nonresistant slave. If the whipping of Aunt Hester acts as his initiation into slavery, his confrontation with Covey restores him to manhood. He cautions readers, "You have seen how a man was made a slave; you shall see how a slave was made a man" (47). Jal is likewise extremely concerned with earning and asserting his manhood. He tells elder officers that he wants "to kill Arabs"

(145) and is eager to join the *jesh a mer*, or boy soldiers noted for their fierce bravery. Like Douglass, Jal links manhood to physical strength and the ability to combat his enemies. Though he comes to regret and hate many of the actions he committed while a soldier, Jal actively embraces his identity as a child soldier.

However, Jal's relationship to the SPLA leads to various forms of bondage; he is placed in a prison for disobeying orders and is forced to fight and kill when he is not even a teenager. Despite these traumas, Jal never attempts to deny or suppress his violent past. When he leaves Sudan and enters school in Nairobi, he does not revert to the child self that Beah insistently claims in *A Long Way Gone*. Beah allows himself to effectively pass among his uncle's children by never mentioning his war experiences and hiding his trauma from others. By contrast, Jal admits to "finding it difficult to concentrate and never catching up with the other children my age" (199). He affirms, "I knew I was different because I was a soldier," suggesting that his war experiences can never be separated from his core identity.

Beah's memoir closely mimics the transformation evident in Douglass's narrative, moving from a state of bondage and corruption to return to a fundamental humanity. Jal, however, offers a more complex journey that incorporates the identity he developed as a soldier into his efforts to stop the kind of violence he experienced as a child. He explains at the end of his memoir how he has redirected his efforts, fighting another kind of battle with new weapons: "I'm still a soldier, fighting with my pen and paper" (254). While Beah finds resolution only by returning to his identity as a child, Jal evolves beyond his child self. He actively resists imagining himself as a child or wallowing in nostalgia for his previous life. At the end of the memoir, Jal is reunited with one of his sisters, but he refrains from speaking too much about the past with her since to do so "would have taken me back to my childhood—a place to which I could never return" (231). For Jal, there is no catharsis as there is with Beah in telling his story. While *A Long Way Gone* positions the reader as a healing witness to the traumas Beah endured, Jal refuses such a tidy resolution. His writing is yet another kind of battle. As he explains, his individual story is less a personal burden than a collective responsibility he shoulders: "Everyone in my country has a story to tell, but I am telling mine to speak for all those who can't" (254). If Beah returns to childhood in part by distinguishing himself from other child soldiers, Jal adamantly maintains his group identity in order to continue fighting.

Rather than looking to the past for redemption, Jal focuses his energies on developing his music career and finding support for the Consolidation Association for Southern Sudanese Youth, a group he forms to better the lives of Lost Boys. Jal discovers that the perseverance he developed in his youth helps him become a more successful musician and antiwar spokesperson. When he encounters an obstacle in promoting his music, he explains, "But Lost Boys are good at finding ways around rocks in the road—we learned well as we fought for food and life in the camps—and we came up with a new plan" (228). Unlike Beah, Jal does not cordon off his war experiences. Instead, he transforms them into a strength, ever mindful of the guilt and hope that propel him to speak out against arms proliferation and the continued suffering in Sudan. Rather than escape into an idealized childhood, Jal incorporates the skills and insights he gleaned as a soldier into his life outside of Sudan. Noting that "childhood in Africa does not hold the same romance that it does in Europe and America" (256), Jal implicitly rejects using childhood as a resource of strength and wisdom. War remains for Jal a useful way of conceptualizing the work that he does, especially given the ongoing injustices in Sudan and more recently in Darfur. The war that defined so much of his life has not ended but only transformed onto other battlefields. Jal concludes his memoir not with his joyful reunion with his sister or with his astounding success as a rap star. Instead he observes, "Today poverty is what scares me—the poverty of my family, my people, and my country. I pray that one day we will not live on aid, because poverty is like a virus that torments you mentally and emotionally. It is a slow and painful death of hope, humiliating and degrading, a parasite that sucks life from everyone it touches. That is why the best investment is human life—either spiritually or physically" (257). Jal's concern for other forms of suffering beyond war links his memoir to the end of Harriet Jacobs's *Incidents in the Life of a Slave Girl*. While many slave narratives conclude with the triumph of emancipation or escape to the North, Jacobs ends her text with continued longing: "The dream of my life is not yet realized. I do not sit with my children in a home of my own. I still long for a hearthstone of my own, however humble" (201). Like Jal, Jacobs does not envision a simplistic end to her life's work. Rather, various forces of oppression and injustice abide, demanding continued vigilance and work from these authors. Readers are thus implicated in such efforts as both Jal and Jacobs implicitly urge their audiences to join their struggle for justice.

2 · UNCANNY REMEMORIES IN TEJU COLE'S *OPEN CITY*

Jal's invocation of Douglass's 1845 narrative represents one way of responding to Achille Mbembe's influential pronouncement in 2001 that there is "no African memory of slavery" (25). If slavery is "the great unspoken subject" in African discourse, then *War Child*'s signifyin(g) relationship to Douglass's classic text encourages a deeper consideration of how contemporary conditions in Sudan relate to the Atlantic slave trade. While we must be wary of simplistic conflations that dehistoricize modern-day conflicts, Jal's revision of Douglass's central tropes establishes a literary relationship that makes the memory of slavery part of the pan-African American consciousness. The memory of slavery, or rather its absence, is similarly foundational to Teju Cole's widely acclaimed first novel *Open City*, though in a radically different way. While Jal signifies on Douglass to highlight his own experience of captivity and bondage, Cole presents slavery and its historical afterlives through the uncanny. Julius, the text's Nigerian-born narrator, actively shuns racial identification even as he bears a deep awareness of American atrocities, especially those inflicted on black slaves and Native Americans. However, he keeps this knowledge at a studied remove from himself, which in turn allows him to cultivate a false sense of freedom and innocence.

Such a uniquely American sensibility reflects what Toni Morrison describes as one of the central aims of "literature of the United States"—that is, "the architecture of a *new white man*" (14–15). In *Playing in the Dark: Whiteness and the Literary Imagination* (1992), Morrison demonstrates how this figure of rugged individuality and bold entrepreneurship depends on the fabrication of an Africanist persona that reflects not the reality of black people but the desires and anxieties of its white creators. Referencing texts by Edgar Allan Poe, Willa

Cather, Ernest Hemingway, and many other nineteenth- and twentieth-century writers, Morrison reads figures of blackness and enslavement as the symbolic counterpoint to an idealized and ever innocent whiteness. The new white man of the American frontier exists only through the always abject Africanist presence. Morrison's reading of American literature suggests that identity operates through dichotomous opposition: the new white man relies on the black other to provide form and value.

Such neat binaries are complicated by twenty-first-century American texts that reflect more heterogeneous and transnational conceptions of identity. *Open City* typifies an American experience that is unbound by traditional notions of race, nation, and social mobility. Julius might be understood as a new black man, one who rejects the claims of race even as he remains uniquely aware of the country's history of racial oppression. Like Morrison's new white man, the cosmopolitan Julius prizes freedom and presumes his own innocence even when confronted with Moji's shocking allegation of sexual assault. However, his relationship to his own blackness as well as to the blackness of others transforms a simplistic desire for freedom into a struggle with America's fraught racial past. As a new black man, Julius reflects a new experience of both blackness and Americanness. Disconnected from the history of African Americans yet subject to the stereotypes and expectations associated with blackness, Julius occupies an unsettled place in America's racialized landscape.

A figure of postcolonial alterity, *Open City*'s protagonist is black without the history and community tied to American blackness. His almost obsessive wanderings through the city demonstrate the rootlessness of his particular racial experience. Michel de Certeau characterizes such movement as emblematic of a profound sense of dislocation: "To walk is to lack a place. It is the indefinite process of being absent and in search of a proper. The moving about that the city multiplies and concentrates makes the city itself an immense social experience of lacking a place" (103). Julius is, in many respects, defined by absence. He represses the past, shuns intimacy, avoids racial affiliations, and lacks a stable sense of home. Moreover, as a kind of postcolonial exile, Julius bears a vexed relationship to the United States. In his study of Homi K. Bhabha, David Huddart reminds us that the "post-colonial perspective is an uncanny one" (89). Uncanniness typifies the migrant experience by offering a model of doubling marked by difference.[1] As a black immigrant, Julius confronts such doubling on multiple levels. The novel is full of uncanny traces that define Julius as a man marked by repressions of all kinds.

Although *Open City* does not rely on the kind of racialized binary that Morrison identifies, it describes Julius as specifically haunted by the specter of African American history. If, for Morrison, the Africanist presence operates as "surrogate selves for meditation on problems of human freedom, its lure and elusiveness" (37), then in *Open City* Cole fashions what we might identify as an African Americanist presence. Like Morrison's Africanist presence, Cole figures African American characters and history as imbued with "the rhetoric of dread and desire" (64). Throughout the novel, Julius experiences American blackness as an encounter with the uncanny, a return of repressed memories that are both personal and historical. This link to the uncanny is best represented through his close relationship with his unnamed friend. Though he remains both anonymous and disembodied throughout the novel, Julius's friend is his most intimate confidant and sole source of stable support.

In the final chapters of the book, readers learn that this friend is African American. This revelation enriches the doubling that Cole establishes between these two characters. Julius's friend offers a complex set of possible futures for our solitary narrator. He possesses an acute understanding of American race relations, and more importantly, he cultivates deeper relationships with women. By presenting Julius and his friend as uncanny doubles, Cole reconfigures how we understand the national and racial investments of the text. Julius and his friend do not identify themselves as black, but blackness is clearly one of the most important commonalities between them. Haunted by African American history, Julius absorbs a racialized past he cannot escape even as he attempts to shun immediate claims to his racial identity. The uncanny represents his fraught relationship to race by foregrounding the repression at work in his limited self-conception.

JULIUS AND THE CLAIMS OF RACE

Introspective and enigmatic, Julius is best defined by his capacious cultural knowledge and his aloof approach to others. His self-containment is so pronounced that he often simulates friendliness and concern while masking a degree of irritation if not outright indifference toward strangers and acquaintances. The first chapter of the novel ends with Julius's discovery that a woman who lived with her husband in the apartment next door to him died months ago. Unnerved by the news and the awkward embarrassment of Seth, her widow, Julius is struck by the realization that he "had noticed neither her absence nor the change—there must have been a change—in his spirit." Though disturbed by his ignorance, he refuses to offer Seth comfort because such a gesture "would have been false intimacy." Instead, Julius enters his apartment, trying to recall if the last substantial interaction he had with his neighbors, in which Seth gently complained about the volume of Julius's music, occurred before or after the death of his wife. He concludes, "Eventually I satisfied myself that it was before, and not after, his wife's death. I felt a certain sense of relief at this, which was taken over almost immediately by shame. But even that feeling subsided; much too quickly, now that I think of it" (21).

Julius's recollection of this event establishes many of the central characteristics of this deeply observant but also deeply detached narrator. Throughout the novel, he rejects all those who would lay claim to his identity or sympathies. This is especially true of the African and African American characters he encounters who all, with the notable exception of his friend, expect some degree of solidarity or connection from him. These depictions present blackness as a form of neediness, an identity ever hungry for continued validation. Louis Chude-Sokei observes a striking contrast between the text's depiction of African Americans and its more engaged approach to a host of other individuals: "For a novel so deliberately worldly in its intellectual explorations and cross-cultural collisions, and so committed to the random interactions of multiple types of individuals emerging from interlacing diasporas, its curiously stand-offish relationship to black Americans is notable" (66). In fact, Julius's worldly cosmopolitanism depends on his deliberate detachment from all aspects of African American culture and history.

Julius treats almost all of the African Americans he meets with disdain, usually a form of quiet condescension that suggests his own intellectual superiority. While buying stamps, he meets a postal worker who asks, "Say, brother, where are you from?" Julius selects a booklet of stamps depicting quilts from Gee's Bend, Alabama, rather than a set involving flags. Julius's preference for the striking geometric quilts over symbols of nation-states highlights his cosmopolitan aesthetic. He admires the quilts for their beauty, not because they honor a particularly African American artistic tradition. Though he often provides detailed historical information about various communities or monuments he encounters, he is notably silent about the impoverished female quilt makers, suggesting a refusal to engage or even acknowledge this particular history. Despite this seeming indifference, the postal worker reads a racial meaning in Julius's selection as he says, "I know . . . I know, my brother." Assuming that a common understanding exists between them, the postal worker continues, "'Cause, see, I could tell you were from the Motherland. And you brothers have something that is vital, you understand me. You have something that is vital for the health of those of us raised on this side of the ocean. . . . Brother Julius, the thing is, you're a visionary. It's the truth. I can see that in you. You're someone who has traveled far. You're what we call a journeyer" (187). The postal worker then recites a poem he wrote called "The Unconquered" and invites Julius to the Nuyorican Poets Cafe. Julius replies, "Sure thing," but makes "a mental note to avoid that particular post office in the future" (188). Though the postal worker means to sincerely reach out to Julius, his idealized conception of his brother African reflects stereotypes that are as racist as they are romantic. Julius is no visionary, and though he has traveled far, he has no wisdom to share for "those of us raised on this side of the ocean."

This incident typifies Julius's response to African Americans throughout the novel. Though he does not directly criticize them, his silence suggests contempt for their attempts to forge some degree of racial solidarity. When a depressed World War II veteran tells him "with sudden emotion in his voice, Doctor, I just want to tell you how proud I am to come here, and see a young black man like yourself in that white coat, because things haven't ever been easy for us, and no one has ever given us nothing without a struggle" (210), Julius again falls silent. This usually voluble and thoughtful narrator has nothing to say about such racial appeals and gestures toward intimacy. Though Julius is not averse to speaking intimately with strangers as evident in his conversations with Dr. Maillotte and Farouq, he refuses to engage with people who approach him through the language of race. This extends to Africans as well. In one incident, Julius endures a bitter harangue from a black cabdriver who criticizes him for not acknowledging him when he enters the car. The driver exclaims, "Hey, I'm African just like you, why you do this? He kept me in his sights in the mirror. I was confused. I said, I'm so sorry about it, my mind was elsewhere, don't be offended, ehn, my brother, how are you doing? He said nothing, and faced the road. I wasn't sorry at all. I was in no mood for people who tried to lay claims on me" (40). Just as Julius lies to the postal worker about meeting later at the Nuyorican Poets Cafe, he tries to appease the cabdriver with a flimsy apology. These weak conciliatory gestures mask a deep well of emotion. Sitting in the cab while the driver listens to an irritating talk-radio show, Julius admits, "Anger had welled up within me, unhinging me, the anger of a shattered repose" (41). Julius indicts the cabdriver for destroying his repose, a repose built on the disavowal of racial commonality. Julius is most at ease when he does not have to confront the complications of race or consider himself a part of any community.

Such troubling disregard for racial affiliation is complicated by the one person in the narrative who Julius describes as a trusted source of support and counsel. This unnamed character is identified only as "my friend," and in a first read of the novel, it is difficult to discern if this term always refers to the same person. However, the scattered allusions to this character do cohere into a unified whole. Julius's friend is an assistant professor of earth sciences at Columbia University. In the first description of his friend, Julius notes,

> His interests were broader than his professional specialty suggested, and this was part of the basis for our friendship: he had strong opinions about books and films, opinions that often went against mine, and he had lived for two years in Paris, where he'd acquired a taste for fashionable philosophers like Badiou and

> Serres. In addition, he was an avid chess player, and an affectionate father to a nine-year-old girl who mostly lived with her mother on Staten Island. We both regretted that the demands of work kept us from spending as much time together as we would have liked. (23)

Julius identifies most of the people he encounters by their first name, but his closest friend remains anonymous throughout the novel. This absence is paralleled by Julius's failure to identify his friend racially. Although Julius often notes the race of the people he meets, nothing in this opening description clearly links his friend to a specific racial group. As in Julius's own self-presentation, intellectual activity and reading habits are the most important means of defining the self.

While the intensity of his friend's interest in the arts and humanities seems to match Julius's vast cultural knowledge, they differ in one important way. Unlike Julius, his friend is "especially passionate about jazz," a form of music that Julius finds "sweet . . . cloying even," though his friend promises that if he could only understand the difference between blues notes and swung notes "the heavens would part and my life would be transformed." As with his vague concern that his shame over his neighbor's death subsided too quickly, Julius suggests an uneasiness with his dislike of jazz. He admits that he "would even occasionally worry about why I seemed not to have a strong emotional connection with this most American of musical styles" (24). As with the earlier scene involving his recently widowed neighbor, Julius recognizes that he should have a stronger intuitive or emotional response; he should be moved by the passing of Seth's wife just as he should be impressed by jazz music. Julius does not explain why jazz should inspire him—because it is a complex art form with a fascinating, uniquely American history? Because he trusts his friend's passion? Because he is black? Our normally voluble narrator is silent on this issue. Instead of genuine feeling, there is only absence and the recognition of a kind of inadequacy that is notable for not being regretted.

These two incidents also establish a certain congruity between racial identification and emotionality. Julius criticizes jazz because it borders on the sentimental. Similarly, Julius would rather be seen as cold and unfeeling than risk the "false intimacy" of a kind or even courteous gesture toward his neighbor. Race is here subtly linked to emotion and intuition as opposed to the educated, contemplative aesthetic of Julius and the novel as a whole. This formulation extends as well to his encounters with African and African Americans. The postal worker, the World War II veteran, and the cabdriver all demand a form of recognition based on an identity that Julius conceives as superficial if not irrelevant. Just as the postal worker endows him with false power and wisdom, race for Julius is a misleading sign, a signifier without meaning. From his perspective, those who invest race with significance thus demonstrate a kind of anti-intellectual baseness that breeds sentimentality and false solidarity.

The emptiness that Julius attaches to race as a sign is especially important because as a psychiatrist, he is tasked with reading human signs. Reflecting on the work of fifteenth-century German wood carvers, Julius recognizes the impulse to glean meaning from material realities:

> Riemenschneider, Stoss, Leinberger, and Erhat brought a complicated material knowledge of lindenwood to bear on their carving of it, and their attempts to marry the spirit of the material with its visible form, craftlike though it is, is after all not so different from the diagnostic struggle that doctors are engaged in. This is particularly true in the case of those of us who are psychiatrists, who attempt to use external Signs as clues to internal realities, even when the relationship between the two is not at all clear. So modest is our success at this task that it is easy to believe our branch of medicine is as primitive now as was surgery in Paracelsus's time. (238)

Julius's reference to these early woodcarvers is striking because while such artists and craftsmen create representations of the human form, psychiatrists are confronted with the human form itself. His conflation of sculpture with diagnosis endows the psychiatrist with the power to create the patient rather than to simply respond to the patient. Julius extends this metaphor in a comment he makes to his friend: "For the troubles of the mind, diagnosis is a trickier art, because even the strongest symptoms are sometimes not visible." What does it mean for psychiatry to be understood as a form of art? Julius extends the comparison, noting, "as in the case of artists, unless the work of art addressed the question of inner life, its external Signs would be empty" (237).

If art involves the ordering of experience into an aesthetic and meaningful whole, then diagnosis is a way of bringing clarity to chaos, beauty to madness. As a psychiatrist, Julius must distinguish between signs endowed with meaning and others that signify nothing or mislead. He provides examples of the dangers of such false signs by referring to "the debased forms of phrenology, eugenics, and racism" (237). These theories fail by mistaking certain bodily signs as meaningful indicators of human characteristics. Although Julius indicts racism rather than race, any mention of race in the text reflects some form of prejudice. The postal worker, the World War II veteran, and the cabdriver all read Julius's black skin as a sign of kinship, but as his relationship with his friend demonstrates, kinship for Julius does not derive from a common racial identity. Instead, it involves cultural affinities and thoughtful discussions about art, philosophy, and history.

Given Julius's disdain for the claims of race, it is no surprise that he does not identify his friend racially. Only toward the end of the novel does the reader learn that his friend is African American. This information is communicated through Moji, who responds to the horrific tales Julius's friend relates about his family. His father descended into madness and drug addiction while his mother had six children with five different men. He further adds that his brother was incarcerated for selling drugs and his uncle committed suicide. This family history reads as a compendium of the worst stereotypes about African American life. After a long silence, Moji replies, "The things black people have had to deal with in this country—and I don't mean me or Julius, I mean people like you, who have been here for generations—the things you've had to deal with are definitely enough to drive anyone over the edge. The racist structure of this country is crazy-making" (203). Moji's comments are especially striking because they follow Julius's discussion of his "craziest" patients. Entertaining his friends with stories of alien visitations and conspiracy theorists, Julius plays the suffering of his patients for laughs. Although he admits to himself that, regarding his worst patients, "within the parameters of their own realities, these worlds were remarkably consistent: they looked crazy only from the outside," he announces to his friends that "some people, in fact, are simply nuts, and that's what we write down in the chart" (202). Julius's flippant attitude toward these patients sharply contrasts with the more compassionate reflections of his friend who opines, "Everyone just finds a way to cope, no one is completely free of mental problems, so I say let everyone sort themselves out." While Julius establishes clear lines between the sane and the insane, his friend recognizes a more permeable border. He then proceeds to describe the "real insanity" of his family, stories that elicit none of the laughter that Julius generates from his anecdotes.

Moji's response to these tales suggests that racism is the cause of such tragedies. If, as she claims, "the racist structure of this country is crazy-making," then the drug addiction, promiscuity, and criminality that Julius's friend describes can be explained through entrenched forms of inequality. Julius does not directly respond to Moji's declaration. Instead, Lise-Anne, his friend's girlfriend, exclaims, "Oh man . . . don't give him excuses," to which Julius notes, "Lise-Anne was immediately likable" (203). Julius's sudden praise of Lise-Anne suggests that he disagrees with Moji's comments, though he does not state such an opinion directly. For Julius, it would seem that race and racism are not defining factors. They are issues that remain almost unspeakable as if to admit one's racial identity is to admit a kind of defeat. Race is a sign without meaning or, more specifically, a sign overdetermined with false signification. Unlike the newly likable Lise-Anne, Julius finds himself irritated by Moji: "In contrast, I was struck by Moji's brittleness, the defensiveness she seemed to have so readily at hand. Speaking of her boyfriend, whom I had not met yet, she'd demanded of me: Are you trying to find out if he's black? I was startled. I assured her that no, I had no such interest. It was trite, it suggested a sort of unformed mind to me. But I found it appealing, and even sexual, and I suddenly imagined us together in a sexual situation" (203). According to Julius, to identify someone by race is to engage in an unsophisticated form of thinking; it is to read the wrong signs and thus to participate in a false art. Taste in music or recently read books are certainly better indicators of character for our intellectual narrator.

And yet, Julius finds himself sexually aroused by Moji's "trite" approach to race. Again, the invocation of race inspires a nonrational, deeply intuitive response from him. Julia Kristeva explains that there is an uncanny quality to the body because, as Freud notes, the body remains alien to the self due to its irrepressible biological drives: "Foreignness, an uncanny one, creeps into the tranquility of reason itself, and, without being restricted to madness, beauty, or faith any more than to ethnicity or race, irrigates our speaking-being, estranged by other logics, including the heterogeneity of biology" (170). From this perspective, Julius's abrupt shift from the seriousness of how race impacts the lives of African Americans to sexual fantasies exposes an uncanny eruption that affirms his lack of interest in the structures of racism and prejudice. Uncertain if he can even call his response to Moji "attraction," he struggles to identify the "something interesting in the mood she gathered around her like a robe" (204). His sudden focus on her sexual appeal obviates any meaningful inquiry into the relationship between race, sanity, and inequality. Sex and the immediacy of his attraction foreclose such considerations, making race a matter of passing curiosity rather than of substantive meditation.

Julius follows this encounter with Moji and his friend with further reflections on the work of his profession:

> The practice of psychiatry is partly about seeing the world as a collection of tribes. Take a set of individuals who have brains that, with regard to how they map reality, are more or less equal: differences among brains in this set, this ostensibly normal group, this control group, which constitutes the majority of humanity, are small. . . . But take another set of individuals, a more distant tribe, and among these the brains differ from those of the first set in some chemically and physiologically significant way. These are the mentally ill. The mad, the crazy: people who are schizophrenic, obsessive, paranoid, compulsive, sociopathic, bipolar, depressed or some grim combination of two or more of these: these people all belong together, they ought to be classed with each other. Or so we think—and this is the rationale for the medical practice of psychiatry. . . . But within this tribe, it has often struck me, the differences are so profound that, really, what we are looking at is many tribes, each as distinct from the others as it is from the tribe of the normal. (204–205)

Julius's ordering of people into "tribes" resonates with an ethnographic approach to human difference that speaks to early forms of racial discourse. The language of race has long been implicated in delineating people according to "tribes," in which difference is measured against a group labeled normal or more specifically white. Julius clarifies that those identified as nonnormal constitute a separate group but reminds us that there is so much diversity among these others that each of these individuals is best understood as a separate tribe. If we read this passage as a commentary on race and racial difference, then all those who are nonwhite are best defined as a set of individual tribes. From this perspective, racially Julius is not black; he belongs instead to the tribe of Julius.

These theoretical musings do little to mitigate the fact that while wandering through the city or engaging with patients, Julius is perceived through his black skin. Although the history of slavery is not Julius's personal or familial history, as a black man in the United States, he cannot escape the racialized projections imposed on him by blacks and nonblacks alike. In a moment of calm reflection, apart from the immediate irritation he experiences when confronted with the racial claims of others, Julius recognizes a certain unity between all people of African descent living in America:

> From where I stood, the Statue of Liberty was a fluorescent green fleck against the sky, and beyond her sat Ellis Island, the focus of so many myths; but it had been built too late for those early Africans—who weren't immigrants in any case—and it had been closed too soon to mean anything to the later Africans like Kenneth, or the cabdriver, or me. Blacks, "we blacks," had known rougher ports of entry: this, I could admit to myself now that my mood was less impatient, was what the cabdriver had meant. This was the acknowledgment he wanted, in his brusque fashion, from every "brother" he met. (54–55)

Neither the slaves who arrived in America nor later African immigrants passed through Ellis Island. That landmark of promise and hope is not part of the experience of American blackness. Instead Julius notes that "rougher ports of entry" unite "we blacks." It is not clear what rough ports of entry Julius has experienced. He does not describe a difficult process of immigration to the United States, and his encounters with racism in the novel are few and relatively mild. Instead we might understand Julius's reference to "rougher ports of entry" as entry into the racialized landscape of America.

At the end of chapter 2, Julius encounters a teenage girl and her younger brother on a subway platform. The children assume that because Julius is black, he must be some kind of ghetto thug. Out of earshot of their parents, who remain absorbed in their own conversation, the children try to provoke Julius to respond to their offensive gestures:

> The little boy wore an imitation Chinese peasant's hat. They had been mimicking slated eyes and exaggerated bows before they came to where I was. They now turned to me. Are you a gangster, mister? Are you a gangster? They both flashed gang signs, or their idea of gang signs. I looked at them. It was midnight, and I didn't feel like giving public lectures. He's black, said the girl, but he's not dressed like a gangster. I bet he's a gangster, her brother said, I bet he is. Hey mister, are you a gangster? They continued flicking their fingers at me for several minutes. Twenty yards away, their parents talked with each other, oblivious. (31–32)

When the train arrives, Julius enters a distant car. He does not speak to the children nor to their parents. Instead, he quite abruptly begins thinking about his oma, or maternal grandmother. Though he is not sure if she is still alive, he resolves to go to Brussels to visit her. Julius's sudden shift in thinking again indicates his refusal to engage with issues of race. He is certainly not responsible for giving the children or their parents a public lecture. However, his refusal to even contemplate how this incident links him to a legacy of blackness in America demonstrates a distinct form of racial repression. By thinking about his Belgian oma, Julius seems to emphasize his distance from black Americans. He is not black as the girl declares but a mixed-race citizen of the world. If to be black is to enter into America through "rougher ports of entry," Julius affirms his ability to leave the country and thereby align himself with other forms of identity.

THE UNCANNY AFRICAN AMERICANIST PRESENCE

Soon after the encounter with the children on the subway platform, Julius travels to Brussels for three weeks. Although he does not find or even attempt to find his oma, he has extended conversations with Dr. Maillotte and Farouq, developing a surprising intimacy with them both. His interlude in Brussels offers a respite from racist and racialized encounters. While he is abroad, no one makes racial or racist claims on him. However, race is not entirely absent from this European escape. "With mischief in his eye," Farouq's friend, Khalil, asks Julius, "The American blacks—he used the English expression—are they really as they are shown on MTV: the rapping, the hip-hop dance, the women? Because that's all we see here. Is it like this?" Julius responds by noting that like European Muslims, American blacks are victim to negative representations in the media. Despite these false images, he explains, "American blacks are like any other Americans; they are like any other people. They hold the same kinds of jobs, they live in normal houses, they send their children to school. Many of them are poor, that is true, for reasons of history, and many of them do like hip-hop and devote their lives to it, but it's also true that some of them are engineers, university professors, lawyers, and generals" (119).

Farouq and Khalil treat Julius as both an outsider and an expert on American race relations. They do not include him among those defined as "American blacks," and though Julius and Farouq speak at great length on issues of injustice, oppression, and difference, they do not return to a discussion of American race relations. Nonetheless, many of Julius's thoughts in response to Farouq's commitment to a Palestinian state have direct application to Julius's relationship to race in the United States. Though wary of Farouq's rage, he also admires his passion: "It seemed as if the only way this lure of violence could be avoided was by having no causes, by being magnificently isolated from all loyalties. But was that not an ethical lapse graver than rage itself?" (107). Julius can be understood as committing this very ethical lapse as he is in many ways "isolated from all loyalties"; neither an American nor a black American, he also lives in exile from his parental homelands.

What loyalties does Julius honor in the novel? While he shuns affiliation to any organized entity or identity group, he is committed to his unnamed friend and to Professor Saito. But perhaps more obviously, Julius is committed to the life of the mind through his aesthetic and intellectual meditations. This would seem to be a solitary endeavor, but close consideration of his reading practices suggests his alignment with a uniquely African American literary tradition. In the first chapter of the novel, Julius admits that he often reads aloud to himself. He cites St. Augustine's belief that "the weight and inner life of sentences were best experienced out loud, but much has changed in our idea of reading since then." He continues, "We have for too long been taught that the sight of a man speaking to himself is a sign of eccentricity or madness; we are no longer at all habituated to our own voices, except in conversation or from within the safety of a shouting crowd. But a book suggests conversation: one person is speaking to another, and audible sound is, or should be, natural to that exchange. So I read aloud with myself as my audience, and gave voice to another's words." Although the books that Julius reads are all non-American (Roland Barthes's *Camera Lucida* [1980], Peter Altenberg's *Telegrams of the Soul* [2005], and Tahar Ben Jelloun's *The Last Friend* [2006]), the image he presents of a man reading aloud to himself resonates with one of the most important tropes in the African American literary canon. Analyzing a scene from *A Narrative of the Most Remarkable Particulars in the Life of James Albert Ukawsaw Gronniosaw, an African Prince* (1770), the first full-length black autobiography, Henry Louis Gates Jr. and Nelly McKay explain how the Anglo-African literary tradition emerged as a way to demonstrate the complex humanity of people of African descent. Gates and McKay draw attention to Gronniosaw's momentous encounter with a book. Gronniosaw places his ear on its pages, hoping it will speak to him as it speaks to his white master: "With Gronniosaw's *An African Prince*, a distinctively 'African' voice registered its presence in the republic of letters; it was a test that both talked 'black,' and, through its unrelenting indictment of the institution of slavery, talked back" (xxxviii). Although the book refuses to speak to Gronniosaw, his narrative demonstrates how he has made words speak through him. The text gives voice to the talking book Gates and McKay identify as one of the foundational tropes of the Anglo-African and then African American literary tradition.

Open City's invocation of the trope of the talking book links the novel to the African American literary canon even as Julius favors European authors, philosophers, artists, and musicians. Orality also helps explain a possible audience for the text as Cole has mentioned that the novel can be understood as an account of Julius's personal therapy sessions.[2] His narration thus takes on a spoken quality as he describes his disjointed thoughts and memories to an invisible psychiatrist. In this way, the text figures as a literal kind of talking book, a written chronicle of the talking cure even if cure may remain a dubious prospect for a patient like Julius. It also bears noting that Julius recognizes that the image of a man speaking aloud to himself is commonly linked to "eccentricity or madness." This association suggests a degree of embarrassment on Julius's part, or a recognition at least of the solitude necessary for him to comfortably read aloud to himself. Such privacy or reticence resonates with Julius's approach to matters of race and blackness. He never mentions a single African American author, except to note in chapter 4 that a man on the subway was reading Octavia Butler's *Kindred* (45), a novel deeply invested in the racialized uncanny. Despite this absence of direct literary allusions, Julius is profoundly affected by the African American characters he meets and is often haunted by aspects of black history. These pivotal encounters establish a powerful if submerged figural presence with links to Freud's uncanny as well as Morrison's notions of the ancestor and rememory.

Julius's first experience in the novel with a black man he meets on the streets of Harlem highlights the unsettling impact African Americans have on him: "An old man with an ashen face and bulbous yellow eyes, passing by, raised his head to greet me, and I (thinking for a moment that he was someone I surely knew, or once knew, or had seen before, and quickly abandoning each idea in turn; and then fearing that the speed of these mental dissociations might knock me off my stride) returned his silent greeting. I turned around to see his black cowl melt into an unlit doorway. In the Harlem night, there were no whites" (18). Julius's encounter with this man is best described through Freud's theory of the uncanny and the return of the repressed. The uncanny provokes a form of dread by combining the new with the familiar. In his discussion of the uncanny, Freud analyzes the linguistic origins of the German word *heimlisch*, which means both "homely" and "concealed." This union of the known with the secretive may also refer to repressed material involving experiences that evoke earlier psychic stages or that threaten the ego. The man that Julius meets is both familiar and strange. Disturbed by his inability to identify the man or even to know for certain if he can identify him, Julius returns his greeting as if they are connected. Though the old man is in fact a stranger, Julius acknowledges him as a familiar by nodding back at him. This gesture of racial solidarity indicts Julius in a form of identification that he clearly disparages, but the power of the man's presence effectively forces him to perform this racialized role. The old man evokes a part of Julius's past that he cannot clearly identify or, more specifically, that he does not want to identify.

In this way, the old man may also reflect Morrison's conception of the ancestor. For Morrison, the ancestor is a figure of blackness and as she explains:

> How the Black writer responds to that presence interests me. Some of them, such as Richard Wright, had great difficulty with that ancestor. Some of them, like James Baldwin, were confounded and disturbed by the presence or absence of an ancestor. What struck me in looking at some contemporary fiction was that whether the novel took place in the city or in the country, the presence or absence of that figure determined the success or the happiness of the character. It was the absence of an ancestor that was frightening, that was threatening, and it caused huge destruction and disarray in the work itself. ("Rootedness" 62)

Julius is not an especially happy character, and though he has achieved some degree of professional success, his personal life demonstrates significant problems sustaining close relationships. At the start of the novel, he has recently broken up with his girlfriend, is estranged from his mother, and is having some difficulty at work balancing the stories of his patients with his meditative nature. While it would be far too simplistic to attribute these difficulties to racial alienation or a refusal to recognize and embrace his ancestors, much of African American history, especially involving the slave trade, manifests for Julius as signs of the uncanny. These images suggest a past repressed not only by the nation as a whole but by Julius as well.

Julius's relationship to the uncanny is made most explicit during one of his long walks through the city. He describes that cold afternoon as a time "during which I flitted in and out of myself, when time became elastic and voices cut out of the past and into the present" (74). Awash in memories and sensations that seem not to be his own, Julius imagines himself transported to an earlier time involving draft riots. He then has a terrifying vision: "What I saw next gave me a fright: in the farther distance, beyond the listless crowd, the body of a lynched man dangling from a tree. The figure was slender, dressed from head to toe in black, reflecting no light. It soon resolved itself, however, into a less ominous thing: dark canvas sheeting on a construction scaffold, twirling in the wind" (75). Julius's reference to draft riots and the specter of a lynched man evoke the 1863 Draft Riots, in which mobs of mostly Irish and German immigrants targeted free blacks in New York City as a way to protest the passage of a mandatory lottery for military service in the Civil War. William Jones, a black man walking home in Greenwich Village, was beaten and hanged from a tree on Clarkson Street. His body was then set on fire. Though at various points in the novel Julius offers scrupulous accounts of historical incidents, he mentions none of these details when he mistakes the canvas sheeting for the lynched man. Instead, his vision seems to arise from the place itself and a vague commotion seemingly from another time.

This encounter with the past, somehow derived from the space Julius inhabits, recalls Toni Morrison's notion of rememory outlined in her masterpiece *Beloved* (1987). Escaped slave Sethe explains to her daughter Denver how certain memories exist outside of individual recollections:

> Some things just stay. I used to think it was my rememory. You know. Some things you forget. Other things you never do. But it's not. Places, places are still there. If a house burns down, it's gone, but the place—the picture of it—stays, and not just in my rememory, but out there, in the world. What I remember is a picture floating around out there outside my head. I mean, even if I don't think it, even if I die, the picture of what I did, or knew, or saw is still out there. Right in the place where it happened. (35–36)

When Denver asks if others can see rememories, Sethe replies, "Oh, yes, yes, yes. Someday you be walking down the road and you hear something or see something going on. So clear. And you think it's you thinking it up. A thought picture. But no. It's when you bump into a rememory that belongs to somebody else" (36). Julius's vision of the lynched man is an encounter with a rememory. He does not need any of his treatises on history and memory to access this visceral confrontation with the past. Instead, it appears to him spontaneously as if it is part of his inheritance of the city or of the nation more broadly. The vision of the lynched man operates as an uncanny rememory by transporting Julius to another time and reminding him of America's inescapable racial traumas.

Freud's notion of the uncanny also does much to clarify Julius's peculiar relationship to his unnamed friend. In their one conversation that touches on racial matters, his friend is presented as a liminal figure who may not even be alive. This discussion begins when Julius arrives at his friend's apartment after an especially frustrating conversation with his dying mentor Professor Saito. Appearing weaker than ever before, the former teacher of early English literature tells Julius, "I don't know what you do in Africa, but I must say, I'm ready to go into the forest. I am ready to go in. It is time for me to enter the forest and lie down, and let the lions come for me" (179). Julius explains his irritation to his friend: "I had hoped for grace. I said, not for immortality. I had hoped for a graceful, strong exit for this professor of mine. I so badly wanted the old man to give me words of wisdom. I said, not this nonsense about lions" (180). Although Julius does not accuse Professor Saito of racism, the reference to lions clearly relies on conceptions of savage Africa defined by wildlife rather than civilization. His friend urges him to look past the talk of lions and not to take "it as an insult to Africans"; instead, Julius should realize that his professor just longs for "a better world" in which "the delirium and pain could be avoided" (182). This exchange with his friend is notable because it presents Julius as disturbed and seeking counsel. His typical self-contained posture is replaced by irritation and doubt. Moreover, his reference to Professor Saito's comment about lions is a reminder that Julius is impacted by racial matters and that his African heritage does indeed have meaning for him. Despite his scorn for racial claims, Julius is not immune to race.

As mentioned before, this conversation between Julius and his friend is unique because it is the only time they talk about racial matters. The singularity of this scene is further heightened by Julius's unusual description of his friend. While Julius offers physical descriptions of most of the people he encounters, throughout the novel his friend is presented with no distinctive bodily features. He appears to lack any clear corporeal presence. Although this absence of physical descriptors adheres to all of the scenes involving his friend, it is especially acute in this passage, which carefully presents him as an otherworldly figure. As Julius listens to his friend's comments on Professor Saito and his own reflections on death, he states "that it almost seemed as if I were being addressed by his shadow, or his future self" (181). Toward the end of the conversation, Julius offers another unsettling description of his friend: "Then, in a low voice, almost as if he were talking to himself or regarding his body from a posthumous point of view, he said, The reality, Julius, is that we are alone out here" (182). Both of these descriptions suggest that his friend is dead or exists as some kind of ghostly presence. This is underscored by his friend's concluding comment. Perhaps Julius is already alone—that is, alone in this conversation with his friend who is not a living person but some other subjective projection. What would it mean for Julius's friend to exist as a ghost or as a construction of Julius's imagination? And more to the point, why is the most important African American character in the text presented with such puzzling ambiguity?

Throughout the novel, African American figures appear as manifestations of the uncanny, which Freud further defined as "a hidden, familiar thing that has undergone repression and then emerged from it . . . everything that is uncanny fulfills this condition" (15). Julius's friend is the most poignant example of various anxieties that Julius represses. In this conversation, he reflects not only Julius's frustration at a racial slight but concerns about his own mortality as well. He effectively combines the dread of death with the dread of racial classification that permeates the novel. It is especially significant that Cole presents this figure of the uncanny as African American. Nameless and disembodied as well as a sophisticated jazz aficionado, he appears as another iteration of Ellison's Invisible Man. However, Julius's friend is also far more socially agile and personally confident than Ellison's protagonist. The insecurity and instability of identity associated with the Invisible Man are instead more evident in Julius, who like Ellison's narrator has severed ties with his family.

By contrast, Julius's friend is a voice of calm counsel and support. As a single father to his nine-year-old daughter Clara, he also offers a portrait of caring, engaged fatherhood. Cole's depiction of Julius's friend signifies on Morrison's conception of the ancestor by providing his protagonist with a guardian of black identity who is not an elder but a more equal companion. By dismantling the hierarchical relationship implicit in Morrison's definition of the ancestor, Cole suggests that the most productive relationship between his immigrant narrator and an African American figure is one defined by mutuality and friendship, not a passing down of generational knowledge. But why is Julius's friend so strongly associated with the uncanny? Why can't their friendship exist as an unambiguous flesh and blood exchange?

As an African American, Julius's friend is a descendent of slaves and those Africans who endured the horrors of the Middle Passage. Freud reminds us that the uncanny also represents a double of the self. Julius and his friend share many similarities—they are both single black men devoted to the arts and the life of the mind. His friend's namelessness suggests that he does not exist as an independent agent in the world but instead relies on Julius to give him life and voice. In one scene, Julius's friend expresses ideas that reflect Julius's own mind-set. While at the park, Julius and his friends observe a group of people parachuting to the ground. The police charge the group and arrest them. Julius marvels at the grace and bravery of the parachutists, but it is his friend who speaks first, capturing his own ideas: "My friend, who seemed to have read my thoughts, said, You have to set yourself a challenge, and you must find a way to meet it exactly, whether it is a parachute, or a dive from a cliff, or sitting perfectly still for an hour, and you must accomplish it in a beautiful way, of course" (197). This comment distills the challenge of Julius's journey in *Open City*: to find a meaningful objective and then complete it in an aesthetically meaningful way.

Despite the many similarities that unite Julius and his friend, their personal histories are markedly different. As an African American, Julius's friend has experienced race and the legacy of slavery in ways that remain unimaginable to our narrator. As a result, his friend embodies what his life might have been had his ancestors been traded to white slaveholders. Freud explains that the double is endowed with "all those unfulfilled but possible futures to which we still like to cling in phantasy, all those strivings of the ego which adverse external circumstances have crushed, and all our suppressed acts of volition" (10). Julius's friend represents a number of possible futures for our narrator: a life involving a beloved child, a passion for jazz, an appreciation for the array of African and African American literature Julius notes on his friend's bookshelf, but perhaps most notably, a deeper awareness of how race operates in American society and culture.

These possible futures also speak to another key difference between Julius and his friend: how they relate to women. At the start of the novel, Julius has recently ended his relationship with his girlfriend, Nadege, and at no point does he suggest a desire to have children. By contrast, though estranged from his daughter's mother, his friend is "an affectionate father" (23). However, if his friend exists as an ephemeral presence throughout the novel, Clara is even more absent from the text. When Julius arrives at his friend's apartment following his last conversation with Professor Saito, he is told that the nine-year-old girl is "out wandering" (179), an unusual and even dangerous activity for a child so young. But the presence of a spirited girl would surely make their conversation on death and mortality impossible. Instead, we must understand Clara, like her father, as a rhetorical figure that highlights the possibilities of Julius's doubled life. Unlike Julius, his friend also has an "ideal companion" in Lise-Anne. Julius observes that the two "were well matched. . . . There was a balance in his seriousness and her natural lightness. She already understood him, which was more than could be said for his several girlfriends" (197). Given Julius's reticence and the lacunae in his personal history, it is almost inconceivable for any person to understand him, much less a woman who would have to further contend with his latent misogyny. Julius's friend thus offers the possibility of a more socially connected and emotionally rich life.

REPRESSION, RAPE, AND PAIN

The sharp difference in how Julius and his friend relate to women becomes especially important with the revelation of Moji's rape accusation. Notably, the final mention Julius makes of his friend occurs in the early morning following his critical exchange with Moji. After attending the party at John's home where Moji confronts him, Julius returns to his apartment building. Before narrating this pivotal encounter with Moji, Julius describes finding Seth, his widowed neighbor, outside his apartment, dragging bedbug-infested mattresses into the street. He remembers his friend who had also tried to get rid of the pests before leaving for a job at the University of Chicago following his failure to win tenure at Columbia. Julius notes, "And it was at that particular moment, speaking with Seth in the front of the infected mattresses that I had an inkling of how acutely I would feel the absence of my friend" (243). Initially, Julius's desire for his friend seems to be derived from the annoyance of having to think about the bedbug infestation as well as how Seth reminds him of his lack of connection to those around him. However, the very next paragraph begins Julius's brief meditation on his response to Moji's revelation. This juxtaposition suggests a longing if not an actual need for a confidant and friend to help him sort through the implications of Moji's story. However, it is important to note that Julius frames his friend's absence as something he "would feel" rather than something he currently feels. Julius is so removed from his own emotional life that he cannot inhabit his own desires; they surface only as "inklings" figured in the conditional tense. Finally, the absence of his double following Moji's accusation implies the singularity of Julius's responsibility in this situation. His friend is suddenly missing because Julius cannot admit to himself his own culpability.

The ordering of this sequence of events is peculiar because Julius describes in great detail what he does after he leaves the party—he stops by a diner for a coffee, then walks down to the George Washington Bridge, passing by the scene of a recent car accident, watches the sunrise, and then walks back to his apartment through Harlem and the campus of Columbia University—before he mentions his conversation with Moji. This narrative deferral parallels the late disclosure of his friend's racial identity especially as in both cases Moji is the source of these important pieces of information.

Julius introduces Moji's disclosure with a brief meditation on the nature of sanity and storytelling: "Each person must, on some level, take himself as the calibration point for normalcy, must assume that the room of his own mind is not, cannot be, entirely opaque to him. Perhaps this is what we mean by sanity: that, whatever our self-admitted eccentricities might be, we are not the villains of our own stories. In fact, it is quite the contrary: we play, and only play, the hero, and in the swirl of other people's stories, insofar as those stories concern us at all, we are never less than heroic" (243). Julius's reference to sanity implies that for him to understand himself as the villain is to sacrifice his own peace of mind. He cannot maintain his sanity and accept the story that Moji tells. And yet he does not deny her claims. Instead he listens to her story with seeming no response, leaving John's apartment and returning to his perambulations with no significant emotional reaction. Moji describes in detail a party that her brother hosted when she was fifteen. At this party, Julius raped her. She states that Julius "had acted like I [Julius] knew nothing about it, had even forgotten her, to the point of not recognizing her when we met again, and had never tried to acknowledge what I had done. This torturous deception had continued until the present" (244). She concludes by demanding that he respond, "But will you say something now? Will you say something?" (245). Julius says nothing and leaves Moji alone on the terrace.

Julius's response to Moji reflects the silence he adopts when confronted with racial appeals. Just as the World War II veteran looks for confirmation of their common racial identity, Moji asks for confirmation of her story. In both instances, Julius rejects the version of himself they each proffer through the power of his silence. By refusing to engage both of them directly—that is, by refusing to speak—Julius denies their claims even more forcefully than if he were to talk back to them. But while the veteran confronts Julius with a form of identity that he simply does not embrace, Moji presents Julius with a version of himself grounded in their shared past. If silence is a way for Julius to disavow the claims of race, then his silence following Moji's story is a rejection of her story. His opening remarks to his encounter with Moji further demonstrate that he cannot accept her version of events and maintain his sanity. He cannot be both hero and villain.

Before leaving the party, Julius recalls a story from one of Camus's journals in which he describes a young Nietzsche telling his schoolmates how Scaevola, an ancient Roman hero, placed his right hand in the fire rather than give up his accomplices. When his schoolmates scoff at the story, Nietzsche took a hot coal in his hand, holding it so long that it left a lifelong scar. The story has no obvious corollary to Moji's revelation. Is Moji to be understood as Nietzsche, the bearer of a story, that Julius, like the skeptical schoolmates, doubts? Does she attempt to prove its veracity by scorching herself with its painful memory? Later Julius looks up the story of Nietzsche and discovers an incongruity in Camus's account; it was not with a piece of coal that Nietzsche burned himself but with several lit matchsticks. As the matchsticks began to burn his hand, a prefect knocked them to the ground. Did they even leave a scar? This revision demonstrates the failures of memory and the ways in which stories lose their truth in their retelling. If Camus's version of the story was wrong, perhaps Moji's story is as well, even as neither may be aware that they are promulgating inaccuracies.

Julius concludes that Nietzsche's action involving either a piece of coal or a set of matchsticks demonstrates the philosopher's "contempt for pain" (246). This reading of the story suggests that he recalls this account as a way for him to express his own contempt for pain. The salient difference then lies in how such pain is directed. Nietzsche literally embraces pain, showing off to his schoolmates that he can withstand the scalding heat of the coal or the matchsticks. By contrast, Julius proves his contempt for the pain of another person. He leaves Moji's questions unanswered, relieved only that she does not burst into tears or mar the quiet moment they share gazing at the Hudson ("Anyone who had come out onto the porch at that moment could not have imagined that we were doing anything other than enjoying the play of light on the river" [246]). His contempt carries through to the end of the novel as he never mentions Moji or her accusation again. Silence again becomes the sign of his rejection and his refusal to acknowledge not only pain but the very subjectivity of another person.

Where does such callousness come from? What accounts not only for Julius's rape of Moji but for his refusal to respond to her? While her accusation may be read as an implausible reversal of the cultured, observant narrator we have come to know, I contend that Julius's immediate response to Moji confirms his guilt. This is a man who as an adolescent stole power from a teenage girl and as an adult denies that same woman a basic recognition of her experience. In order to understand Julius's repression, it is helpful to return to Morrison's conception of rememory. Like the uncanny, rememory also connotes memories that have been repressed. Before the arrival of Beloved, Sethe works diligently to "beat back the past" as a way to control the traumas she endured as a slave. However, certain smells, images and sounds trigger her memory, forcing her to remember "something she had forgotten she knew" (61). In this way, rememory suggests a repressed past that is both individual and collective. While Julius appears open to rememories that exist outside of him, the kind with a geographic origin and linked to African American trauma, he is less receptive to exploring his own past. Significantly, the vision of the lynched man leads to the only chapter in the novel that offers some explanation of Julius's rape of Moji.

This section describes his experiences at the Nigerian Military School and his father's death. Throughout the chapter, Julius describes a growing tension between him and his mother, but this conflict is never made explicit. He states that he sided with his father regarding an argument between his parents but admits that the details of their rift were never disclosed to him. A few months following his father's death, his mother tells him about her childhood in Magdeburg and the privations she suffered having little money and no father. Growing up in the aftermath of World War II and most likely one of the children born of the Red Army's systematic rape of Berlin women, Julius's mother experienced "an unspeakably bitter world, a world without sanctity" (80). Though Julius appears to recognize such horrors intellectually, he "listened with only half an ear, embarrassed by the trembling and the emotion." He recalls this exchange as the closest thing to "an intimate conversation" (81) he ever had with his mother, noting as well that soon after they retreated into "an easier silence" that in turn nurtured the unbridgeable divide between them.

It is also significant that the only character in the novel to ask about Julius's mother is Moji: "Once, she [Moji] had abruptly asked me how my mother was doing. I was silent, then told her that I didn't know, that we weren't in touch. Oh, that's too bad, she said, in a weirdly cheerful tone of voice. I remember meeting her. She was such a nice person" (231). Although Moji's positive recollection of Julius's mother says little about her actual character, the question establishes an important connection between these two key female characters. Just as Julius has repressed the history of his relationship with Moji, he has likely repressed much of the dynamic that existed between him and his mother.

Julius's mother's account of her childhood mirrors the psychiatric sessions he later conducts with his patients. His somewhat indifferent response to his mother suggests that his profession may have been chosen to redeem his peculiar refusal to empathize or even thoughtfully listen to her stories. Or, if this scene is any harbinger of his future career, Julius is a decidedly mediocre psychiatrist. In either case, it is impossible not to draw a link between his interest in psychiatry and trauma with his strained relationship to his mother. Julius then recounts an incident at his military academy that both solidified the distance between them and established his adolescent character. After taking what he believed to be a discarded newspaper, Julius is accused of theft by a second-class warrant officer and caned in front of his classmates. He concludes this story by stating that he "could say nothing about any of this to my mother" and noting that because of the incident he "gained a reputation for fearlessness." Such fearlessness calls to mind the story of Nietzsche and his contempt for physical pain. Careful readers of *Open City* will also realize that Julius's rape of Moji occurs soon after this incident, just as Julius was becoming "popular with the girls at some other schools in the town, and had developed a somewhat callous self-confidence" (84). This chronology, which Julius suppresses through his nonlinear narrative, helps explain how our seemingly benign narrator could be guilty of sexual violence. Alienated from his mother and extolled by his peers for his stoicism, the young Julius gains power by maligning women and mastering his emotions. While the initial cause of his break from his mother remains opaque, these incidents reveal a young man contemptuous of female pain and eager to assert his own authority.

Although as an adolescent Julius prides himself on his ability to master pain, the violent mugging he endures in chapter 18 is a reminder that excruciating physical pain cannot be easily transcended. Julius is attacked by three boys whom he identifies as "no older than fifteen" (213). This estimate places them at the very same age as Julius when he rapes Moji. Their similarity in age implies an especially violent male adolescent impulse. As the boys beat Julius, he senses that the attack is impersonal: "I was being beaten, but it was not severe, certainly not as severe as it could be if they were truly angry." He further notes that the language they use is not specific to him but bound to some other encounter: "And the words, fluent, spiking in and out of their laughter, seemed somehow distant from the situation, as if they were addressing someone else, as if this were like all the other times I had encountered those words: never hostile, never directed at me" (213). Julius is the object of their violence but not its source. Despite the intensity and even intimacy of this encounter, he is wholly replaceable. Nothing about the attack is personal. This experience provides an important corollary to his history with Moji. Just as Julius is a convenient target for the boys' aggression, Moji was less a premeditated victim than a ready object of his lust and power. Though violence leaves its greatest impress on its victims, they do not inspire attack so much as withstand it.

There is no trace of Julius's contempt for pain following his attack. Though two chapters later he refuses to even acknowledge Moji's pain, here he is overwhelmed by the immediacy of his wounded body: "I had felt only the fear of pain and the love of being free of pain. But how could I have missed this! I'd thought, lying in the dirt. How could I have been less than completely aware of how good it was to be injury-free?" (215). Julius's failure to appreciate his earlier condition mirrors his later inability to sympathize with Moji. The experience of being "free of pain" seems to make him an amnesiac to his own immediate past. He is unable to remember the intensity of his pain and therefore the impossibility of Nietzsche's performative contempt. While still curled on the asphalt, an elderly man walks past him. The man "did not notice, or did not care to notice, that I had just been beaten" (214). The man's indifference or desire for indifference suggests that those free of pain cannot enter into the experience of those in pain.

Julius's mugging is also significant because of the racial dynamics it exposes. Immediately before he is attacked, he believes himself to be safe because he recognizes two of his soon-to-be assailants from an earlier encounter.

> My jumpiness hadn't been necessary, and I smiled and relaxed when I saw who it was: the two young men at whom I had nodded earlier. They didn't return the smile, but loped toward me, their every step seemingly calculated to save energy. They walked past me on either side without speaking to each other and as though they hadn't seen me. Each appeared to be intent on his own thoughts. There had earlier been, it occurred to me, only the most tenuous of connections between us, looks on a street corner by strangers, a gesture of mutual respect based on being young, black, male, based, in other words, on our being "brothers." These glances were exchanged between black men all over the city every minute of the day, a quick solidarity worked into the weave of each man's mundane pursuits, a nod or smile or quick greeting. It was a little way of saying, I know something of what life is like for you out here. They had passed by me now, and were for some reason reluctant to repeat that fleeting gesture. (211–212)

In "The Black Man's Nod," Mukoma Wa Ngugi, an American writer born of Kenyan parents, describes the gesture that Julius exchanges with the two men who assault him. For Ngugi, the nod acts as a way to bridge the divide between African Americans and the descendants of recently immigrated Africans. It is an expression of solidarity and recognition. Julius understands the import of the nod, but his use of quotation marks around the word "brother" reveals his skepticism of such a gesture. The nod represents "only the most tenuous of connections" because to be "young, black" and "male" represents for him no connection at all. Julius participates in the nod for the same reason that he tries to appease the African cabdriver and tells the postal worker that they will meet at the Nuyorican Poets Cafe: because it is an easier, simpler response than expressing his skepticism of racial solidarity. Julius's nod to the men who assault him may also reflect his fear of them. Nodding might be a way of establishing some degree of familiarity, which will in turn protect him from their violence.

As previously mentioned, the age of the boys links them to Julius when he was a student at the Nigerian Military School. In this way, they can also be read as his uncanny doubles. The violence that Julius inflicts on Moji is in part visited on him through the mugging. This interpretation of course leaves out the sexual trauma of Julius's attack on Moji. In the hall of mirrors that Cole creates in *Open City*, there is no way to reflect sexual difference. It is especially notable that Julius never encounters or, perhaps more accurately, never mentions African American women. His uncanny and often frustrating experiences with American blacks involve only men. While this observation underscores how these encounters serve as confrontations with a doubled self, they also expose a significant failure to engage with female subjectivity. This gap may explain Julius's return to his adolescent approach to pain after he listens to Moji's story. Though weeks before he had been the victim of horrific violence, he cannot move outside himself to acknowledge her pain. Like the elderly man, when confronted with her story, he too walks by wordlessly.

The chapter in which Julius is mugged closes with his reflections concerning an area used in the 1700s as a burial ground for blacks.

> What I was steeped in, on that warm morning, was the echo across centuries, of slavery in New York. At the Negro Burial Ground, as it was then known, and others like it on the eastern seaboard, excavated bodies bore traces of suffering: blunt trauma, grievous bodily harm. Many of the skeletons had broken bones, evidence of the suffering they'd endured in life. . . . How difficult it was, from the point of view of the twenty-first century, to fully believe that these people, with the difficult lives they were forced to live were truly people, complex in their dimensions as we are, fond of pleasures, shy of suffering, attached to their families. . . . Bending down, I lifted a stone from the grass and, as I did so, a pain shot through the back of my left hand. (221–222)

The physical pain Julius still bears from his attack merges here with his thoughts on the pain inflicted on the former slaves and free blacks buried beneath the city. What links his trauma to theirs? Although the novel does not equate one pain with the other, Julius's meditation isolates the violence directed at black bodies. Though he spurns appeals to racial solidarity, he recognizes a history that makes the experience of blackness unique. His abiding physical pain, borne through and on black bodies, is part of a complex, continuous history.

DELAYED ILLUMINATION

Although Moji's accusation comes in the penultimate chapter, it is, as Cole has stated, "the heart of the book."[3] Following this episode, the narration changes to the immediate past (Julius references a concert he attended "last night" [249]), and though Julius does not directly mention Moji again, a significant change is evident in the last chapter. Bereft of his unnamed African American friend, Nadege, and Moji, Julius is at last completely alone. With no one to accompany him, he buys a single ticket to a performance of Mahler's Ninth Symphony. Art remains his final and only source of consolation and communion. However, during the concert, Julius is frustrated to note that he is the only black man at the event:

> I can't help noticing; I notice it each time, and try to see past it. Part of that is a quick, complex series of negotiations: chiding myself for even seeing it, lamenting the reminders of how divided our life still remains, being annoyed that these thoughts can be counted on to pass through my mind at some point in the evening. . . . I am used to it, but it never ceases to surprise me how easy it is to leave the hybridity of the city and enter into all-white spaces, the homogeneity of which, as far as I can tell, causes no discomfort to the whites in them. The only thing odd, to some of them, is seeing me, young and black, in my seat or at the concession stand. At times, standing in line for the bathroom during intermission, I get looks that make me feel like Ota Benga, the Mbuti man who was put on display in the Monkey House at the Bronx Zoo in 1906. I [am] weary of such thoughts, but I am habituated to them. But Mahler's music is not white, or black, not old or young, and whether it is even specifically human, rather than in accord with more universal vibrations, is open to question. (251–252)

Julius's observations are a marked departure from his previous meditations. He confesses that he always notices that he is the only black man in concerts like these, suggesting that for all his disdain of racial matters, he remains uniquely attuned to his status as a minority. Race has never been invisible to him but has instead been an integral part of his vision. This unprecedented focus on race may also reflect his new solitude given the abrupt departure of his friend. His absence leaves Julius unmoored from any semblance of racial community. He is alone as never before. "Chiding" himself "for even seeing it"—that is, his racial isolation—Julius clearly aspires for a world that mimics the transcendence of Mahler's music, which "is not white, or black, not old or young."

But Julius cannot easily escape the racialized world in which he lives, a conclusion underscored by what happens to him immediately after listening to the final movement of the symphony. He inadvertently uses the emergency exit and finds himself locked out on the fire escape. In the rainy evening, Julius experiences a "solitude of rare purity" (255). To live outside of racial constructs requires him to live in complete isolation. Although there is beauty to be had in such a condition as he admires the stars, sharp and bright in the night sky, they are also a reminder of his own limitations:

> I wished I could meet the unseen starlight halfway, starlight that was unreachable because my entire being was caught up in a blind spot, starlight that was coming as fast as it could, covering almost seven hundred million miles every hour. It would arrive in due time, and cast its illumination on other humans, or perhaps on other configurations of our world, after unimaginable catastrophes had altered it beyond recognition. My hand held metal, my eyes starlight, and it was as though I had come so close to something that it fallen out of focus, or fallen so far away from it that it had faded away. (256–257)

Julius ends *Open City* aware that his whole self is "caught up in a blind spot," unable to see the light of stars that will take lifetimes to arrive on earth. Illumination will come only for other generations whose world will be radically changed from the one he knows now. The only revelation to be had is the impossibility of revelation, the impossibility of his own self-knowledge. Cole frames this epiphany as a function of physics; starlight indeed takes generations to arrive on earth, and the stars we perceive now in the night sky may in fact already be extinguished. This metaphor naturalizes Julius's failure to confront Moji's accusation as well as his own embattled relationship to race. While he remains a guardian of historical trauma, he fails to face his own struggles as if the contemporary moment cannot bear to acknowledge its own inhumanities. The light of revelation is ever delayed, creating a temporal displacement that illuminates the past but leaves our immediate present obscured. This formulation further explains the text's emphasis on the uncanny past as history retains a sharpness impossible for present traumas.

The novel ends as Julius boards a boat bound for the Upper Bay. He gazes at the Statue of Liberty, the perennial symbol of immigrant dreams and the promise of America. Rather than reflect on an emblem that has meant very little to America's African immigrants, both voluntary and forced, Julius muses on the death of birds lured by its seductive light. He notes that in 1888, hundreds of birds "lost their bearings when faced with a single monumental flame" (258).

The light blinds the birds, and disoriented, they fall dead on the balcony of the torch. Even as Julius longs for the light of revelation (it's worth noting that he describes Mahler's final works including the Ninth Symphony by stating, "The overwhelming impression they give is of light" [250]), the story of the birds suggests that too much illumination may be fatal. Moji's accusation offers a kind of light that Julius cannot bear to confront because it will overwhelm his sight and his fragile conception of himself. There is a limit to his insight. Like the starlight he observes, illumination may exist only for later generations. Julius abides, culpable and blind, and, perhaps most tragically, not even aware of his own blindness. This willed innocence makes him an heir to the new white man Morrison identifies. Like that earlier literary figure, Julius claims innocence on the repressed shadows of an abject other. As he gazes at the Statue of Liberty in the final scene, this postcolonial exile becomes an American, blind to his own crimes and free of his own dark past.

3 · THE IMPOSSIBILITY OF INVISIBILITY IN THE NOVELS OF DINAW MENGESTU

For Teju Cole's Julius, innocence is a willed condition made possible through the repression of past atrocities that are both personal and national. The narrators of Dinaw Mengestu's three novels are also eager to escape their traumatic pasts, derived largely from violence witnessed in their home country of Ethiopia. In *Open City*, Cole presents black identity and history as figures of Julius's troubled relationship with his own past. His attempts to evade the complications and burdens of race in America reflect in part his educational and economic privilege. Annoyed by the racist heckling of the children on the subway, Julius books a flight to Brussels. As a psychiatrist at a prominent New York City hospital, he appears not to consort with African Americans as colleagues or peers, instead enjoying a rarefied social world of his own creation. By contrast, the protagonists of Mengestu's fiction cannot escape the consequences of their blackness so easily. This is largely due to their lower socioeconomic status. Although these men are quite educated, as recent immigrants to the United States, or in one case the son of recent immigrants from war-torn Ethiopia, they face financial struggles unknown to a cosmopolitan man like Julius. Due to their working-class status, Mengestu's narrators have a more intimate relationship to blackness and African American identity. Sepha lives in an all-black neighborhood, Jonas is married to an African American woman, and the midwestern residents of Laurel understand Isaac's blackness only through their experience with the civil rights movement. While Julius ambles through and past African American neighborhoods in New York, Mengestu's protagonists interact in close proximity with struggling and impoverished blacks of diverse backgrounds.

The blackness of Mengestu's immigrant protagonists is often mistaken or conflated with African Americanness, causing profound miscommunication between his characters. As Americans, both black and white, project racialized fantasies onto Mengestu's African characters, his newly arrived immigrants in turn struggle to understand themselves as racial subjects in the United States. Such deep disjunctures have significant consequences for creating lasting relationships between Americans and Africans. Mengestu suggests that individuals can move past the misconceptions of race and color only by sharing their stories with one another. However, the personal histories of Mengestu's cagey narrators are often muddied by fantasies and desires that make truth illusory if not entirely inaccessible. His protagonists seek not so much an escape from race as an escape from all forms of identity because they inevitably make one vulnerable to the expectations and thus disappointments of others. As he examines how identity is both mutable and deceptive, Mengestu engages with the trope of invisibility, one of the most important motifs in the African American literary tradition. However, his version of invisibility presents a marked departure from the kind of invisibility made famous by Ralph Ellison's groundbreaking masterpiece. For the narrators of Mengestu's three novels, invisibility is an adopted strategy used to escape personal trauma. It provides a form of safety, albeit one that is largely imagined.

Perhaps the most obvious difference between Ellison's Invisible Man and Mengestu's narrators is that all of the latter have actual names: Sepha Stephanos, Jonas Waldermain, and Isaac Mabira. These are men who exist with particularized histories, who have identities that move them beyond the universal abstraction of Ellison's novel. While they each exhibit aspects of invisibility, they are never able or willing to escape their families, responsibilities, and communities as completely as the Invisible Man. His underground lair is ultimately a luxury that the hardworking and often bewildered immigrants of Mengestu's fiction never enjoy or sustain for themselves. Even if we read the Invisible Man's underground retreat more as a metaphor than as an exercise in realism, his complete separation from others and apparent contentment with that separation distinguish him from Mengestu's lonely but still deeply connected narrators. This difference suggests that while Ellison sought to create a generalized metaphor for black subjectivity, Mengestu recognizes the impossibility of such a totalizing structure due to the unique circumstances of his characters' journey to and arrival in the United States. Although all of his novels are concerned with newly arrived Ethiopians in contemporary America, his characters are not interchangeable. Instead, they are marked by distinctive experiences of migration and assimilation. And yet, despite differences in age, political commitment, class status, and education level, his three black male narrators all cultivate a profound form of invisibility. By examining the invisibility of Sepha, Jonas, and Isaac, we may better understand how Mengestu changes the terms of Ellison's influential trope to enlighten the diverse experiences of African immigrants.

ESCAPING INTO INVISIBILITY: *THE BEAUTIFUL THINGS THAT HEAVEN BEARS*

Like many immigrants to the United States, Sepha Stephanos bears the hopes and ambitions of his family. When he first arrives in Washington, DC, his uncle Berhane, who works as a cabdriver, expects his nephew to become an engineer or a doctor. Sepha recalls how "tears would well up in his eyes sometimes as he spoke about the future, which he believed could only be filled with better and beautiful things." His uncle further laments that he "only wish[ed] your father could have lived to see it" (41). Berhane projects the familiar dream of the successful immigrant onto Sepha, leaving himself out of such fantasies as if aware of their ultimate impossibility. Berhane's invocation of his nephew's father underscores how Sepha's life in the United States is to serve as compensation for his father's early death. He is to honor and fulfill the life cut short during Ethiopia's genocidal Red Terror. In this way, Sepha's journey to the United States as well as his response to his new homeland is never his own but a reflection of his family's history and trauma.

Overwhelmed by such expectations, Sepha soon disappoints his relatives and, in many ways, himself by dropping out of school and moving to Logan Circle, where he opens a modest convenience store. He reflects on the diminished expectations he comes to have for his future and admits that the immigrant's quest for a better life is a fantasy mapped onto his far more desperate life story:

> Here in Logan Circle, though, I didn't have to be anything greater than what I already was. I was poor, black, and wore the anonymity that came with that as a shield against all of the early ambitions of the immigrant, which had long since abandoned me, assuming they had ever really been mine to begin with. As it was, I did not come to America to find a better life. I came here running and screaming with the ghosts of an old one firmly attached to my back. My goal since then has always been a simple one: to persist unnoticed through the days, to do no more harm. (41)

After a lifetime of upheaval and struggle, Sepha craves nothing more than invisibility, to slip into the background of life and make no impression on the world around him. In this way, being poor and black is an asset since it affords him the kind of anonymity that allows him to disappear into the urban landscape of Logan Circle. Invisibility is here presented as a type of shelter, a way to escape the ghosts of the past and the fraught expectations of his family. It shifts Sepha's narrative away from that of the immigrant and toward the blighted poverty of African Americans even as that poverty is not actually shared by Sepha. As a store owner, he clearly has resources that belie his identification as "poor." This incongruity reveals how Sepha is effectively passing as "poor" and "black" to further his personal aims.

As a result, we must read Sepha's invisibility not simply as a form of racialized subjectivity but instead as a choice and more specifically a site of desire. Ellison's Invisible Man eventually comes to understand how he nurtured his own invisibility; this proves to be one of the key revelations of the novel. By contrast, Sepha is explicit in selecting and cultivating invisibility as a way to deal with the hardships of his life. Choice is the original condition of his invisibility, rather than the racism incurred by his blackness. Invisibility for Ellison's narrator is inextricable from his skin color. Although his adoption of false and destructive identities fosters his invisibility, Ellison emphasizes that blackness is the foundation of his condition. If, for the Invisible Man, blackness produces invisibility, for Sepha invisibility is made possible through his blackness.

Sepha uses his social identity—that is, his race and class standing—as a shield against confronting the disappointments of his life. In this way, he exploits the low expectations attached to blackness to his advantage. Sepha seems to renounce his own immigrant identity here and instead claims the anonymity Ellison identified with African Americanness. By using black invisibility as a cover for his personal shame and repression of the past, Sepha hides in a preestablished form of self-erasure. Instead of being a disappointment to his hopeful family, he becomes yet another poor black, unencumbered by lofty ambitions. However, this approach to African American identity proves dangerous as Sepha effectively wields black subjectivity according to his own desires and indulges stereotypes that conflate blackness with inferiority and low achievement. Moreover, this pursuit is ultimately futile; he does not become invisible, for as his neighbor Ms. Davis reminds him, he is neither African American nor invisible. Despite his best attempts, he, like the original Invisible Man, cannot escape himself. But while Ellison's protagonist became invisible as a way to cope with America's exhausting racial imaginary, Sepha's desire for invisibility is deeply rooted in the trauma he bears from his homeland. Unable to confront his guilt in his father's execution, Sepha opts for invisibility as a way to erase or at least contain the past. However, just as Sepha is hardly invisible, he cannot evade the memories that continue to haunt him.

Mengestu resists Sepha's desire for anonymity by emphasizing again and again the particularity of his protagonist's experience. Unlike the Invisible Man, Sepha cannot retreat underground or effectively abandon all of his family and friends, as Ellison's narrator seems to have done. The kind of isolation that the Invisible

Man creates for himself is impossible for an immigrant like Sepha, whose journey to the United States depends on the generosity of many relatives and friends. Sepha craves invisibility, but such anonymity proves to be an abstraction, not a meaningful or viable way of living and relating to others. As Sepha discovers, someone has to mind the store; someone has to pay the bills and keep the shelves stocked. Even when Sepha attempts to abandon his livelihood, to quite literally disappear from his own life, his friend Kenneth calls to make sure he is still manning the counter and Mrs. Davis arrives to fend off potential looters. Sepha cannot slip into invisibility because others will not allow him to disappear.

This representation of the impossibility of invisibility acts as a potent critique of Ellisonian invisibility. The Invisible Man neatly abandons his family and community; only the memory of his grandfather's dying words haunt him as if his other relatives, including his parents and possible siblings, made no lasting impression on him. Such an isolated character is troubling if not wholly unrealistic. By contrast, Sepha consciously if futilely beats back the traumas of his past, suggesting that the Invisible Man's lack of intimate memories reflects a hollow core or at least a character devoid of meaningful connections to others. While Ellison powerfully operates on the level of metaphor, exploring invisibility as a dynamic cognate for black subjectivity, Mengestu returns us to the inescapable details and peculiarities of his characters. There is no generalized condition for his immigrant characters, and as evident in how the trope of invisibility unfolds in his later two novels, this single theme leads to notably different consequences for his protagonists.

Even within the world of *The Beautiful Things That Heaven Bears,* African immigration is portrayed as complex and diverse. Sepha's two friends, Joseph from the Congo and Kenneth from Kenya, are not versions of himself but instead exist with distinct histories and desires. Kenneth, with his well-tailored suits and dented Saab, refuses to fix his bent teeth in order not to forget where he came from, while Joseph, a master at chess, gets drunk on the leftover drinks he cleans up as a waiter at the Capitol Hotel. None of these men are reducible to a single way of being, even as they are all immigrants, all black, and all, as they sing together, "children of the revolution."[1] Although they bear the disappointments of the intense political and social changes of their respective African homelands, they do so in radically different ways. Notably, Kenneth and Joseph do not opt for the kind of invisibility that inspires Sepha. While Sepha views his convenience store as a gateway to anonymity, Kenneth and Joseph enthusiastically celebrate its opening. Joseph proclaims, "This is the beginning. . . . Today, right here with Stephanos's store. We begin new lives. No more of this bullshit" (144). Sepha again hides behind the aspirations of others, allowing his friends to project their fantasies onto him just like his uncle did. He has no intention of owning an entire grocery store or expanding his business into other neighborhoods, as Kenneth suggests. But just as the Invisible Man allows others to define his identity, so Sepha quietly yields to the dreams of others rather than state his true desires.

Despite his malleable identity, Sepha allows himself to be grouped among "the children of the revolution." The phrase comes from a song that he and his African friends heard when they all worked at the Capitol Hotel together during their first years in the United States. Sepha explains, "We had been in America for only a couple of years when we first heard it, and we did believe that we were children of a revolution, and not only because we were willing to be grand. We all had stories of families we missed and would never see again. We spoke in our broken English of Africa's tyrannies, which had yet to grow tedious. And we had our own stories of death and violence to match" (48). Importantly, the novel never provides stories of death and violence for Kenneth and Joseph though they surely exist. This absence suggests that Sepha may not have shared his own traumatic past with his friends. The story of his father's death remains a deeply private incident, a memory he recounts while alone in his uncle's apartment, never in conversation with a friend or family member. Not even his uncle knows all of the details surrounding his brother-in-law's death. Sepha's desire for anonymity is premised on the need "to do no more harm." This comment makes sense only when the reader learns much later in the novel about Sepha's role in his father's execution. For Sepha, to be invisible is to escape the trauma of his past and his familial ties. The soldiers who kill Sepha's father arrive at the house because of the revolutionary flyers the young Sepha collected. His father tells the soldiers that the flyers belong to him, protecting his son from violence and even death. Soon after watching his father die at the hands of the soldiers, Sepha leaves for the United States.

Sepha passes his first two months in his new homeland in almost complete isolation. He speaks only to his uncle, and "even then our conversations were brief and strained. I rarely left the apartment, nor did I want to. Any connection, whether it was to a person, building, or time of day, would have been deceitful, and so I avoided making eye contact with people I didn't know, and tried to deny myself even the simplest of pleasures" (140). Although not invisible, Sepha rejects a normal existence due to the responsibility he feels for the death of his father. Sepha's retreat from the world reflects his horror and shame at his family's tragedy. However, his uncle eventually forces him to engage again with the world. Ironically, by making Sepha get a job, Berhane actually deepens his nephew's sense of invisibility. Berhane tells the manager at the Capitol Hotel that "he could call me Sepha, or even Steven for short, if he found that more convenient." Sepha observes the scene, noting, "The two men discussed my background while I stood there, mute." The manager goes so far as to feel Sepha's right bicep to make sure he is strong enough to serve in the kitchen. Both Berhane and

Sepha are embarrassed by the exchange with the manager as they both recognize the roles they must play before a more powerful white audience. The layers of performance are compounded as they exit the hotel: "After we walked out of the office, I heard my uncle mumble under his breath just loud enough so only I could hear, 'Fucking bastard.' Yes, it was a show of pride, halfhearted, but necessary nonetheless. It was one thing for him to 'sir' his way through the day on his own, and an entirely different matter to have me there as his witness to it" (141).

Sepha's description of his uncle's behavior bears a striking resemblance to how the Invisible Man recalls his grandfather's response to white people. On his deathbed, he declares, "Son, after I'm gone I want you to keep up the good fight. I never told you, but our life is a war and I have been a traitor all my born days, a spy in the enemy's country ever since I give up my gun back in the Reconstruction. Live with your head in the lion's mouth. I want you to overcome 'em with yeses, undermine 'em with grins, agree 'em to death and destruction, let 'em swoller you till they vomit or bust wide open" (16). Like the Invisible Man's grandfather, and like the Invisible Man himself, Berhane performs an abject form of blackness before whites. Sepha follows the model of his uncle, though rather than just obey his new white boss, he also becomes subservient to Berhane and the dreams he has for his nephew: "I worked at the job my uncle found for me, and later on I attended the school he had picked. I hardly remember making any decisions of my own, until one night, three years later, when I realized I couldn't continue living like this any longer" (142). Sepha decides to quit school and his job at the Capitol Hotel. Soon after, he moves out of his uncle's apartment and opens his store in Logan Circle with a small business loan. There he hopes to indulge his desire for anonymity, content "to sit in my high-backed chair behind a counter and read as silent as a god until the world came to an end" (146). Despite Sepha's rejection of his uncle's grand ambitions for his future, Sepha effectively replaces one form of invisibility with another. As a worker at the Capitol Hotel, Sepha is a shell of a self, simply fulfilling the mandates and orders of others. And as the owner of his modest convenience store, Sepha seeks not self-fulfillment but anonymity and even a form of self-erasure.

Sepha does not explicitly state that he wants to become invisible through the operation of his store. Instead he craves the opportunity to sit alone and read. Reading bears a special resonance in the text that is intimately linked to Sepha's pursuit of invisibility. He describes how he has always kept a book behind the counter of his store "so that every hour of even the quietest days has been filled with at least one voice other than my own" (39). As in *Open City*, this description of voices emerging from texts resonates with the trope of the talking book. Mengestu evokes this figure to emphasize Sepha's isolation. Unlike Gronniosaw's longing to make pages speak, Sepha easily animates the books he reads, but they do little to mask his abiding sense of loss. His talking book is not an expression of his life, not a testimonial as with Gronniosaw or Cole's Julius, but yet another form of repression that in turn fosters his invisibility. Sepha uses reading as a retreat from the world and the fears surrounding his expatriation to the United States. He reflects, "Left alone behind the counter, I was hit with the sudden terrible and frightening realization that everything I had cared for and loved was either lost or living on without me seven thousand miles away, and that what I had here was not a life, but a poorly constructed substitution made up of one uncle, two friends, a grim store, and a cheap apartment" (40). Rather than confront the emptiness of his life, Sepha fills the silence of the store with the narratives of others such that "the real world in which you live begins to fade into a past that you have tried to put to rest" (40).

As previously mentioned, Sepha cannot go underground like Ellison's Invisible Man. Instead he uses reading as a way to hide from himself and the world around him. But this ostensible mode of escape ultimately leads him back to others and to the intimacy extolled in the books he reads. Sepha befriends Naomi, the eleven-year-old daughter of his new neighbor Judith. The young girl visits his store after school and together they read long sections of *The Brothers Karamazov* (1880). Sepha discovers that it is impossible to read such a novel without applying its insights to his own life and therefore to Naomi's as well. He memorizes one of the most important passages of the novel in which the youngest of the Karamazov brothers, Alyosha, gathers a flock of young boys around him at the funeral of the innocent Illusha: "People talk to you a great deal about your education, but some good, sacred memory, preserved from childhood, is perhaps the best education. If a man carries many such memories with him into life, he is safe to the end of his days, and if one has only one good memory left in one's heart, even that may sometime be the means of saving us" (188).

Like Mengestu, Ellison was a close reader of Dostoevsky. He originally modeled the voice of the Invisible Man on that of the Russian writer's Underground Man. Both isolated protagonists rage against the conventions of their day, and just as the Underground Man cannot surmount his own self-hatred, the Invisible Man lacks the courage to end his self-imposed hibernation. The two succumb to cowardice and shame rather than risk emerging from the safety of their isolation. They lack the education that Alyosha imparts to the boys, "some good, sacred memory" that will provide them with renewed confidence in their own character and goodness. For Alyosha, such a memory requires loving another person, or as he tells the boys, "let us never forget how good we once felt here, all together, united by such good and kind feelings as made us, too, for the time that we loved the poor boy, perhaps better than we actually are" (774). There is not a single moment in Ellison's long novel that demonstrates the Invisible Man's ability to provide the kind of love that Alyosha honors here.

The community Alyosha nurtures and celebrates in this critical scene is entirely absent in *Invisible Man.*

Sepha, though ever troubled by his role in his father's death, at least finds some solace and peace through his relationships with others. Though he and Judith are unable to sustain their tentative affair, he remains steadfast in his tender feelings for Naomi. Sepha recalls, "Sometimes while I read, Naomi would lay her head against my arm or in my lap and rest there, wide awake and attentive, until forced to move. It was just enough to make me see how one could want so much more out of life" (105). United with Naomi through reading, Sepha dares to hope for a life beyond his calculated anonymity. However, Sepha's friendship with Naomi is cut short when Judith enrolls her daughter in a boarding school. During Sepha's last encounter with Judith, she gives him a letter from Naomi. He cherishes the two pages of "carefully scripted letters," and then "hid the letter under the cash register. I imagined that if I ever wanted to read it again, it would be while I was standing here, behind the counter" (215). Sepha's placement of the letter recalls his desire to spend his days in his store, "read[ing] silent as a god until the world came to an end." Naomi's letter suggests that Sepha may at last give up his habit of reading only books from the library. A future correspondence with Naomi promises a form of reading that is not an escape from life but an embrace of the vulnerabilities and visibilities required of genuine intimacy.

If reading was once a way for Sepha to cultivate his own invisibility, it at last prompts him to reengage with life and move beyond his isolation. On the final page of the novel, he reflects, "What was it my father used to say? A bird stuck between two branches gets bitten on both wings. I would like to add my own saying to the list now, Father: a man stuck between two worlds lives and dies alone. I have dangled and been suspended long enough" (228). Sepha's suggestion that he will not live and die alone recalls the Invisible Man's implicit promise that he will at last leave his underground lair "since there's a possibility that even an invisible man has a socially responsible role to play" (581). But while many critics have rightly argued that the Invisible Man may never actually emerge into the world, Sepha ends the novel walking through his neighborhood, admiring how his store "looks more perfect than ever before." Explaining that he "can see it exactly as I have always wanted to see it," Sepha replaces his desire for invisibility with the satisfaction of identifying his store "neither broken nor perfect . . . as entirely my own" (228). As an extension of his tentative claim to the United States, his store symbolizes the beginning of Sepha's visible life in America. Unlike the underground lair of Ellison's Invisible Man, Sepha's store represents a commitment to engaging in a complex social world and becoming part of the fabric of black life.

NARRATING YOUR OWN FATHER IN *HOW TO READ THE AIR*

The Beautiful Things That Heaven Bears ends with Sepha adding to his father's wisdom. Building on his father's saying, Sepha asserts the wisdom of his individual experience. This constructive dynamic is further explored in *How to Read the Air*, which extends Mengestu's critique of Ellisonian constructs through its concern with the legacy of absent black fathers. This motif again connects Mengestu's novel to *Invisible Man* while also providing a way to differentiate its two main characters: Angela, an African American, and Jonas, the son of African immigrants. Like Sepha, Jonas Woldermariam, the novel's narrator, resorts to a form of invisibility as a way to cope with his traumatic past. Born to Ethiopian parents but an American by birth, Jonas is similarly haunted by the history of his father. However, while Sepha was a witness to his father's execution, Jonas can only speculate on the experiences that shaped his father's violent temper. This history is largely inaccessible to Jonas, but his need to understand his parents' conflicted marriage is so great that he imagines their story, creating a narrative that reflects his anxieties as much as their actual experiences.

Jonas represents an important evolution from Sepha who found meaning through reading and the consumption of narratives about other people. Jonas is very much a storyteller even if his tales are built on an unsettling mixture of imagination and fact, or as the title of the novel suggests, little more than air. While employed at a refugee resettlement center, Jonas is tasked with embellishing the narratives of recently arrived immigrants. By adding drama and vivid descriptions to their stories, he increases their chances of receiving asylum. These lies are tied to a very specific kind of material gain, the opportunity to live and prosper in the United States, which directly corresponds to the form of black identity that Jonas adopts in the novel. While Sepha hides in the anonymity associated with those who are "poor" and "black," Jonas aligns himself with the upward mobility of his wife Angela. As part of a "black power couple," Jonas becomes defined by his wife's aspirations. By hiding in her fantasies, he attempts to escape his family's traumas.

Like Jonas, Angela has a conflicted relationship with her father, who abandoned his family when she was a child. Although Jonas's father was physically present during his childhood, he invoked such terror as to make any intimacy or affection between them impossible. Jonas responds to his father by willing himself into a kind of invisibility in order to avoid his anger and violence. Invisibility is for Jonas the starting point of his relationship with Angela as he effectively becomes the black husband she needs to ease her racial and class anxieties. Both *How to Read the Air* and Mengestu's third novel, *All Our Names*, explore the ways in which women project racialized fantasies onto African men. Because these fantasies are derived from the experiences of African Americans, they prove to be awkward if not impossible translations for Mengestu's Ethiopian characters. Jonas and Angela's marriage ends in divorce because Jonas cannot sustain the deceptions that initially drew Angela to him. He cannot at last align his story with her own in part because he is not even aware of his family history and, more importantly, because he refuses to admit his tenuous relationship to the past. He prefers to let Angela project her fantasies on him rather than reveal his flawed, incomplete self to her. While Angela actively grapples with her difficult childhood and in particular her father's absence throughout the novel, Jonas is largely silent about his past, sharing almost nothing about his family with his wife. This silence proves to be deeply destructive, as it prevents any long-standing intimacy between them.

Like Jonas, Angela must fill in the gaps of her childhood. She tells Jonas multiple versions of how her father left. In one instance, she states that he went out for cigarettes and never returned; in other moments, she describes his arrest for petty crimes. She first mentions her father when Jonas comes home late from work one evening. Worried after calling him multiple times to no avail, she states, "You know that's how my father left us." Having heard "at least a half-dozen ways this imaginary father of hers had left," Jonas understands that Angela "turned to him whenever she felt she needed to prove that she hadn't actually been worried" (47). Jonas's reading of Angela's invocation of her father is peculiar because it elides the issue of her actual worry; rather than address her very real concern, he focuses on the image she wishes to project. This failure to address his wife's anxiety reflects his refusal to explore how her past structures her present. Angela's concern about Jonas clearly reignites her childhood fear of abandonment and the specter of her absent father. Jonas, however, is unable to consider the consequences of her fear and, most importantly, his role in fostering her anxiety. By creating multiple versions of her father's departure, Angela makes the past conform to the particularities of her present moment. In this way, she affirms how this early trauma continues to impact her life even as her husband remains impassive to his part in this dynamic.

Angela's contradictory narratives indicate that, like Jonas, she has no idea what actually happened to her father. This ambiguity becomes a dark joke when, after listening to a former roommate describe her plans to go to Mexico for Christmas, Angela states, "That's funny. . . . That's exactly what my father did. He went to Mexico just before Christmas, but then he never came back. I guess he must have really liked it. Maybe you'll see him down there. Tall black guy" (48–49). Jonas and Angela spend the rest of the evening trying to interject the phrase "that's the same thing my father said just before he left us" into other people's conversations. Although they arrive home still laughing, their antics prompt only stares from the other partygoers. Angela understands such consternation as explicitly racial, commenting, "If I was white, everyone would think I was joking. . . . Instead everyone thinks it's true" (49). Angela's observation highlights the racial dynamics at play in the trope of the absent black father. This is especially important because although Jonas is not African American, he too must contend with his own troubled paternal legacy. Though united by their absent fathers just as they are united by their blackness, Jonas and Angela differ considerably in how they respond to their family histories and their racial identities.

Although Angela's malleable approach to the past would seem to be an ideal fit with Jonas's own vivid imagination, he proves unable to share any part of his family's story, speculative or not, with her. Angela's fungible relationship to the truth provides a model for the story Jonas eventually tells about his parents. This parallel relationship suggests an important similarity between their personal histories. As the children of absent fathers, they must effectively create their own fathers. This necessity resonates with one of the key quests of Ellison's Invisible Man, who is told by the wise vet at the Golden Day, "Be your own father, young man" (156). The Invisible Man must become his own father in part because no father exists for him in the novel. Instead, he is confronted with a series of failed fathers, including Mr. Norton, Bledsoe, and Jack, whose misguided examples emphasize the importance of the vet's admonition.

Mengestu's characters demonstrate the impossibility of being one's own father. Neither Angela nor Jonas can renounce the profound sorrow that their fathers have wrought in their lives. Just as Sepha cannot retreat underground and cut off ties with his friends and community, Jonas and Angela cannot take the place of their own fathers. Such a substitution would negate the enormity of their loss. If the Invisible Man ever becomes his own father, it is only because he has no father to begin with. By refusing to sever or deny such a fundamental bond for his characters, Mengestu explores the generative aspects of loss. Rather than serving as their own fathers, Jonas and Angela create their fathers through experimental narratives. They do not supplant their fathers as the Invisible Man seeks to do. Instead, they create stories about their fathers that allow them to make sense of their own lives and relationships. This approach again refigures the hierarchical relationship implicit between parents and children or, in Morrison's terms, ancestors and descendants. Mengestu takes seriously the absence of his characters' fathers and the profound, irrevocable loss this incurs. But rather than present a neat substitution for Angela and Jonas, even one involving a heroic repositioning of them as their own fathers, Mengestu uses the narratives they tell as gateways to other forms of creation. There is no triumphant return of the father here, only the stories Jonas and Angela imagine, stories that generate both laughter and sorrow and, most importantly, the love that draws them together.

Jonas's fraught relationship with his father is the reason that he cultivates his sense of invisibility. From a very early age, Jonas tries to make himself disappear in order to cope with his difficult home life. He reflects how "for so long I had concentrated my efforts on trying to appear to be almost nothing at all—neither nameless nor invisible, just obscure enough to blend into the background and be quickly forgotten" (101). Jonas develops this strategy as a response to his violent father. He recalls how "one evening he came home from work and didn't notice me at all. I was sitting near the end of the couch, with my knees lifted to my chest and the lamp next to me deliberately turned off, and I realized then that all I had to do to avoid him was blend into the background. That knowledge followed me from there so that eventually I thought of my obscurity as being essential to my survival." Although Jonas states that he does not aim for invisibility, he later comments, "Whoever can't see you can't hurt you. That was the reigning philosophy of my days." A form of embodied invisibility is his goal. Even if he does not aim to disappear physically from the world, he masks himself so thoroughly that his emotions and desires become opaque, not just to others but to himself. If no one can see him, then no one can hurt him. Identifying this state as "neither nameless nor invisible," Jonas seems to acknowledge the impossibility of ever fully escaping his name and his body and thus himself. Again, Mengestu points to the limitations of Ellisonian invisibility by emphasizing the inescapable particularities of Jonas's identity. This version of invisibility also departs from Ellison's conception by operating not as a response to a racist society but instead as a defense mechanism against personal trauma. And yet in both Ellison's masterpiece and Mengestu's novels, invisibility provides a secretive haven, a way of removing oneself from the world in order to protect the self.

One might argue that Mengestu here deracializes invisibility as a trope by making it a consequence of Jonas's history of domestic abuse. There is nothing particularly black about a man who physically assaults his wife or a child who is afraid of his father's temper. But Jonas's racial identity is as inescapable as his childhood trauma. Moreover, the invisibility he cultivates as a child has a profound effect on his later approach to race. His father's rage is derived in part from his escape from Africa and his difficult marriage to a woman who does not recognize her husband when she joins him in the United States years after they first meet. Jonas's fear of confrontation impacts how he relates to his racial identity as an adult. He opts for invisibility or at least a form of calculated ambiguity rather than claim his own blackness, as either an African or an African American. Throughout the novel, Jonas is deliberately cagey with people who question him about his origins. When one of his students asks him where he is from, he insists only that he is from Illinois, though he understands that he is being questioned about where in Africa his parents were born. Rather than simplistically map

Ellisonian invisibility onto Jonas, Mengestu provides his protagonist with a history of invisibility that is particular to his experience. Mengestu does not have Jonas merely inherit one of the most important metaphors of black subjectivity; instead, this son of African immigrants experiences a form of invisibility that is informed both by his family's migration story as well as by his own encounter with American forms of race and racism. Jonas is a new kind of invisible man, one who bears the burden of black skin in an ever-racialized America and who wields invisibility as a strategic mode of survival.

Jonas's childhood need to hide himself from his father helps contextualize his approach to racial matters. Like Ellison's Invisible Man, Jonas gains coherence and identity by interacting with others; both characters need the expectations and directives of others to define themselves. The Invisible Man becomes a model student and an obsequious worker when confronted with whites and blacks alike who demand he be a "credit to his race" (255). Jonas, however, is more discerning of the company he keeps, and he quickly pairs himself with Angela, the only other black person working at the refugee resettlement center. Like Jonas, Angela understands herself apart from the social roles she is expected to play though she proves to be far more settled in her identity than her future husband. Angela has worked hard to build a professional career. She tells Jonas "how she felt the first time she looked in the mirror and told herself that she was a lawyer. 'It was strange,' she said. 'I had to say it three times before I really began to believe it'" (15). Angela does, however, convince herself that she is a lawyer, and as the novel progresses, it becomes clear that she has a stronger relationship to the truth and her own identity than Jonas. This is especially evident in their differing approach toward race, an issue that Jonas largely evades just as he evades his past history.

As a black woman, Angela is keenly attuned to matters of race and gender. Her first question to Jonas is if he is bothered that the only other black people at the center are clients. He replies that he never thinks about this. She confesses that she too doesn't give it much thought though "I wonder sometimes if it should" (18). Angela's response highlights one of the key differences between the soon to be lovers. While Jonas largely ignores distinctions of race and color, Angela sees race as defining much of her life. This is demonstrated in particular by her awareness of how her class mobility has isolated her from her racial community. As she and Jonas celebrate their marriage over dinner, the two view their surroundings in significantly different ways. Jonas notes, "the restaurant was crowded with a dozen other couples in suits." By contrast, Angela observes, "Don't look now . . . but we're the only black people here" (73), to which Jonas replies, "Don't worry . . . I don't think anyone's noticed," as he playfully covers his face with the menu. Angela clearly perceives racial difference as a defining part of her surroundings. Jonas, however, seems indifferent to race, noticing only the clothing of the other couples. His comment that "I don't think anyone's noticed" subtly undermines Angela's observation. Even if others did not notice, she certainly did, and his failure to affirm her comment demonstrates how little meaning he assigns to race. In a similar way, Angela ignores Jonas's comment, replying, "Someone is probably wondering why they don't see more black people here, especially since we've all supposedly come so far."

There's a deep bitterness to Angela's statement even as it also exposes her anxiety toward her own upward mobility. Angela is one of the people who has "come so far," escaping an impoverished childhood to become a corporate lawyer. Despite her achievements, she is clearly ambivalent about a form of success that isolates her from other African Americans. When Jonas tells her that the other restaurant patrons must be "grateful to see us," Angela adds, "As long as it's just the two of us, trust me. They're delighted." Jonas does not respond to Angela's final comment and thus fails to delve into the racial dynamics at work in his wife's life and consequently in his own as well. Though she struggles to understand herself as a lawyer and an upwardly mobile woman, Angela recognizes the ways in which race shapes her social world. Jonas's reluctance to acknowledge race is not deceitful or fraudulent, but it does suggest a refusal to accept certain truths in Angela's life.

While Sepha longs for the anonymity of those who are poor and black, Jonas loses himself in another trope of African American identity. By marrying Angela, he ties his future to her aspirations and anxieties. Jonas notes, "For a woman who had grown up deep on the side of poverty . . . the line that separated the two halves of her life, in her mind, could be moved at any time, and she was convinced that only increasingly larger sums of wealth could protect her from a return to the poor, rootless childhood that she had known" (71). Class mobility is essential to Angela's hopes. When Jonas is laid off from his job at the resettlement center, she is first concerned about how they will pay their monthly bills, but Jonas notes that "even worse, I now figured into someone's statistic—the twenty-five-to-thirty-five-year-old black male without a job; Angela had come too far in life to bear that for long" (52–53). Jonas threatens to become a stereotype of black underachievement, and thus she urges Jonas to apply to graduate school even after she helps him get a teaching position at a private prep school. He adopts her dreams without clearly acknowledging his own desires: "We began to think of ourselves as a black power couple in a city full of aspirants, the kind who would someday vacation for an entire month in the summer and whose children would attend elite private schools" (56). With Angela, Jonas finds purpose and a way to define himself racially.

Jonas, however, is able to sustain Angela's fantasy for only a brief period of time. He sabotages his teaching position at the academy by ignoring his lesson plans and instead telling his students the story of his father's harrowing escape from Ethiopia to the United States. It is impossible to know what parts of Jonas's story are based in fact and what are complete fabrications. The truth of his narrative is less important than the effect this storytelling has on Jonas. After the first day describing his father's life to his students, Jonas returns home to Angela with the news that he has been invited to teach at the academy full time. His jubilation at his new narrative power can be translated to Angela only through a lie that demonstrates her version of success. He describes talking with the dean who promises him tenure in two years and a doubling of his salary. The encounter is a total falsehood, though Jonas notes, "However imagined that conversation may have been, the effect was nonetheless real. I was going to move forward in life" (189). Despite lying to his wife, Jonas is moving forward by beginning to grapple with his father's past. His excitement over his classroom storytelling only highlights how he and Angela have very different conceptions of progress. Jonas's lie to Angela demonstrates his understanding of the value she places on financial stability and social status. She wants a husband with a professional career and respectable salary. By contrast, Jonas measures progress through his understanding of his parents and their stories.

Jonas tells the story of his father to his students rather than to Angela due to his overwhelming fear of intimacy. For Jonas, knowledge of his origins equates with a form of possession, or as he explains, "What I didn't understand until I began teaching was that knowledge, or perhaps intimate knowledge I should say, was the first step toward possessing anything" (95). Angela's lack of knowledge about her husband's country of origin and his past in general suggests that she does not possess him at all. However, with his students, Jonas is never in danger of being possessed. No doubt he tells his father's story to them knowing that it will lead to the end of his employment. To tell Angela his story would require a level of visibility he cannot sustain. Moreover, before his students Jonas is an undisputed authority, able to provide a definitive account even though much of what he relates is a product of his imagination. To tell Angela his version of his father's story would be to admit that he is like her, unaware of the real details of his family's history. Rather than acknowledge their similarities, he performs for an audience that never questions his hold on the truth. Jonas's refusal to share with Angela his imaginative storytelling might also be read as a reluctance on his part to identify himself with his absent black father. Just as he fails to acknowledge the racial dynamics at play in their lives, Jonas also fails to see himself as impacted by this notable black trope.

Jonas must eventually leave the academy after the dean catches him in his lie about being offered a permanent teaching position. When he returns to his wife after his last day at the academy, she explains that she already knew he had been lying. Angela decides not to confront him with the truth in order to dwell a little longer in the fantasy world of his deception, stating, "We were suddenly happy. I probably would have done almost anything to have kept that going for as long as possible. I even began to fantasize on the train that maybe you really would find something great, at the school or someplace else, and that everything we talked about would still be possible" (294). The dream to be part of a "black power couple" is so overwhelming that truth, as in Jonas's story of his father's life, falls away. Angela proves to be just as dependent on Jonas's false version of himself as he is on her aspirational vision. United by their common need for a certain kind of racialized identity, they become invisible to each other.

In the final pages of the novel, Jonas relates how in one of their last conversations before their divorce, Angela confessed her fear of disappearing: "'If we're not together,' she said, 'then I wonder what's left. I'm afraid to find someday that there's no one who knows me anymore. I could disappear and who would care.'" Jonas reflects on his wife's fear: "Once I would have had a hard time finding fault in that. I would have thought that there was little else that one could look forward to in life other than being set free from others' demands and the obligations they placed on both your time and heart. The invisibility that came with that freedom was a small price to pay for all the damage and pain that could be avoided as a result. By the time I had packed my bags and was preparing to leave Angela, I was grateful I no longer believed that" (304). Angela's fear shifts invisibility from a site of desire for Jonas to a site of danger. What had once been a coveted condition becomes a threat to his very self. The ultimate consequence of invisibility is not freedom and the elimination of pain but absence. Angela's comment also suggests that only Jonas truly saw her, that to the rest of the world she is invisible. While this conclusion affirms how invisibility remains an important facet of African American life, Angela also implies that meaningful intimacy is possible between members of the wide pan-African American diaspora. Jonas comforts Angela with the promise that she will not disappear because "we're going to remain a part of each other's lives for much longer than we think." Reflecting on the influence of his parents as well as of his wife, Jonas concludes, "We do persist, whether we care to or not, with all our flaws and glory" (305). Jonas's final comments again affirm the impossibility of invisibility. His dead father and distant mother persist through him and the stories he weaves. And despite their failed marriage, Jonas and Angela remain deeply connected, proof that fantasies and their racialized roots offer as much insight into the self as historical truths.

BECOMING VISIBLE: *ALL OUR NAMES*

Sepha and Jonas both use invisibility as a way to protect themselves from the dangers of intimacy. Rather than asserting their unique experiences, they hide in versions of African American identity that do not adequately reflect their own desires and histories. Isaac, one of Mengestu's dual narrators in his latest novel,

All Our Names, also escapes into the identity of another—but in a far more literal manner. A refugee of Uganda, Isaac has adopted the name and identity of his closest friend and comrade in order to begin a new life in the United States. A literal fugitive of his past, this new Isaac must further contend with American expectations of race that complicate his relationships with others. As in *How to Read the Air,* this African immigrant becomes a site of racialized fantasies for his lover. These projections reflect the long-standing historical anxieties of Helen, a white social worker assigned to help Isaac adjust to the United States. *All Our Names,* like Mengestu's second novel, alternates between two narratives. However, while Jonas struggles to make the story of his parents merge with his marriage and eventual divorce, the stories of Helen and Isaac at last converge in their decision to build a new life together in Chicago. *All Our Names* represents the culmination of Mengestu's exploration of invisibility by presenting a romantic relationship grounded in the intimacy of mutual storytelling. Both Helen and Isaac are made visible to each other through their shared narratives; to be seen is to be heard. By recognizing the deceptions that structure their behavior, they move past the fear and hesitation that so limited Sepha and Jonas.

Born and raised in the Midwest, Helen has never before encountered someone like Isaac. Upon seeing him for the first time, she comes to realize "two assumptions I wasn't aware of possessing: the first that Africans were short, and the second that even the ones who flew all the way to a college town in the middle of America would probably show signs of illness or malnutrition" (14). Tall and as Helen concludes not "bad-looking," Isaac exposes and challenges her unconscious prejudices. Though hardly racist, Helen discovers that she is not as open-minded as she expected. Unable to identify or categorize this mysterious man, she finds that "compared with others, Isaac was made of almost nothing, not a ghost but a sketch of a man I was trying hard to fill in" (21). While Mengestu's first two novels explore invisibility from the perspective of those who are or want to be invisible, *All Our Names* examines the process by which an invisible man is made visible to another. This unusual narrative approach emphasizes how invisibility is a condition born of both the seen and the seer. In *Invisible Man,* Ellison stopped short of exploring how characters like Mr. Norton and Jack make the novel's protagonist invisible. Though he ventures, "Who knows but that, on the lower frequencies, I speak for you?" (581), neither author nor narrator dares to imagine how this mutuality of experience works for white characters. By structuring the novel through chapters that alternate between Helen and Isaac's perspectives, Mengestu makes Isaac's invisibility the responsibility of both narrators. While Isaac must be willing to share his story with Helen, she must rid herself of her ingrained prejudices. Helen, despite her best intentions, cannot help but bear the marks of her racist society. As she attempts to "color in the missing parts" (21) of Isaac, she inevitably applies, though at last rejects, racial constructs derived from her own experiences and her acute sense of white guilt.

Through Isaac, Helen attempts to work through her failure to take part in the civil rights battles of her youth. As a witness but not a participant in this history, she has been content to observe the complacency of her fellow townspeople. Isaac's presence, and most importantly his black skin, forces her to reevaluate her relationship to forms of discrimination. Raised in a world that defines race through black/white relationships, Helen is bewildered by Isaac's presence. He is both black and not black; though he has dark skin, he bears none of the history that Helen identifies with the African American community. While watching a group of black students on the steps of the university library, she notes that she "couldn't have pictured him among that crowd" (99). Although Helen instinctively associates Isaac with these black students, she does not seem aware of how this categorization ignores the profound cultural and historical differences that exist between them.

The affair between Helen and Isaac begins in private. She notes, "No one watched us draw closer, and no one was there to say that we made for a great or poorly matched couple" (18). This absence of observers applies just as well to Helen and Isaac as they seem not to fully see or even believe in the presence of one another. After their first kiss, Helen pinches his fingers, stating, "I'm making sure you're really here" (20). In trying to make Isaac real to herself, Helen maps the racial history of her hometown onto her new lover. Although she describes Laurel as "middle of the road, never bitterly segregated," she knows "that certain risks had to be taken if Isaac and I were going to have any sort of life together" (33). Helen understands the political stakes of making her relationship with Isaac more public, but in doing so she fashions herself as a kind of integrationist crusader. Reflecting on her shopping ventures with Isaac, she imagines, "Had Isaac and I touched each other once, I would have said we dealt an important blow against segregation" (34–35). Aware of her own cowardice since she and Isaac "never touched except by accident," Helen decides that "what I needed next were new targets" (35)—that is, locations where she can put her relationship with Isaac on display. This dangerous approach both fetishizes their affair and ignores Isaac as he effectively becomes a tool to her misguided schemes. She invites him to lunch at a diner she frequented as a child with her father. By not telling Isaac about her political and personal motives, she uses him to assuage her white guilt.

Though he offers to meet her at the diner, Helen insists on picking him up "so everyone could see us walk in together." For Helen, the scene is to unfold according to a "scripted version that had played in my head." In this fantasy, "All eyes turned toward us, and we ignored them. We didn't hold hands—that would have been too provocative—but we did pause to look at each other with what I thought of as an abundance of affection" (36). Even in her dreams, Helen does not have the courage to touch Isaac and "deal[t] an important blow against segregation." Her imagined version of events reflects her abiding cowardice, while also robbing Isaac of any agency of his own.

Immediately aware that he is a prop in her activist charade, Isaac recognizes Helen's miscalculation upon arriving at the diner and asks her why they are here. Helen brushes off Isaac's question but soon realizes that she has made a grave mistake. The waitress suggests that the couple take their food to go. Isaac responds faster than Helen, insisting that they stay. Helen, however, requests that they leave. Confronted with Isaac's determination to stay, Helen "felt bold again" and she quickly returns to her elaborate fantasies: "I saw myself adding this lunch to my column of victories once I returned to the office. If we made it through this, then perhaps there was nothing in the world we couldn't conquer, from post offices to movie theaters and the all-too-perilous family dinner at home. I was imagining what my mother would say if Isaac were to show up one Sunday evening, when his lunch arrived" (38). Overwhelmed by her self-congratulatory visions, Helen becomes blind to the man sitting across from her. He disappears in her noble, solipsistic fantasies. Helen's boldness fades almost instantly and she grabs their young waitress to tell her to cancel her order. Isaac remains steadfast, insisting they finish their lunch because "that's what you wanted, isn't it?" (39).

Helen again escapes into her fantasy world rather than confront the difficult reality before her: "In this story, Isaac and I were still heroes. The fact that we chose to sit there and linger when every part of me wanted to run was proof of the sacrifices we were willing to make" (39–40). Ignoring her childish desperation to leave as well as Isaac's "slightly cruel" insistence that they finish their lunch, Helen fashions a story that finds virtue in her escapade, not shame and fear. Neither she nor Isaac is a hero. They have not sacrificed in the name of integration; instead, Helen has sacrificed Isaac's trust in order to play out her racial fantasy. Using him to enter into the progressive narrative of civil rights, she ignores his history as well as her own racial insecurities.

Two weeks pass before Helen again sees Isaac after the incident at the diner. While before she had thought of him as a "sketch of a man," she now hopes that she will have faded in his memory: "A part of me hoped that, given enough time, he might begin to forget what I looked like, that my chin and nose and eyes might begin to blur with the images of a million other women" (50). Like Sepha and Jonas, Helen appears to long for a kind of invisibility that will erase the past. This instinct is hardly specific to any racial group but instead reflects a desire to escape her embarrassment. Though she wants to call Isaac, she is too ashamed to do so. He instead surprises her one day by appearing at her office. Helen's response again demonstrates both her cowardice and her sheer ignorance about the man she has been fantasizing about: "I'd never felt afraid of him before, but seeing him in that chair that morning I was reminded of how little I knew about him, and for a few seconds I considered turning around and running away" (51). Helen's fear exposes how Isaac's physical presence undermines the safe fantasies she has conjured for herself. In fact, Helen admits to herself while alone one day at Isaac's apartment that he is an impediment to the romance she imagines them having. Lying on his bed, she reflects, "Isaac was so much easier to be with when only the ghost of him was around, and I remember thinking that if he were dead or never came back, I'd probably learn to care for him more than if he were to walk through that door right then and never leave" (71). Helen prefers to have a relationship with "a sketch of man" rather than confront Isaac's messy, complicated reality.

Isaac, however, does little to make himself accessible to Helen—that is, to allow her to see him for who he really is. Without notice, he disappears for three weeks and just as abruptly returns with small presents for Helen collected on his travels to various American cities. This physical absence reflects Helen's struggle to see and know Isaac even when he is present. Before Helen meets Isaac again after his trip, she returns to the university where she took him on his first day in town: "I tried my best to draw a solid image of Isaac, first alone, and then together with me, and when that wasn't enough, I drove to the university and parked near the library, where I hoped the memory of him on his first day in Laurel would remind me of who Isaac 'really' was when I wasn't part of the picture" (98). Helen's search for the real Isaac requires that she erase herself from the image she has constructed of him. For the first time, Helen tries to envision Isaac without her influence or through the complications of her desires and regret. Helen recalls the final weeks of her senior year at the university "when the entire campus had been closed off and traces of tear gas could be seen from blocks away. I had watched that on television, from the safety of my mother's living room, convinced that I was missing out on something important" (99). She concludes, "It wasn't nostalgia but regret that guided me through the campus that afternoon. All that time lost—not to have done more, but to have seen better" (100). To understand her own relationship to history and to Isaac, Helen must see others in a new way.

As she observes a group of black students, she notes, "Had Isaac been younger, I still couldn't have pictured him among that crowd." Although he shares their black skin, Isaac does not share their history and sense of community. This recognition of Isaac's fundamental difference from the black students represents Helen's first step to seeing Isaac clearly. Impressed by their "cool confidence" (99), she considers what battle would have been worth her effort and thus her regret: "If it were possible to grant the small measure of entitlement that was theirs to others, then that would be worth fighting for. I didn't have the words to explain it at the time, but as soon as the thought crossed my mind, I knew it was wrong. There wasn't a protest in the world that could have done that for them. The right to claim their small share of this country had always been theirs; they knew that long before the rest of us. I wondered if the same would ever be true for someone like Isaac" (100). Initially, Helen seems to believe that the battle for civil rights was a battle for "the small measure of entitlement" she perceives among the black students, as if the change that was required was a change in their own sense of self-esteem. But Helen quickly realizes how this misguided conclusion places responsibility on African Americans rather than on the benighted whites who denied them access to the university and other public institutions. The struggle Helen must embrace is the one that allows her to understand her complicity in forms of discrimination. Through Isaac, Helen begins this difficult process by observing how her fantasies work to assuage and erase her white guilt. Instead of aligning herself with social protest, Helen focuses on Isaac, wondering if he will embrace his right to the United States. If there is a difference between Isaac and the African Americans it lies here: while the students Helen sees belong in this country, Isaac continues to search for a place to which he belongs. Armed with her new vision, Helen then spots Isaac walking to the campus parking lot. She is amazed to see him get into a car and drive away because he earlier told her that he had never learned how to operate a vehicle. Although Helen knows that she "had been lied to" (101), she finds herself smiling. At last she sees Isaac shorn of her fantasies and desires.

This clarity does not last long for Helen. The night that she is to meet with Isaac following his sudden return to Laurel, she circles his neighborhood, looking for the car she saw him enter outside the university. Unsettled by Isaac's ability to drive, Helen at last understands that her lover is full of secrets. This knowledge excites her as she relishes the possibilities of his mysterious identity. "Was he friend, or foe? I had a hard time deciding. There was something classically romantic about falling for the enemy—the risks were greater, and so were the odds against a happy ending. But I could see a possible happy ending if Isaac was on our side; I could be not only his lover but his confidante, and who could ask for a better cover than a woman like me? Adventure versus romance—not being alone won out every time" (112). Helen's thoughts demonstrate how she again uses her fantasy of Isaac to fuel her own desires. She craves a narrative that ends in her ultimate wish—not to be alone like her mother. His mystery becomes a prop used to support the story she wants to tell about herself. His truth—his identity, history, and desires—is made invisible by her demand for a "happy ending." She even believes that her uneventful life will be an asset to him as if her passivity and political detachment will at last prove to be sources of strength rather than emblems of her shame. However, Helen quickly recognizes that her fantasies are childish and even cowardly. While waiting outside his apartment, deciding if she should leave, Helen is surprised by Isaac who grabs her arm and leads her back to her car. Helen feels her body "recoil" at his touch. When he apologizes for surprising her, Helen replies, "You didn't surprise me. You just never know who's watching" (113). Helen's statement suggests that they may be in danger as an interracial couple publicly displaying signs of intimacy. But in her narration, she admits that her excuse is a lie. She recoils not because she fears the racists in her town but because the man who grabs her is a complete mystery to her.

Immediately after this episode, Helen reflects, "I wonder whether, if before meeting Isaac I had tried to challenge the easy, small-time bigotry that was so common to our daily lives that I noticed it only in its extremes, I might have felt a little less shame that evening" (113). Helen's shame emanates from her recognition of how she has used Isaac to evade her white guilt. If he is indeed an African spy, her lack of civil disobedience becomes an ideal cover, a way for her to become part of a larger liberation movement without having to risk anything of her own. Helen must admit that she has done nothing "to challenge the easy, small-time bigotry" that circumscribes Isaac's American life. As Isaac leaves her to return to his apartment, Helen "wished that there were some way I could vanish or simply slip out of my skin, keep my flesh but without the exterior that came with it" (114). Helen's desire to disappear is explicitly racial. She longs to be rid of the shame and guilt of her whiteness.

Helen's relationship to Isaac shifts more definitively when she learns that his friend Isaac has died and that the man she knows adopted the deceased's identity. She admits that she "had known all along that there was something fraudulent about the man sitting next to me" (149). The truth about Isaac's identity almost seems to vindicate Helen; even as she projected fantasies onto him, he was passing himself off as another. Neither Isaac nor Helen had allowed the real Isaac to be seen. If invisibility is a result of the seer and the seen, then both Helen and Isaac are responsible for his absent self. With the original Isaac now gone, Isaac allows Helen to see him for who he really is. Before he starts to tell her his story, they go to a motel where for the first time they have sex slowly, able to carefully study one another's bodies: "Isaac and I had the whole night ahead of us, and so, for once, we took our time. We kissed just on the other side of the door until our legs were tired, and then fell onto the bed; in another first, Isaac was the one to undress me. . . . We finished just as we had begun, unashamed and nearly laughing. We had left the lights on and could finally see each other with our eyes, not just our hands, and for what felt like hours all we did was stare at each other's bodies" (151). The tentative nature of their earlier encounters falls away as Isaac and Helen explore each other's bodies. Rather than hide in the dark, they see each other clearly. This scene anticipates the emotional intimacy to come as Isaac begins to narrate his story to Helen, and she in turn takes him to meet her mother. Just as Helen and Isaac need time to understand one another's physical bodies, Helen needs time to absorb his story: "Just as I had wanted him to talk, I needed him to stop. I didn't know it earlier, but this was what had governed our silence—not that we couldn't understand each other but that we could lay ourselves bare and in the end each find a stranger sitting on the other side" (188). Helen recognizes that listening to Isaac's story may not be enough to understand him. Afraid of this possibility, she leaves early in the morning and drives to speak with her friend and boss David. He tells her that he hoped to see her with Isaac, and she asks him why he never left Laurel. He replies by telling her how when he was a child he asked his father why the black people of Mississippi did not leave. His father said, "maybe they didn't believe anything would change, or maybe they were waiting for the world to change around them and they wanted to be home when it did." David continues, "It was the most eloquent thing he had ever said to me, and I knew he must have asked that same question himself and that was the best answer he could come up with. I would say both reasons are equally true" (192). Regardless of the reason that the black people stayed, Helen resolves to leave. She returns to Isaac and they make preparations to go to Chicago together. By embracing change and movement, Helen defines herself and Isaac against the black people who stayed in Mississippi. The history of African Americans that she had so intently tried to map onto her relationship with Isaac at last proves to be a story far removed from their own.

The final chapters of Helen's narration describe their journey to Chicago. Both are strangers to the city, and thus for the first time they are equally overwhelmed by their new surroundings—the enormous height of the Hancock building, the expanse of Lake Michigan. As they explore the city, Isaac takes Helen's hand: "We hesitated, looking at our hands, not each other, then gathered our strength and moved forward. We walked. It didn't feel like a victory over anything, but I was proud and, to an equal degree, scared. After walking one block like that, I was grateful for the feeling of his hand in mine, and even for the anxiety that came with it. After two more blocks, the gratitude had turned to sorrow that we hadn't had this sooner. All this time, I thought, we've been at best only half of what was possible" (237). At last, Helen recognizes this moment of physical intimacy not as a blow against segregation but as a personal comfort. Free from the demands of a political imperative and aware of her past failings, Helen experiences Isaac's touch as the thrill of love, not the performance of righteousness. As they stand together on the beach, swinging their arms like birds about to take flight, Helen concludes, "We had to invent new rules, phrases, and axioms to live by" (243). The old models don't hold. Together she and Isaac must discover ways of being that exceed the histories they have known.

Isaac's narration, which focuses on the story of his friendship with the original Isaac and the political upheavals in Kampala, ends the novel. He at last mentions Helen and his new life in the United States. He recalls the last sentence his friend wrote in his notebook, a sentence he "read again after saying good-bye to Helen on a street in Chicago, and which was what I said to her before she left with a promise to return: No one will have ever loved each other more than we did" (256). Isaac's repetition of this sentence makes it both a lie and a part of the "new rules, phrases, and axioms" that Helen envisions. For Isaac to tell Helen that "no one will have ever loved each other more than we did" threatens to demote the love he shared with the original Isaac. However, the peculiar use of the future perfect verb tense envisions a looking back from the future. In the future, love may exceed what has come in the past or even the present. Every new iteration may be more than what has come before. If signifyin(g), the black trope of tropes, is repetition with a difference, then Isaac's invocation of this sentence makes new his love with Helen even as it builds on the stories of his past.

Mengestu's treatment of invisibility subverts Ellison's guiding trope by emphasizing how individuals, especially newly arrived immigrants and their children, depend on families and communities for both survival and identity. This affirmation of the impossibility of invisibility resonates with Toni Morrison's response to Ellison's masterpiece: "Invisible to whom?" she said upon reading the novel, "Not me" (Houston 253). While Ellison's text encodes an awareness of a white observer into its very title, Morrison's works operate from the assumption that a community already exists for her characters. Invisibility marks an escape from intimacy and from forms of identity created through relationships with others. Mengestu's novels similarly demonstrate how invisibility is less a trope of blackness than of escape. By choosing invisibility, his narrators attempt to evade not only race but their very pasts as well.

4 · REFIGURING THE ANCESTOR IN THE FICTION OF CHIMAMANDA NGOZI ADICHIE

Americanah, the third novel by Chimamanda Ngozi Adichie, chronicles the process by which Nigerian-born Ifemelu becomes black by living in the United States. In her popular blog, *Raceteenth or Curious Observations by a Non-American Black on the Subject of Blackness in America*, Ifemelu delineates between two categories of black people: American-born blacks and non-American blacks. However, Ifemelu ultimately comes to occupy a third category; she is an African who chooses not to be black. Despite her interest in America and its complex social relationships, unlike Mengestu's protagonists, she remains a visitor, an outsider who refuses to commit herself to the dynamics she observes. Ifemelu's understanding of blackness is based entirely on geography. She is black only in the United States; once she returns to Nigeria, she is no longer subject to the ramifications of racial identity. This conception of blackness challenges how African Americans experience race. For Ifemelu, blackness is primarily an issue of image and representation. It is a condition she passes through, just as she passes through the United States; it is not an essential part of her ancestry. Though she recognizes the reality of slavery, she lacks a historical awareness of how the legacy of institutionalized discrimination impacts current social dynamics in America. Ifemelu is unavoidably black while living in the United States. However, her understanding of what blackness means offers a stark contrast to how African Americans experience their racial identity. She is effectively black without the history of blackness.

While there is no monolithic history of blackness, Toni Morrison describes the ancestor as a literary figure imbued with an understanding of the racialized past. The ancestor represents awareness and continuity with an individual's black history. Tracking an ancestral presence in Adichie's fiction elucidates how African immigrants relate to history and family in significantly different ways than African Americans. For Morrison, the ancestor is a specifically black construct. By contrast, Adichie presents the ancestor as preracial, existing far earlier than the historically specific adoption of racial categories. In "Rootedness: The Ancestor as Foundation," her most direct discussion of what constitutes the "blackness" of black literature, Morrison highlights the presence of an ancestor as key to understanding textual blackness. As I have cited previously, she explains of African American literature, "There is always an elder there. And these ancestors are not just parents, they are sort of timeless people whose relationships to the characters are benevolent, instructive, and protective, and they provide a certain kind of wisdom" (61–62). Although Morrison refers specifically in this essay to what blackness means in literary texts, her comments also apply to a more generalized understanding of what black identity signifies for African Americans. Exemplified by such figures as Morrison's own Pilate from *Song of Solomon* (1977) and the Invisible Man's grandfather from Ellison's masterpiece, the ancestor reflects familial legacy and historical continuity. The ancestor affirms blackness as a form of community and an identity based on commitment to others. Morrison further notes, "the presence or absence of that figure determined the success or the happiness of the characters" (62), as if personal fulfillment is possible only through a reconciliation with blackness. This formulation presents the racialized self as a precondition of identity and thus challenges how recent African immigrants experience racial ascriptions.

The ancestor is also of vital importance in Adichie's fiction, but this figure operates in almost complete opposition to Morrison's formulation. While Morrison understands the ancestor as foundational to African American identity, Adichie suggests that recent African immigrants have the strongest tie to an ancestral presence. Moreover, while Adichie's African American characters long for a meaningful tie to the ancestor, this desire is largely presented as not only unfulfilled but woefully misguided. In the short story "On Monday of Last Week," Tracy, an African American visual artist, claims that "the motherland informs all of my work," yet her Nigerian nanny Kamara cannot detect any traces of Africa in her painting, which "looked like haphazard splashes of bright paint to her" (*The Thing* 88). Tracy proves to be less interested in the motherland than in capturing the beauty of her son's various caretakers. While American-born blacks in Adichie's fiction either invent their relationship to an ancestral presence or languish without one, recent African immigrants like Ifemelu are portrayed as possessing a more fundamental tie to an African past and thus a firmer sense of self. Ironically, this connection counters the racial identity foisted on them in the United States and powerfully reimagines Morrison's understanding of the ancestor; for Adichie, to be connected to the ancestor is to escape the imposition of blackness.

In *Americanah*, Michael, an African American man Ifemelu meets at a party, expresses his envy of her connection to Nigeria: "It must be good to have that . . . to know where you're from. Ancestors going way back, that kind of thing" (328–329). Ifemelu replies in the affirmative, unable to say more or even meaningfully relate to Michael's longing: "He looked at her, with an expression that made her uncomfortable, because she was not sure what his eyes held, and then he looked away" (329). Here and throughout *Americanah*, African American characters are portrayed as struggling to assert a rooted form of racialized identity that is not merely a response to injustice. Blaine, Ifemelu's boyfriend for many years, and his activist friends continually define blackness through forms of discrimination; to be black is to protest racial oppression and bemoan the state of race relations. This constant vigilance and agitation is at odds with Ifemelu's self-assured calm and her reluctance to align herself with any defined community. As Michael observes, Ifemelu knows where she is from and has a strong relationship to her family. However, this does not signify as a racial trait for her. Though crucial to her identity, her rootedness bears no relationship to the geographic determinant that defines race for Ifemelu.

Michael's comment poses a striking contrast to Morrison's formulation of the ancestor. While for Morrison the ancestor is a cornerstone of African American identity, here the ancestor is presented as the province of the African alone. Moreover, the ancestor here is raceless; it instead connotes a sense of self that is rooted in family and history, not one that is linked to blackness. Throughout *Americanah*, African American characters are portrayed as lacking any meaningful connection to an ancestor. Blaine, a political science professor, is defined primarily through horizontal relationships. He has many close friends and colleagues and especially cherishes his older sister, Shan. However, he is seemingly devoid of parents or older relatives, and despite his success as a young Ivy League professor, he seems to have no mentors. The absence of ancestral figures in his life suggests a lack of rootedness. His blackness is not linked to a historical or familial community; instead, his racial identity emerges as a series of complaints about American society. Though these complaints are rigorously historicized, Blaine derives a connection to the past only through academic study as if race constitutes a body of knowledge he has dutifully mastered. Ifemelu is initially impressed by Blaine and his sophisticated style, but she ultimately leaves him, unable to share his righteous principles and commitment to racial causes. The novel portrays him as charming and intellectual but so bound to the cause of racial injustice as to be without joy, humor, and depth. He embodies blackness as prescription, a devoted conformity that denies a wide spectrum of intraracial difference.

Ifemelu's rejection of Blaine highlights her general approach to the United States. America is never her home, only a curious land of misleading opportunities and unresolved paradoxes. After more than a dozen years living in various cities on the East Coast, Ifemelu returns to Nigeria. The final hundred pages of the novel describe her reintegration into life in Lagos as well as her reunion with her first true love, Obinze. By leaving the United States, Ifemelu escapes all of the contradictions, inconveniences, and confusions of race. This conclusion neatly circumvents the problems of blackness as the novel falls back on the conventions of popular romance. Ifemelu's return to Obinze transforms her American experiences into a series of distracting escapades, a diversion from the essential truth of her decades-long love. Moreover, in Nigeria, Ifemelu begins a new blog titled *The Small Redemptions of Lagos*. Only in her homeland can Ifemelu focus on small redemptions, for as the title of her American blog suggests, race is an overwhelming preoccupation in the United States and redemption an impossible consideration.

Raceteenth is especially concerned with how African immigrants experience race differently than American-born blacks. Adichie does not draw inexorable distinctions between these two groups. Rather, race is presented as a kind of education that immigrants must master. African immigrants, or at least those with considerable financial freedoms, are presented with a kind of choice: to become black like African Americans or, as Ifemelu demonstrates, to escape racial categorization entirely. Ifemelu understands America to be the birthplace of her blackness. She explains in her blog, "Dear Non-American Black, when you make the choice to come to America, you become black. Stop arguing. Stop saying I'm Jamaican or I'm Ghanaian. America doesn't care. So what if you weren't 'black' in your country? You're in America now" (222). For Ifemelu, coming to America is a choice but becoming black is not.

This opposition highlights one of the salient differences between her experience of blackness and the way that race operates for African Americans. While she can choose to leave the United States and return to a country where blackness does not exist, African Americans are born into an inescapable racial identity. Ifemelu's wealth allows her to choose between Nigeria and America, but other American Africans, like her teenage nephew Dike, lack such a convenient respite from race. He must instead find a way to be both black and not black—that is, to contend with the consequences of his dark skin while also recognizing like Ifemelu that race need not be the foundation of his identity. As Adichie's immigrant characters navigate the largely silent but powerful codes of race, they learn that they are not African Americans and at times they seem to share more qualities with middle-class whites. Caught in a society that prefers simplistic binaries, they struggle to understand themselves as black, but not American, often privileged but not white, and strangers to a national history that determines how they are treated or, as is too frequently the case, mistreated.

Dike's attempted suicide and uncertain future in the United States highlight the need for African immigrants to affirm some kind of black identity and forge alliances with African Americans. Although *Americanah* effectively abandons Dike and his struggles in the United States by focusing on Ifemelu's long-anticipated reunion with Obinze, a handful of stories in Adichie's 2009 *The Thing around Your Neck* explore the ways in which African immigrants adjust to life in the United States. "The Arrangers of Marriage" offers the most promising portrait of how African Americans and African immigrants can learn from and support one another. Adichie suggests that American blacks may be just as lost and confused as their recently arrived brethren. However, this shared disorientation can be a point of strength, especially for women who, whether born in Africa or in the United States, must endure similar forms of sexism and vulnerability.

BLAINE AND THE MISEDUCATION OF IFEMELU

Americanah charts Ifemelu's education into the protocols of race. In addition to coming to understand what blackness signifies, Ifemelu must also learn to distinguish American-born blacks from immigrants like herself. Her education is as much intraracial as interracial. Initially, she is unable to perceive the difference between these two groups: "But the longer she spent in America, the better she had become at distinguishing, sometimes from looks and gait, but mostly from bearing and demeanor, that fine-grained mark that culture stamps on people" (178). Adichie seemingly presents the difference between American-born blacks and African immigrants as a matter of culture and thus something that can be learned, adopted, and therefore discarded. And yet the language here exposes a degree of ambivalence in this neat formulation. For culture to "stamp" people and leave a "mark," however "fine-grained," implies the creation of an immutable difference. A stamp or mark cannot be easily removed. Culture seems to impact individuals so intensely as to create permanent differences. As Ifemelu becomes more attuned to the ways in which African Americans and African immigrants differ, she comes to bear the mark that she perceives in others. She becomes implicated in the very structure that she finds so confounding and limiting.

Although Ifemelu states that blackness originates upon her arrival in the United States, she addresses audience members that may not have yet made the trip abroad. In this way, she constitutes blackness as a category simply through her writing and the creation of a readership identified as "Non-American Black."

To put the matter another way, Ifemelu establishes blackness through her community of readers, perpetuating the very identification she finds so vexing. The ultimate aim of her blog is to educate non-American blacks in the ways of race. Here race operates as a set of learned practices, or as Ifemelu explains, "here's the deal with becoming black: You must show that you are offended when such words as 'watermelon' or 'tar baby' are used in jokes. . . . You must nod when a black person nods at you in a heavily white area. It is called the black nod. It is a way for black people to say, 'You are not alone, I am here too.'"

Ifemelu's focus on "the black nod" emphasizes the importance of community to racial identity. Blackness is a performance conducted for other blacks, not for whites. Ifemelu is expected to feel kinship with a group of people simply on the basis of skin color, not because she shares with them a common sense of self. While the black nod is, as Mukoma Wa Ngugi explains, a way to express solidarity and support, Ifemelu perceives it as prescriptive, a requirement rather than an affirmation of community. This difference underscores one of the primary ways in which the experiences of African immigrants depart from those of African Americans. Ifemelu does not identify with a racialized collective the way that African American characters in the book unite through their blackness. Though she is perceived as black, it is not an identity she ultimately embraces. If coming to the United States is a "choice" but "becoming black" is not, Ifemelu ultimately chooses not to be black by returning to Nigeria. However, while she is in the United States, there is no escape from blackness, only a grudging reluctance to become entangled in the commitments racial identification engenders.

Ifemelu's primary identification with blackness occurs through her relationship with Blaine. Initially, Ifemelu seems eager to acknowledge herself as black in part because of the attractive, cultured image her future boyfriend radiates. An earnest activist who tutors inner-city children and fluently code switches between English and Ebonics, Blaine is quick to name race as the defining factor in American society. His profession affirms the student-teacher dynamic between the two lovers, and in fact, when they first meet, Ifemelu is still an undergraduate. They begin dating years later when they reconnect at a conference. Although by then Ifemelu is an established and well-respected blogger, in her posts she always refers to him as "Professor Hunk," a title that reifies the imbalance between them, or as she muses, "Sometimes she felt like his apprentice" (313). As their relationship develops, Ifemelu comes to model Blaine's behavior and even his language. He effectively teaches her how to identify the problems of race and even attempts to influence her aesthetic choices: "When he played selections from his complete John Coltrane, he would watch her as she listened, waiting for a rapture he was sure would glaze over her, and then at the end, when she remained untransported, he would quickly avert his eyes." Ifemelu's lack of passion for Coltrane demonstrates an inability to connect to one of the greatest African American art forms, jazz, and as in *Open City* casts doubt on her racial authenticity. However, even when she expresses admiration for black American writers like Ann Petry and Gayl Jones, Blaine critiques her choices, noting, "'They don't push the boundaries.' He spoke gently, as though he did not want to upset her, but it still had to be said" (314). Blaine treats Ifemelu like a bright but misguided student who has yet to perceive the truths readily apparent to him. And yet the brilliant professor remains blind to his own self-righteous superiority and a latent misogyny that permeates his thinking.

Ifemelu largely acquiesces to her boyfriend's political and social beliefs but at last grows tired of his arrogant anger and pious activism. Blaine eventually accuses Ifemelu of approaching race and her blog as "a game that you don't really take seriously, it's like choosing an *interesting* elective evening class to complete your credits" (346). By comparing Ifemelu's relationship to race to an elective class, Blaine furthers the trope of Ifemelu's education into racial practices. However, if race is indeed a course of study for her, she proves to be a skeptical student, never quite accepting the principled assumptions of her professor boyfriend. While he understands race to be the dominant feature of American social life, she resists his suggestions to provide additional details "about government policy and redistricting" in a post for her blog titled "Why Are the Dankest, Drabbest Parts of American Cities Full of American Blacks?" (313). He reminds her that her writing is "a real responsibility" and thus she cannot be "lazy" like "students who did not hand in work on time" or "black celebrities who were not politically active." This conflation between distracted undergraduates and politically quiescent African Americans characterizes Blaine's critique of Ifemelu's approach to race. She fails to be a sufficiently rigorous student by preferring to opt out of material that according to him requires more commitment, more historical understanding, and more active participation. Moreover, by framing Ifemelu's relationship to race as a "choice" rather than an imposed and inescapable identity, Blaine anticipates how Ifemelu abandons the problems of race by returning to Nigeria. Although he too could leave the United States, his comments emphasize how he has internalized notions of racial identity that Ifemelu finds not only strange but variable. She is black due to geography—that is, by living in the United States. His blackness, however, has nothing to do with choice. It is an irrevocable condition of his homeland and thus of himself.

Blaine is the first person that Ifemelu correctly and enthusiastically identifies as African American. She first meets him on a train to Haverhill, observing how he was "a man with skin the color of gingerbread and the kind of lean, proportioned body that was perfect for a uniform, any uniform. She knew right away that he was African-American, not Caribbean, not African, not a child of immigrants from either place." "The color of gingerbread" is one of many descriptions of dark skin that Adichie uses rather than rely on binaries of black and white. A Senegalese professor is described as "sable-skinned" (340), while another character has "skin so dark it had an undertone of blueberries" (342). Blaine's gingerbread skin affirms Ifemelu's resistance to polarized descriptions of race; people are not black and white to her but a rich spectrum of colors. However, even as she appreciates such diversity in skin colors, Ifemelu identifies in Blaine a certain restrictiveness. Her sense that Blaine's body "was perfect for a uniform" suggests that he is a person who easily fits into set categories. By then identifying him as African American, she implies that American racial categories function as prescribed uniforms, garments that clearly fit some better than others. Moreover, Blaine's "lean, proportioned body" presents a striking contrast to Ifemelu's shifting physique. While he maintains a stable physical presence through almost obsessive attention to his diet and exercise, Ifemelu notes how her body, like that of other immigrant women, changes in America. Aunty Uju puts on considerable weight while her friend Ginika welcomes her to the United States looking "much thinner, half her old size, and her head looked bigger" (123). These physical changes reflect instabilities of identity that simply do not pertain to the ever-disciplined Blaine. While Ifemelu and Aunty Uju may transform from Nigerian to black and back again, Blaine will never cross such boundaries. His adherence to race makes such mutability impossible.

Upon hearing Ifemelu's name, Blaine immediately identifies her as Nigerian, even noting that she is "Bourgie Nigerian." For the intellectually sophisticated Blaine, class is a key aspect of identity much like race and country of origin. Ifemelu replies that she is "just as bourgie as you," suggesting that what unites them is less blackness than the privileges of their elite class status. As in her description of his skin color, Ifemelu pivots away from race to find other modes of social identification. However, Blaine quickly references an implicitly racialized hierarchy that pits people like him and Ifemelu against others. When she asks if Africa is the focus of his research, he replies, "No. Comparative politics. You can't just do African in political science graduate programs in this country. You can compare Africa to Poland or Israel but focusing on Africa itself? They don't let you do that." Ifemelu then muses, "His use of 'they' suggested an 'us,' which would be the both of them" (179). Though she initially resists race as a way to connect with Blaine, Ifemelu is seduced by this suggestion of intimacy. If blackness and its opposition to whiteness can be the foundation of a relationship with this alluring man, she may readily embrace its possibilities. With Blaine's resonant "us" in mind, she begins "to imagine a relationship, both of them waking up in the winter, cuddling in the stark whiteness of the morning light." Significantly, her fantasy operates through images of black and white—their dark cuddled bodies against the whiteness of winter and the morning light. Ifemelu is so taken by Blaine that she concedes to the terms of racialization; she will happily be black to be with him. From the start of their relationship, she understands that embracing blackness is the key to Blaine's heart.

Ifemelu thus continues her conversation with Blaine by focusing on specifically racialized issues. Embarrassed that she is reading a magazine and not a literary text, she pushes it away, noting "that it was absurd how women's magazines forced images of small-boned, small-breasted white women on the rest of the multi-boned, multi-ethnic world of women to emulate" (180). With this comment, Ifemelu extends the racial unity between her and Blaine. As a black man, he too is marginalized from the pages of fashion magazines and other popular media. Despite their different backgrounds and her scorn for the protocols of race, Ifemelu uses blackness as a common experience to forge a connection with Blaine. She is not above using race if it will get her what or who she wants. For her, blackness is indeed a choice or, more specifically here, a strategy.

Just as the absence of black women in fashion magazines serves as a point of connection with Blaine, this issue proves to be a source of tension in her relationship with Curt, her rich white boyfriend. Ifemelu is Curt's first black girlfriend, and while he treats her with remarkable devotion, he is also wildly childish and naive. Paging through a copy of *Essence* that he finds in Ifemelu's apartment, Curt deems the magazine "kind of racially skewed." Ifemelu immediately takes him to a nearby bookstore where they page through a stack of women's magazines looking for pictures of black women. They find three and exasperated, Ifemelu declares, "Now, let's talk about what is racially skewed." Cowed, Curt replies, "I didn't mean for it to be such a big deal" (298). What Blaine understood implicitly, Curt has to learn.

This exercise in education leads Ifemelu to begin blogging after she describes the incident to a friend. Although Ifemelu states that her blog is born of a longing to know "How many other people had become black in America?" the inspiration for her writing originates in the need to educate Curt. Prior to her arrival in the United States, Ifemelu had already been aware of the racial bias apparent in fashion magazines. What is new in America is the presence of people like Curt who are ignorant of such problems. Is blackness thus derived from the obliviousness of white people? Does she become black when she must explain such racial dynamics? The origin story of Ifemelu's blog indicates that race for Ifemelu is fundamentally about image and representation as opposed to more pressing political and social inequalities involving forms of violence and injustice. Moreover, Ifemelu discovers that to be black is to express discriminatory dynamics to ignorant others. To be black is to voice what is already obvious to her. Though she claims to have become black only once she arrived in America, Ifemelu's frustration with fashion magazines reveals that she has long been aware of racism. What is new is having to explain these dynamics to people like Curt.

Blaine understands without question the bias of fashion magazines. Despite sharing with him a disdain for white ideals of beauty, Ifemelu soon discovers that her blackness is not the same as that experienced by American-born blacks. Their relationship begins to erode when they discover how differently they respond to racial issues. When an older white woman asks to touch Ifemelu's hair, she agrees much to Blaine's horror. While he is outraged that Ifemelu allows herself to be, as he claims, the white woman's "guinea pig," Ifemelu asks, "How else will she know what hair like mine feels like?" The narrator concludes, "He expected her to feel what she did not know how to feel. There were things that existed for him that she could not penetrate" (314). Just as Ifemelu lacks the historical knowledge to understand how references to watermelon and tar babies can be insulting to African Americans, she does not find the white woman's request to be an offensive intrusion. It exists for her as a discrete encounter, not the culmination of centuries of white appropriation and objectification of black bodies. Ifemelu's ignorance of such history parallels Curt's initial response to *Essence*. However, while Curt accepts Ifemelu's lesson in racial representation in fashion magazines, she bristles at Blaine's condescending remarks and feels alienated by his group of politically conscious friends. Unlike the affable Curt, she will not be so easily schooled for this would require accepting that she may be ignorant of some things.

Ifemelu at last affirms her difference from Blaine and other American-born blacks by changing the name of her blog. Originally titled *Raceteenth or Curious Observations by a Non-American Black on the Subject of Blackness in America*, it later becomes *Raceteenth or Various Observations about American Blacks (Those Formerly Known as Negroes) by a Non-American Black*. By switching her focus from blackness to American blacks, Ifemelu distances herself from African Americans. They are a population to be studied rather than an intrinsic part of her own community. However, both titles of her blog include the word "Raceteenth," a derivation of Juneteenth, the day celebrating the end of slavery in the United States. Ifemelu's reference to June 19, 1865, the day that the abolition of slavery was announced in Galveston, Texas, at last realizing the promise of the Emancipation Proclamation issued two and a half years earlier, signifies on one of the most important dates in African American history. By citing the end of slavery, *Raceteenth* implies that the end of race has yet to arrive. This formulation suggests that race is a divisive problem rather than a possible point of celebration, community, and identity. Such a conception is supported by Ifemelu's tendency to conflate race with racism. In one of her posts, she writes, "Race matters because of racism" (338). By ignoring the historical legacy of how racial difference united an oppressed group, Ifemelu fails to recognize the ways that racial difference can be a progressive force of social change. Moreover, by shifting attention from blackness to American blacks, Ifemelu seems to indict

African Americans for contributing to their own racialization. Because race largely equates to racism for Ifemelu, she implies that American-born blacks are complicit in their own oppression.

Shan, Blaine's glamorous and opinionated older sister, is the first person to question Ifemelu's authority to comment on racial matters. At a dinner party, she proclaims, "You know why Ifemelu can write that blog, by the way? Because she's African. She's writing from the outside. She doesn't really feel all the stuff she's writing about. It's all quaint and curious to her. So she can write it and get all these accolades and get invited to give talks" (337–338). Ifemelu, stung but unable to counter Shan's declaration, replies, "I think that's fair enough" and privately concedes, "It was true that race was not embroidered in the fabric of her history; it had not been etched on her soul" (338). As in the scene in which Ifemelu first encounters Blaine, the text again invokes images of clothing and fabric to conceptualize racial difference. However, while Blaine's body had been described as "perfect for a uniform," Ifemelu is not presented through her physique. Instead her "history" and "soul" are at stake as if she is not as easily reduced to the categories of race that define American life. In many ways, Ifemelu is writing from the outside; she makes explicit what many Americans and American blacks in particular know all too well. The appeal of her blog is to express what is manifest to those people already immersed in the often-contradictory practices and expectations of race. Shan is right that Ifemelu can draw attention to these matters because she is not American, but her claim that "she doesn't really feel all the stuff she's writing about" is suspect. As Shan affirms, Ifemelu is not African American, but her black skin interpellates her into a world already fraught with racial meaning. In the United States, she is read as black and thus she is just as likely as Shan to have a white person ask to touch her hair. However, while Shan would no doubt recognize the historical implications of this request, Ifemelu perceives this encounter as an experience between two individuals shorn of America's past. In short, she lacks sufficient knowledge to be insulted.

Ifemelu elaborates on her difference from American-born blacks in her next blog post titled "Is Obama Anything but Black?" Like Ifemelu, our president is not African American but he too is black. She explains, "Race is not genotype; race is phenotype. Race matters because of racism. And racism is absurd because it's about how you look. Not about the blood you have. It's about the shade of your skin and the shape of your nose and the kink of your hair" (338). For Ifemelu, individuals become instantiated in racial dynamics because of their physical appearance. To appear black is to be black. By suggesting that she too appears black, the blog serves as a response to Shan's comments. However, while Obama, Ifemelu, and Shan all read as black due to the color of their skin, Ifemelu clearly experiences her blackness differently than the African American characters in the book. She understands blackness always as a form of difference involving a set of imposed expectations. As a result, she perceives race as inextricably linked to racism. But must race always involve discrimination? Is it possible for race to exist apart from oppression and forms of violence? Can it serve as a cause for celebration, pride, and community? Ifemelu's comments remind readers that race is indeed a social construction and thus a category that might very well need to be jettisoned in order to achieve a more egalitarian society.

By contrast, the African American characters in *Americanah* do not equate race with racism as Ifemelu does. Instead, race figures as an inevitable but also desired category of identity for them. The history and community associated with blackness have special resonance for Blaine and Shan. They perceive race not solely as a cause of discrimination; it is also a mark of difference that signifies a legacy of survival, resistance, and triumph. Such history is invisible and absent to Ifemelu, who struggles to understand the loaded meaning of seemingly trivial items like watermelon. Because she lacks and arguably refuses a fuller education into African American history, her comments on race continually return to issues of image and representation. She becomes most passionate when demonstrating the paucity of black models in fashion magazines to Curt or when she bemoans the difficulty of finding someone who can style her hair. For Ifemelu, there is no discussion of the black underclass or racial disparities in health care, educational opportunities, and professional advancement. Such entrenched forms of institutionalized racism are not readily felt by an immigrant like herself; though her life is hardly free of discrimination and difficulty, her greatest challenges are posed by her immigrant status, not her dark skin. In this regard, Shan is right to identify Ifemelu as an outsider. Despite her attentiveness to how race operates in America, she lacks the historical awareness that would make blackness more than an irritating signifier of difference and inferiority. Although ostensibly she is the character with the strongest tie to the ancestor, she has the weakest connection to a racialized history. This failure underscores how the story of African Americans is not simply her story but also implies a troubling reluctance to engage with the black community.

ACTIVISM AND LAZINESS

The divide Adichie describes in *Americanah* between African immigrants and African Americans is best demonstrated by the fight that marks the beginning of the decline of Ifemelu and Blaine's relationship. Blaine organizes a protest after learning that Mr. White, a security guard at the university library, is accused of dealing drugs after a white coworker sees him receive money from a black friend. Blaine describes the older black man as "a history book," while Ifemelu perceives him as a slightly lecherous "old black man beaten down by life" (343). She also observes that with Mr. White, Blaine speaks Ebonics, a language Ifemelu does not use. Instead, she finds that the incident with Mr. White prompts her to mimic Blaine's voice. Blaine states that Mr. White "expects this sort of thing to happen," to which Ifemelu replies, "That's the actual tragedy." She immediately "realized she was using Blaine's own words; sometimes she heard in her voice the echo of his. The actual tragedy of Emmett Till, he had told her once, was not the murder of a black child for whistling at a white woman but that some black people thought: But why did you whistle?" Neither the narrator nor Ifemelu comments on Blaine's description of "the actual tragedy," but Ifemelu's use of this line suggests that she does not fully believe her own declaration. This is a borrowed form of thinking, one that emphasizes the internalization of oppression over actual forms of violence and discrimination. Such thinking is foreign to Ifemelu who is always surprised by racism and never assumes that it will govern her life. She has in no way absorbed the ideology of racial hierarchy and thus "the actual tragedy" of these incidents remains peripheral to her own experience. Her parroting of Blaine's words demonstrates the limits of her education in race. She can replicate the language of victimization, but as Shan earlier claims, it may very well be true that at least in some cases Ifemelu "doesn't really feel all the stuff she's writing about."

After learning about Mr. White's questioning by the police, Blaine spends the evening calling media outlets and organizing an elaborate campus protest. When he and Ifemelu part in the morning, he assumes that she will be at the library to take part in the event. But she does not go; she attends a going-away lunch for Kavanagh, a colleague who grew up in the Congo, before heading back to their apartment to lie down. Importantly, she is invited to this lunch while chatting with Boubacar, a Senegalese professor who rankles Blaine. Ifemelu surmises that Blaine "resented how easily she had drifted to Boubacar that day . . . as though to a person who spoke the same silent language as she did" (340). This "silent language" stands in stark opposition to the borrowed language Ifemelu uses when learning about Mr. White's questioning by the police. While she learns how to apply Blaine's words, the language she shares with Boubacar represents a familiarity that Blaine cannot penetrate. Reflecting on Blaine's dislike of Boubacar, she muses, "Perhaps Blaine resented this mutuality, something primally African from which he felt excluded" (341). It is especially notable that Adichie uses the phrase "primally African" to link Ifemelu and Boubacar. While the novel repeatedly presents race as a cultural adornment, here the bond between the two African natives is "primal," somehow essential to their being. In light of Michael's comment about Ifemelu's relationship to her ancestors, she and Boubacar seem to be connected in a way that is deeper than race. In this relationship, Blaine is the outsider, unable to understand the language that leaves his girlfriend "with the feeling of having been fortified" (341).

Ifemelu finds herself "seated in a classroom with Kavanagh and Boubacar and other professors, sipping a bottle of cranberry juice, listening to a young woman talk about her upcoming tenure review, when Blaine's texts flooded her phone" (345). Ifemelu's leisurely lunch among the academic elite is completely at odds with Blaine's grassroots organizing of students, staff, and family members of Mr. White. Delighted with the multiracial crowd he assembled, Blaine describes the protest as a "mini-America." Importantly, Ifemelu does not specify the racial identity of her lunch companions. Though Kavanagh is described as "curly-haired" and "lived in the Congo as a child," he could be either black or white, or something else entirely. Only Boubacar, her African compatriot who is described as "sable-skinned" (340), is clearly identified racially. This absence of racial ascription highlights how Ifemelu does not understand race as the most important mark of social identity. Her perception of the lunch emphasizes class privilege and the rarefied world of the university. Her academic companions could just as well represent the "mini America" that Blaine extols—"Black kids and white kids and Asian kids and Hispanic kids" (345)—but such diversity is not of primary concern to Ifemelu. Where Blaine seeks a multiracial coalition, Ifemelu sees a group notable for its limited singularity. Race makes Blaine attuned to difference while Ifemelu finds commonality in her colleagues.

Although Ifemelu leaves the lunch early, she does not join Blaine at the protest. Instead, she returns to her apartment, and lying in bed, she at last replies to his multiple text messages, apologizing and explaining that she had just awakened from a lengthy nap. Again, Adichie highlights the stark differences between Ifemelu and Blaine; while he is out protesting with others, she enjoys a moment of private repose. As he defines himself by a political community, she remains a solitary outsider. He identifies with the working class, and she indulges a distinctly elite laziness. Blaine soon learns that Ifemelu was not just napping but attended the lunch rather than join the protest. He explodes in anger over her lie and then asserts, "You know, it's not just about writing a blog, you have to live like you believe it. That blog is a game that you don't really take seriously" (346). Blaine is right to accuse Ifemelu of not being interested in the political stakes of racism. She observes how race impacts her daily life, but she lacks an appreciation for how its long history shapes the lives of others. Ifemelu understands Blaine's anger as indicative of the essential divide between them: "She recognized, in his tone, a subtle accusation, not merely about her laziness, her lack of zeal and conviction, but also about her Africanness; she was not sufficiently furious because she was African, not African American" (346). Is Ifemelu's failure to participate in the protest a consequence of her Africanness and her tentative embrace of blackness? Does her "bourgie" background prevent her from empathizing with the black working class? Or has Blaine been right all along to identify his apprentice girlfriend as lazy?

Adichie complicates an answer to these questions by presenting Mr. White as a misogynistic, even repulsive character. Despite Blaine's obvious admiration and respect for the old man, Ifemelu is offended by the sexually inappropriate comments he makes about her to Blaine. Seeing them together, Mr. White asks, "Does she have a sister?" Another time, he notes, "You look tired, my man. Somebody keep you up late?" (343). Both of these comments are directed at Blaine, making Ifemelu a silent outsider to this exchange. She also observes how "whenever they shook hands, Mr. White squeezed her fingers, a gesture thick with suggestion, and she would pull her hand free and avoid his eyes until they left. There was, in that handshake, a claiming, a leering, and for this she had always harbored a small dislike, but she had never told Blaine because she was also sorry about her dislike. . . . She wished she could overlook the liberties he took" (343). Ifemelu's desire to ignore or dismiss Mr. White's behavior indicates how, like Blaine, she wants a simplistic narrative of righteous innocence and heroic triumph. Although Blaine is unaware of how Mr. White touches Ifemelu suggestively, he witnesses the older man's offensive comments. Blaine seems to have no qualms about how Mr. White treats Ifemelu. His male privilege makes him blind to such slights while Ifemelu's silence on the matter quietly reifies such patriarchal structures. Mr. White may be a rich "history book," but his stories remain closed to Ifemelu. Is Mr. White's history available only to men? Does Mr. White's sexism make the racism he suffers less sympathetic? By not attending the protest, Ifemelu can be understood as resisting the older man's inappropriate comments and overtures. However, by not explaining her behavior to Blaine nor telling him about how Mr. White treats her, she implicitly makes the ensuing conflict between her and Blaine about different forms of blackness rather than about gender or class. Ifemelu is ultimately too detached to clarify her decision not to attend the protest. Rather than think through her motivations, she prefers to take a nap. For Ifemelu, the personal may be political, but she is, as Blaine notes, too lazy to make such stakes clear.

The chapter ends with a long quotation from one of Ifemelu's blog posts titled "What Academics Mean by White Privilege, or Yes It Sucks to Be Poor and White but Try Being Poor and Non-White." The subject of the post seems to have little to do with her fight with Blaine. She describes a white man who claims that because he grew up poor in West Virginia he lacks white privilege. Ifemelu counters by explaining that "privilege is always relative to something else," and then asks her readers to imagine the white man in question as black. She concludes, "The Appalachian hick guy is fucked up, which is not cool, but if he were black, he'd be fucked up plus" (347). This discussion of how privilege operates along a spectrum of opportunity and discriminatory practices seems far removed from the fight between Ifemelu and Blaine about the protest. However, privilege and relativity are also at work in how the couple respond to Mr. White's mistreatment.

Ifemelu's blog post encourages a parallel between the "Appalachian hick" and his imagined black doppelgänger and Ifemelu and Blaine. Just as both the poor white man and the poor black man share similar challenges as members of the lower class, Ifemelu and Blaine are united by the difficulties of being black in the United States. Moreover, while the poor black man faces a further level of discrimination due to his race, Ifemelu and Blaine experience different forms of racial treatment. If, as Ifemelu argues, "privilege is always relative to something else," then is she more privileged than Blaine because she is not African American? And what does Blaine's identification with Mr. White suggest about his own class status? Adichie poses these questions by juxtaposing Ifemelu's blog post about white privilege against her fight with Blaine but does not provide an easy answer to this provocative correlation.

It is important to note that both Ifemelu and Blaine are members of a rarefied social elite; they are comfortable in the Ivy League, drinking organic juices and specialty wines while talking about the nuances of various social and political issues. And as they observe in their first encounter, both enjoy the privileges of high-class status. Mr. White's plight does not match Blaine's personal experiences. He is not the one questioned by the police, but nonetheless, Blaine adopts the security guard's fight as his own. No doubt Mr. White is glad to have such an enthusiastic and resourceful supporter, but Blaine's behavior does suggest a troubling appropriation of another man's struggle. Mr. White is not in control of the protest; instead, it is Blaine's creation. This dynamic implies a certain anxiety on Blaine's part as if by taking on Mr. White's fight, he may authenticate his own blackness. Moreover, the novel does not reveal if Mr. White receives some kind of redress or apology from the white employee who assumed he was dealing drugs. The triumph of the event is framed through Blaine and his satisfaction in seeing Mr. White with his family. He tells Ifemelu, "Mr. White's daughter was there, taking pictures of his photos on the placard, and I felt as if that finally gave him some real dignity back" (345). This peculiar conclusion encourages us to consider what has actually been achieved through Blaine's protest and for whom. Blaine admires the sight of Mr. White's daughter taking a picture of a picture as if the proliferation of an image compensates for the insult the security guard endured.

Blaine requires a simplistic narrative of racial discrimination and humiliation followed by the triumph of a collective outpouring of support that restores dignity and pride to the victim. But in fact no crime has occurred, only an offense with no significant long-term damage. Blaine's exaggerated response speaks to a nostalgia for the protests and sit-ins of the civil rights era as well as a series of battle lines that clearly demarcate righteous victims from malevolent enemies. There is almost something laughable in Blaine's outrage as if he can only seize on small injustices to exercise his commitment to the black underclass. Perhaps Ifemelu does not attend the protest because she does not perceive Mr. White's mistreatment as an event that warrants a protest. The absence of further information about the consequences of the protest or any change in Mr. White's situation suggests that the incident is ultimately of little importance. It functions most significantly as a reflection of Blaine and his belief that Mr. White's dignity has been sufficiently restored. The text provides a subtle critique of Blaine in the image that affirms his conviction in the success of the protest. By focusing on Mr. White's daughter taking pictures of his photo, the text implies that the reproduction of an image is more important than the image itself. The picture of Mr. White on the placard is presumably an image that Blaine has chosen of the elderly security guard. As she takes a picture of that picture, Mr. White's daughter seems to value Blaine's image of her father over the actual man. The "real dignity" that Blaine believes has been given back is mediated through the image he has constructed. The protest is ultimately a reflection more of Blaine's need for a racialized cause than of Mr. White's need for dignity.

From this perspective, Ifemelu's failure to participate in the protest acts as a rejection of Blaine's self-serving approach to blackness. While Mr. White with his "history book" knowledge might operate as an ancestral presence for Blaine, their roles are effectively reversed. Mr. White imparts no wisdom to Blaine; instead, the younger man directs his elder, taking control of his experience. Moreover, the novel provides no context by which to understand the significance of the incident. Was Mr. White's questioning a discrete incident or part of a pattern across the university? Just as Ifemelu has little interest in understanding the history of African Americans, the text prevents readers from placing this injustice within a larger landscape. To return to Morrison's formulation, there is no ancestor to guide these young black characters and help them understand how blackness signifies as more than just protest, as more than just discrimination and lost dignity. Morrison explains that in contemporary African American fiction "it was the absence of an ancestor that was frightening, that was threatening, and it caused huge destruction and disarray in the work itself" ("Rootedness" 62). The absence of an ancestor in this episode thus foregrounds the dissolution of Blaine and Ifemelu's relationship. With their differing conceptions of racial identity, they cannot be black together. Though Ifemelu may have a strong ancestral connection, there is no elder for either her or Blaine in the United States.

THE PROMISE OF OBAMA

Ifemelu and Blaine do not break up over the fight about the protest, but this disagreement seriously frays their relationship. Instead, the two are briefly reunited through their support for Barack Obama: "Their union was leached of passion, but there was a new passion, outside of themselves, that united them in an intimacy they had never had before, an unfixed, unspoken, intuitive intimacy: Barack Obama" (353). Ifemelu and Blaine's shared and notably "unspoken" hope for an Obama presidency resonates with the "silent language" that Ifemelu shares with fellow Africans like Boubacar. For the first time, Blaine seems to be a part of a wordless, essential connection with Ifemelu. If blackness might indeed be a shared condition for them, Obama represents the bridge to their common racial identity and the promise of pan-African American community.

Adichie presents Ifemelu and Blaine's passion for Obama as a remarkably physical experience. When Ifemelu first tells Blaine that she hopes Obama will become president, he responds not with language but with "eyes lit," and "she felt between them the first pulse of a shared passion" (354). Watching Obama win the Iowa Caucuses, the couple "clutched each other in front of the television," and as the election nears, both are gripped with worry that something will destroy his campaign. This emphasis on a shared physical experience over verbal communication presents the bond of blackness as an embodied encounter. Blaine and Ifemelu are most intimate when they don't speak, or don't need to speak.

Concerned about Obama's campaign, Ifemelu begins visiting chat rooms that malign the young Illinois senator. The racist comments she reads "made her blog feel inconsequential, a comedy of manners, a mild satire about a world that was anything but mild" (355). Ifemelu's recognition of the trivial nature of her blog bolsters Shan and Blaine's comments. Suddenly her blog really is "quaint and curious" as Shan declared, an "interesting" set of observations that lack the seriousness Blaine ascribes to the lived experience of race. Ifemelu seems unconcerned by this realization because with the excitement surrounding Obama's campaign and the unity he inspires, she "no longer felt excluded" (356). Overwhelmed by the historic consequences of his bid for the White House, Ifemelu stops writing her blog. The seriousness of Obama's campaign and its astounding import effectively silence her. While she once complained about racial expectations, the future president demolishes them all.

Her only contribution to the discussion about Obama is a blog post titled "Is Obama Anything but Black?" in which she counters "lots of folk—mostly non-black" who claim that "Obama's not black" (338). She writes that despite his white mother, "In America, you don't get to decide what race you are. It is already decided for you" (339). Although Ifemelu is right in asserting that Obama looks visibly black and cannot deny the consequences of being perceived as African American, she again makes race a matter of discrimination, noting "Barack Obama, looking as he does, would have had to sit in the back of the bus fifty years ago. If a random black guy commits a crime today, Barack Obama could be stopped and questioned for fitting that profile" (339). In Ifemelu's calculus, blackness is always a liability, and though it certainly is a cause for discrimination, she neglects how Obama also used his blackness as an asset on the campaign trail. Among other factors, the excitement surrounding the prospect of America's first black president propelled him into office, as did a savvy rhetorical style that targeted an especially diverse electorate. Obama is proof that blackness need not be a mark of discrimination and outrage but can instead be a galvanizing force of change and unity.

Just as Obama reunites Blaine and Ifemelu, he also offers the promise of a community for African immigrants in the United States. Ifemelu finds herself among the "true believers" (357), like Blaine and his friends who cling to the hope of his presidency. Ifemelu makes this identification even after Blaine observes that Obama is "a different kind of black. . . . If Obama didn't have a white mother and wasn't raised by white grandparents and didn't have Kenya and Indonesia and Hawaii and all of the stories that make him somehow a bit like everyone, if he was just a plain black guy from Georgia, it would be different. America will have made real progress when an ordinary black guy from Georgia becomes president, a black guy who got a C average in college" (357). Blaine's comments seem to undermine the sheer thrill of Obama's election as if "real progress" is not at all evident in his victory. For Blaine, there is a difference between Obama, who is "somehow a bit like everyone," and "an ordinary black guy from Georgia," who is presumably defined by his particularity. Blaine's comments suggest that the ordinary black guy can never be as relatable as Obama. The experiences of such a man remain unique to African Americans. This description makes American blackness exclusive rather than inclusive, a notion at odds with the expansive approach to the electorate that defined Obama's 2008 campaign. Once again, Blaine is portrayed as limited by his racial assignations rather than attuned to the possibilities of a broader national community.

The physical passion that Obama inspires in Ifemelu and Blaine culminates the day that he wins the Democratic nomination. With this victory, "Ifemelu and Blaine made love, for the first time in weeks, and Obama was there with them, like an unspoken prayer, a third emotional presence" (357). Again, Obama prompts a wordless bond that emphasizes the physical over the verbal. The startling intrusion of Obama into Ifemelu and Blaine's sex life recalls one of her first blog posts. She writes, "The simplest solution to the problem of race in America? Romantic love. Not friendship. Not the kind of safe, shallow love where the objective is that both people remain comfortable. But real deep romantic love, the kind that twists you and wrings you out and makes you breathe through the nostrils of your beloved" (298). The romance between Blaine and Ifemelu should or could provide the foundation for meaningful racial connection. However, the presence of Obama in their bedroom affirms that their love is a sham, necessarily mediated by the future president. Ifemelu is not breathing out of the nostrils of Blaine; instead, both encounter one another through the promise of Obama. Such dependency on a remote third figure ensures the demise of their relationship. While Obama used his blackness as a way to inspire the country and unite disparate constituencies, Ifemelu and Blaine remain at odds with their differing conceptions of what race means.

Obama's victory is followed by a blog post from *Raceteenth* that appears to be unconnected to the thrill of his election. Titled "Understanding America for the Non-American Black: Thoughts on the Special White Friend," the post describes the rare white friend who "not only get[s] it" but "totally understand[s] that they can say stuff that you can't" (361–362). The "special white friend" is someone who recognizes how white privilege operates. Ifemelu concludes by urging her readers to have this person point out how racism continues to influence the lives of black people because such comments from blacks would incur accusations that they are "playing the race card." As with other blog posts inserted into the text, this one does not directly relate to the issues occurring in Ifemelu's life. There is no one in the novel who even remotely correlates with the special white friend described here. Why then does Ifemelu follow Obama's historic election with a discussion of a white figure who doesn't even appear in the text?

All of the things that Ifemelu suggests the white friend should say are things she presents in her blog. She writes,

> Have your white friend point out how the American black deal is kind of like you've been unjustly imprisoned for many years, then all of a sudden you're set free, but you get no bus fare. . . . If the "slavery was so long ago" thing comes up, have your white friend say that lots of white folks are still inheriting money that their families made a hundred years ago. . . . And have your white friend say how funny it is, that American pollsters ask white and black people if racism is over. White people in general say it is over and black people in general say it is not. Funny indeed. More suggestions for what you should have your white friend say? Please post away. And here's to all the white friends who get it. (362)

The insights offered in Ifemelu's blog are precisely what the special white friend "gets." As someone who has had to learn what her own blackness means in the United States, Ifemelu has much in common with the special white friend. Both come to an understanding of race relations and racism through a process of education. In this regard, the novel suggests that Ifemelu is a stand-in for the special white friend; she too understands racial privilege and the impact of slavery on current social dynamics. By establishing such a strong correlation between Ifemelu and the special white friend, Adichie affirms how race operates in America as a series of learned social practices. Moreover, Ifemelu has a certain degree of privilege and freedom that American blacks do not; as Shan notes earlier, her blog is successful and popular precisely because she is an outsider. Though she is not white, she is special, a figure apart from the community of American blacks she has come to know. Ifemelu's reliance on the conceit of the special white friend to describe her own subjective position highlights the limited social categories that exist for her. She is not black like Blaine and Shan but neither is she white. Instead, she bears qualities of both experiences.

The constraints of such preexisting racial categories elucidate why this blog post follows a description of Obama's presidential victory. Adichie quotes from Obama's election night speech: "*Young and old, rich and poor, Democrat and Republican, black, white, Hispanic, Asian, Native American, gay, straight, disabled and not disabled, Americans have sent a message to the world that we have never been just a collection of red states and blue states. We have been and always will be the United States of America*" (361). As Blaine points out earlier (and as many commentators observed), Obama's political success was fundamentally derived from his ability to appeal to a broad multiracial constituency. Though he identified himself as a "black American" in *Dreams from My Father,* Obama does not fit into easy identity categories. With his Kenyan father and Kansan mother, he relates to immigrants and native-born Americans, to whites and blacks, and to people who exist between the margins of settled identities. In this way, Obama reflects Ifemelu's alienation and her struggle to fit within stark racial categories that do not account for experiences of immigration and learned encounters of race. However, Ifemelu shares none of Obama's devotion to public service and community. Like Blaine, he is passionate about making America a more just society, though he is of course committed to more than racial causes. Obama's dedication to the United States is a reminder of how far removed Ifemelu is from the society she inhabits.

Despite Ifemelu's similarities to Obama, following his election, she decides to leave the United States. Reflecting on the termination of her blog, she concludes, "The more she wrote, the less sure she became. Each post scraped off yet one more scale of self until she felt naked and false" (5). Ifemelu's nakedness contrasts with the description of African American history as a fabric. Ifemelu will not dress herself in such clothing nor don the uniform that defines Blaine's stringent approach to racial matters. The blog exposes for Ifemelu the ways in which race is alien to her, a posture she cannot continue to uphold. This sense of her own falsity is made all the more acute by Dike's suicide attempt. Ifemelu traces his depression to his struggle to understand himself racially in the United States. His mother proclaims that he is not black, meaning not African American, yet he continually suffers from racial discrimination. Ifemelu does not challenge Aunty Uju's understanding of Dike's racial identity but explains, "You told him what he wasn't but you didn't tell him what he was" (380). And yet neither can Ifemelu provide a clear form of identity for her nephew. She, like him, is caught in a world defined by categories she resists. Earlier in the text, she wonders "what he would be considered, whether American African or African American. He would have to choose what he was, or rather, what he was would be chosen for him" (142). Ifemelu's recognition that race is beyond Dike's control clarifies her decision to return to Nigeria. In America, she will always be black, ever subject to limiting expectations from blacks and whites alike. Following his suicide attempt, Dike urges Ifemelu to leave the United States; while he has little connection to Nigeria, she at least can return to her homeland and make a life there.

Although Ifemelu is surprised by the changes wrought in her country, there she can at last escape the confounding problems of race. As she explains, "I feel like I got off the plane in Lagos and stopped being black" (475). Ifemelu proceeds to channel her wry observations and humor into a new blog titled *The Small Redemptions of Lagos* that celebrates her homeland: "She was at peace: to be home, to be writing her blog, to have discovered Lagos again. She had, finally, spun herself fully into being" (475). Ifemelu also reunites with Obinze, the love of her life. Obinze once idealized America, but as a successful businessman he reflects, "I realized I could buy America, and it lost its shine" (434). Although they both once longed for the education and opportunities of the United States, they return to Nigeria satisfied with the world they originally left behind. While *Raceteenth* expressed outrage and confusion at the problems of race in America, *The Small Redemptions of Lagos* finds beauty and resilience in Nigeria's changing landscape. The last excerpted post of the novel describes the government's destruction of a neighborhood of shacks:

> They destroy the shacks, reduce them to flat pieces of wood. They are doing their job, wearing "demolish" like crisp business suits. They themselves eat in shacks like these, and if all the shacks like these disappeared in Lagos, they will go lunchless, unable to afford anything else. But they are smashing, trampling, hitting. One of them slaps a woman, because she does not grab her pot and her wares and run. She stands there and tries to talk to them. Later, her face is burning from the slap as she watches her biscuits buried in dust. Her eyes trace a line towards the bleak sky. She does not know yet what she will do but she will do something, she will regroup and recoup and go somewhere else and sell her beans and rice and spaghetti cooked to a near mush, her Coke and sweets and biscuits. (474)

An anonymous commentator whom Ifemelu believes to be Obinze writes, "This is like poetry," and indeed the post is far removed from the sarcastic, frustrated comments of *Raceteenth*. There is a depth and seriousness to Ifemelu's description of the woman that is completely absent in her American blog. When she referred to individuals in *Raceteenth*, they came with nicknames like "Badly-Dressed White Middle Manager from Ohio" or the "Hot White Ex." But here the slapped woman retains a dignity denied to the people Ifemelu wrote about in the United States. The racial slights and provocations Ifemelu chronicled come across as trivial in comparison to the destruction of an entire neighborhood. This post also evinces a sensitivity to class difference largely absent from *Raceteenth*. Although Ifemelu recognized class hierarchies while living in the United States, especially as Curt's ever indulged girlfriend, she never concerned herself with the plight of the poor specifically. This new attention implies that race effectively blinded Ifemelu to class struggle. For example, by emphasizing issues of race and gender in the incident involving Mr. White, Ifemelu failed to recognize how the security guard was also the victim of class bias. The absence of race in Lagos broadens Ifemelu's vision, making her a more empathetic person and arguably a stronger writer.

While Ifemelu escapes the complications of race by returning to her homeland, her nephew Dike cannot so easily abandon racial ascription by a summer visit to the familiar if rapidly modernizing world of Nigeria. Instead Dike falls into a depression and attempts suicide. Ifemelu links Dike's despair to problems of race and identity. She scolds Aunty Uju for telling him, "you are not black." His mother defends herself by stating, "I didn't want him to start behaving like these people and thinking that everything that happens to him is because he's black" (380). For Aunty Uju, blackness is a deplorable form of behavior that links misfortune to victimization. To be black is to believe that one is powerless to racism and to accept that race defines all aspects of life. However, Ifemelu understands that Dike cannot escape the reality of his skin color. As someone who is "recognizably black," he will always be subject to the discriminatory practices that define race relations in the United States. Despite his mother's protestations, Dike is black, and to deny this reality is to deny the root of his depression. Aunty Uju's color-blind statement leaves her blind to the source of her son's anguish as well as to its solution.

Ifemelu's decision to return to Nigeria affirms the privileges of her class status. Dike and many other characters described in *The Thing around Your Neck* lack such freedom. They have no choice but to contend with America's fraught racial categories. Although *Americanah* avoids exploring the long-term complications of race for American Africans, Adichie's short story "The Arrangers of Marriage" suggests that partnership between American blacks and recent African immigrants is possible. While Blaine and Ifemelu were unable to find a way to be black together, the two women in "The Arrangers of Marriage," Chinaza and Nia, bond over their struggle to make an independent life for themselves in America.

"SHE WAS RIGHT": FEMALE FRIENDSHIP IN "THE ARRANGERS OF MARRIAGE"

In "The Arrangers of Marriage," Chinaza arrives in New York to meet the husband her uncle and aunt arranged for her to marry. Raised by her relatives following the death of her parents, Chinaza lacks the rootedness that defines Ifemelu's relationship to Nigeria. As an orphan, Chinaza is an outsider both in the United States and in her home country where her relatives constantly remind her of how grateful she should be for their generosity, especially for finding her a husband who is a doctor. For Chinaza, America represents the promise of a new beginning. However, the story opens with a catalog of disappointments as nothing fits the fantasy Chinaza imagined. Just as her husband's dreary apartment is far removed from the "house like those of the white newlyweds in the American films that NTA showed on Saturday nights" (167), she discovers that there are many things about her husband that her relatives failed to warn her about: "No mention of offensive snoring, no mention of houses that turned out to be furniture-challenged flats" (168).

Chinaza's disappointment and the false information about her husband proffered by her relatives highlight her marginalization from a familial community. Unlike Ifemelu, she has no meaningful connection to an ancestral presence, a quality that aligns her with many of the African American characters in Adichie's fiction. Her family offers no wisdom, no protection, and no kindness, only a demand that she be grateful for the life they have provided. To find freedom and happiness, Chinaza must cut all ties to her family, her husband as well as her overbearing relatives. Any ancestral presence that exists here proves to be an impediment to her self-actualization, not a source of stability and support. This depiction of Chinaza indicates that recent African immigrants have a wide range of relationships to the ancestor. While Ifemelu remains deeply connected to Nigeria, Chinaza longs for the possibilities of a new country. The obvious difference between these two characters is their class status. Educated and "bourgie," Ifemelu need not rely on the favors of relatives to travel to the United States and she is not looking for a husband to provide her livelihood. This difference clarifies the class context at work in depictions of the ancestor; in Adichie's fiction, the sense of rootedness and identity associated with the ancestral presence is exclusive to the upper class.

Upon arriving in the United States, Chinaza learns that her husband has renamed himself Dave Bell. Obsessed with adapting to America in order to advance economically and socially, Dave insists that Chinaza go by Agatha. He admits that he chose her as his wife only because of her light complexion, declaring, "Light-skinned blacks fare better in America" (184). Chinaza is puzzled by the man Dave has become; he "sounded different when he spoke to Americans. . . . And he smiled, the eager smile of a person who wanted to be liked" (176). While Chinaza is unsettled by her husband's transformation in the United States, she is astounded to discover that he had been previously married. He explains that it was a business arrangement, but Chinaza is still devastated by the deception. And as Dave notes, Chinaza would have been unable "to say no to people who have taken care of you since your parents died" (183). Chinaza is as trapped by her relatives as she is by her dishonest husband.

Given her isolation, Chinaza is eager to make friends. She is initially wary of other Africans and African Americans, finding that blackness does not provide a common bond or affiliation: "The people who pushed against us, even the black ones, wore the mark of foreignness, otherness, on their faces" (176). Chinaza sees in other blacks the mark of difference that Morrison identified as foundational to how African Americans are perceived in the United States. As a result, blackness confers no sense of intimacy or community for Chinaza; it is a condition to shun, not embrace. However, she eventually befriends Nia, an African American who lives in the same apartment complex as her and Dave. When she first sees Nia's provocative outfit and heavy makeup, she perceives her through her aunt's admonishments: "Aunty Ada would call her an *ashawo*, because of the see-through top she wore so that her bra, a mismatched shade, glared through. Or Aunty Ada would base her prostitute judgment on Nia's lipstick, a shimmery orange" (180). Nia's genuine warmth and kindness suggest that Chinaza cannot rely on the wisdom of her relatives to guide her in this American world.

The two women soon become friends as Nia offers Chinaza help in finding a job and Chinaza teaches Nia a handful of Igbo phrases. Chinaza is surprised to learn that Nia changed her name after spending three years in Tanzania: "she, a black American, had chosen an African name, while my husband made me change mine to an English one" (180). This shuffling of names demonstrates opposite trajectories of longing. Nia wants a more authentically African identity while Dave is ready to cast his former self aside to embrace the American way of life. Although Chinaza accepts Nia's name, she refuses to call her husband Dave "because I didn't know his name, because I didn't know him" (185). Dave proves to be a sham, but Nia, even with her new name, offers Chinaza meaningful solidarity.

After Chinaza tells Nia that Dave was previously married, Nia confesses that she once slept with him. Chinaza realizes that her marriage has been a lie. Nia comforts her with the promise of the life she can create on her own: "You can wait until you get your papers and then leave. . . . You can apply for benefits while you get your shit together, and then you'll get a job and find a place and support yourself and start afresh. This is the U.S. of fucking A., for God's sake" (186). Nia's conception of Chinaza's future is a uniquely American vision, built on rugged individualism and a belief in self-reinvention. Chinaza returns to Dave's apartment, concluding, "She was right, I could not leave yet." With the single word "yet," Adichie suggests that Chinaza will embrace this American future and in so doing will leave behind both her husband and her relatives. There is no nurturing ancestral presence for Chinaza, only the hope that she can be strong enough to make a life on her own. In this respect, she has more to learn from Nia than she does from her relatives. Nia may not have the wisdom of an elder, but she offers Chinaza a new model of independence. Chinaza notes of her friend, "She sprinkled her everyday conversation with words like the noun 'clitoris' and the verb 'fuck.' I liked to listen to her. I liked the way she smiled to show a tooth that was chipped neatly, a perfect triangle missing at the edge" (182). Nia's comfort with her sexuality and her flawed appearance offer an important way for Chinaza to understand her own femininity. By telling her friend that she and Dave slept together years ago, she warns her against Dave's duplicitous behavior. What might have been a point of rivalry becomes a moment of intimacy between the two women as Chinaza recognizes the importance of leaving her repugnant husband.

Adichie's emphasis on the friendship between Chinaza and Nia offers a new way to conceptualize black identity for African immigrants. While the ancestor is an important means of identification for African Americans, Adichie suggests that female friendship is a more useful way to envision the relationship between blacks of various backgrounds in the United States. For Adichie, the ancestor is a fraught figure, often based in class privilege and beholden to a patriarchal legacy. Her stories also imply that too often the ancestor exists more as a figure of imagination than as a credible source of identity and strength. By contrast, the living exchange between black women provides the kind of community and support necessary to survive the challenges of America. Adichie's de-emphasis on history as a way of understanding blackness suggests that the immediate experience of race presents a powerful point of commonality for black women of all nationalities.

5 · BECOMING HIS OWN FATHER

Obama's *Dreams from My Father*

While *Americanah* concludes with Ifemelu happily settled in Lagos and reunited with her true love Obinze, her nephew Dike remains in the United States, still struggling to understand his relationship to blackness. Ifemelu's neat escape from the expectations of race leaves Dike's story completely unresolved. What will happen to this thoughtful, conflicted young man? How will he identify himself? Will blackness always be a burden to him, or might it evolve into a source of joy and pride? And who will guide him through these fraught personal issues? Will he find elders or at least friends to help him make sense of what it means to be a black man in America?

Adichie leaves all of these questions unanswered as if the problems of race are too overwhelming to be addressed. Though the United States can be mined for amusing ironies and utilized to further various educational and professional opportunities, this country remains a spectacle to observe, not a home to fight for. Adichie's suggestion at the end of "The Arrangers of Marriage" that African American and African immigrant women can unite through a common experience of gender discrimination notably omits any mention of how men are to contend with the vicissitudes of American society. While women like Nia and Chinaza find solace through their shared struggle to establish independent lives, Dike is portrayed as devoid of any meaningful friendships or connections outside of his relationship with his mother and aunt. What happens to a young man like Dike? He lacks the connection to an African homeland displayed by Mengestu's characters as well as the devotion to art and ideas that keeps loneliness at bay for Cole's Julius. Moreover, Dike is much younger than these more established characters. They are men who encounter the United States already formed by African experiences and cultural norms. By contrast, Dike remembers nothing of his homeland and knows nothing of his father, a general whose death precipitates Aunty Uju's flight to the United States.

The silence surrounding Dike's story affirms the challenges ahead. There is no easy way to claim blackness for someone caught between homelands and no American racial identity that reflects the totality of Dike's heritage. However, his experience is not unfamiliar. In fact, much of his story reflects the upbringing of our forty-fourth president, Barack Obama. Like Dike, Obama is the son of an absent African father and was raised in the United States by a single mother. Though he was never driven to attempt suicide, his first book, *Dreams from My Father: A Story of Race and Inheritance*, attests to his long struggle to come to terms with his racial identity. Obama's adolescence departs from Dike's circumstance in a number of key ways; unlike Adichie's character, Obama was born in the United States to a white mother and grew up with a strong tie to his maternal grandparents. However, both must contend with the challenge of reconciling their African heritage with a racial landscape largely defined by African American history.

The comparison between Dike and Obama highlights a key generational shift. Most of the protagonists examined in this study are first-generation immigrants. By contrast, as the son of a Kenyan man who returned to his homeland, Obama is part of the second generation. This fact helps contextualize the significant differences between Obama and other pan-African American writers. Obama is effectively writing from another generation, and thus his fluency and approach to American mores reflect a cultural belonging not seen in other texts. Obama is indisputably American, but what makes him relevant to a discussion of pan-African American literature is how he embraces and is embraced by the African American community. That movement from African immigrant identity to American blackness is foundational to the development of a pan-African American solidarity. Blackness in the United States need not derive from an ancestral history of antebellum slavery but instead reaches out through shared experiences of racialized struggle and a powerful commitment to build a better world.

Like Dike, Obama is caught between multiple identities. For Adichie's character, these identities can be defined through geographic locations, specifically Nigeria and the United States. By contrast, Obama, who was born in Honolulu, Hawaii, is ever an American. However, the seeming stability of this identification belies a complex heritage. As the son of a Kenyan father and a Kansan mother, Obama has no direct access to the history, community, and culture of African Americans. Raised primarily by his mother and his maternal grandparents, Obama discovers that his white family cannot provide the guidance necessary to understand what it means to be a black man in America, even as they encourage this aspect of his identity. Ta-Nehisi Coates writes of our former president, "As a child, Obama's embrace of blackness was facilitated, not impeded by white people." However, there was a limit to the education his white family could provide. Obama told Coates that "part of it is I think that my mother thought black folks were cool, and if your mother loves you and is praising you—and says you look good, are smart—as you are, then you don't kind of think in terms of *How can I avoid this?* You feel pretty good about it" ("My President"). But being cool is not at all the same as being black. Like many of Adichie's African American characters, Obama had no ancestor to impart racial wisdom and identity. Instead, Obama must come to his own self-definition or, to return to Morrison's formulation, craft an ancestral figure in his own image.

Obama writes in the introduction to *Dreams from My Father* that what follows describes "a boy's search for his father, and through that search a workable meaning for his life as a black American" (x). Although Obama begins by searching for his father, he concludes by discovering a definition for himself—the identification "black American." In this brief description, Obama encapsulates the whole of his narrative and the startling metaphoric journey of the text: how Obama will come to supplant his own father and ultimately become the object of his search. It is important to note that Obama describes few direct encounters with his father, who dies in Kenya when Obama is twenty-one. As a result, the search for his father is less about reconciling with Obama Sr. the man than with addressing the outsized expectations Obama sets for himself because of his father's absence. Ultimately, Obama supplants the failed figure of his father by modeling his identity on an image of blackness associated with public achievement and social justice. Obama Sr. operates as a powerful ancestral presence in the text but a presence defined by absence and therefore ripe with the possibility of Obama's own fulfillment. In replacing his father metaphorically throughout the text, he effectively becomes his own ancestor.

Perhaps because he is aware of the rather grandiose leap enacted by his text, Obama concedes in the introduction that while "the result is autobiographical," he has "usually avoided such a description." He explains his unease with this term by noting that an "autobiography promises feats worthy of record, conversations with famous people, a central role in important events. There is none of that here" (xvi). Adding to this disavowal of the term "autobiography," Obama explains that "there are dangers inherent in any autobiographical work: the temptation to color events in ways favorable to the writer, the tendency to overestimate the interest one's experiences hold for others, selective lapses of memory." Obama lightly admits to indulging such temptations as he writes, "Such hazards are only magnified when the writer lacks the wisdom of age; the distance that can cure one of certain vanities" (xvi). Penned when Obama was only thirty-four years old, *Dreams from My Father* deliberately sets out to tie one man's individual experience to the struggles of the nation as a whole. In the preface to the 2004 edition, he describes the context for the book's creation: "I received an advance from a publisher and went to work with the belief that the story of my family, and my efforts to understand that story, might speak in some way to the fissures of race that have characterized the American experience, as well as the fluid state of identity—the leaps through time, the collision of cultures—that mark our modern life" (vii). Obama suggests here that telling his story is a kind of service to the nation. The insights derived from his life might bridge "the fissures of race" and clarify "the fluid state of identity." His book is less an autobiography than a contribution to a necessary national discourse. While this posture might come across as condescending, it reflects one of the key elements of how Obama understands his own blackness. As I discuss further, he conceptualizes blackness as an activist devotion to the struggle for a more just society. By framing his book as an act of public service, Obama prizes nation over self and makes introspection a form of model citizenship.

If we heed Obama's caution not to label his book autobiographical, how are we to classify this text? What genre does it belong to? Obama anticipates this question when he writes at the conclusion of his introduction, "Whatever the label that attaches to this book—autobiography, memoir, family history, or something else—what I've tried to do is write an honest account of a particular province of my life" (xvii). Though Obama seems to abdicate responsibility for categorizing his book by genre, inevitably "the label" will attach itself, regardless of his apparent preference to dispense with one altogether. But more importantly, his qualification posits a distance between autobiography and "honest account," implying that honesty may exist apart from a simple recitation of factual events. We might read this as the semantic play of a candidate eager for higher office, but I contend that there is far more than political spin at work here.

In highlighting Obama's distinction between autobiography and an "honest account," I am not concerned with questioning the factual basis of Obama's written narrative of his life. He admits in the introduction to creating composite characters and altering the chronology of actual events, common memoir techniques that can preserve and even emphasize a certain emotional or psychological truth. Rather, I am interested in exploring how his discomfort with the term "autobiography" reflects on the central concerns of the text, which he explicitly identifies in the book's title as race and inheritance. Obama's book does not lend itself to easy categorization, much as Obama does not fit into simplistic categories of race. Identifying himself at the beginning of *Dreams from My Father* as a "black American," Obama takes his race from his father and his nationality from his mother. However, this seemingly simplistic merger of differences masks a unique inheritance—a childhood spent in Hawaii and Indonesia, a father known primarily through the stories of others, and a maternal family characterized more by rootlessness than by a settled geographic homespace. The term "black American" is certainly an appropriate description of Obama, but like the label "autobiography," it elides a far more intricate history. And importantly, this is an identification that Obama claims for himself in a way that he does not ascribe a genre to his book. The label "black American" represents a chosen identity because given his background he could just as easily describe himself as biracial, white, Kenyan, or Hawaiian. Moreover, as he implies in the book's introduction, this is an identity fundamentally derived from the absence of his father.

The generic instability of *Dreams from Father* is inextricably bound to the elusive, often malleable image of Obama's father. Just as Obama adopts a novelistic style, recounting in minute detail conversations that are decades old, he describes his search for his father as a controlling trope that undergirds a more fundamental engagement with himself and his anxiety concerning his racial identity. Obama does not at last find his father at the book's conclusion. In fact, the testimonies of Obama's half siblings who had a much closer relationship to their father reveal a man far more complicated and mysterious than Obama's initial conception of Obama Sr. Instead, Obama's search for his father leads him to discover and embrace a self-fashioned and especially rigorous form of blackness. This conception of racial identity, established as much through Obama's tireless work as a community organizer on Chicago's South Side as through the color of his skin, reflects the amalgamated aspects of his text. For Obama, both race and textual production are sites of dynamic creation.

Dreams from My Father is divided into three sections: "Origins," "Chicago," and "Kenya." The first section describes Obama's childhood in Hawaii and Indonesia, ending with his first years after college when he lived in New York City and struggled to decide what to do with his life. The second section offers a detailed account of his work as a community organizer in Chicago, and the third focuses on his first trip to Kenya, where he meets many of his paternal relatives and learns important details about the history of his father. There is no clear transition between the second and third sections. "Chicago" ends with Obama crying during his first service at Trinity United Church, where he at last discovers not only his faith but also a deep sense of belonging among the black community. This powerful scene could just as well be the end of the book as it offers a resolution to the journey that has defined the text as a whole: Obama embracing and being embraced by other black Americans. But instead, the text shifts abruptly to Kenya, where Obama once again confronts a deeply personal struggle rooted in the search for his father: "Stripped of language, stripped of work and routine—stripped even of the racial obsessions to which I'd become so accustomed and which I had taken (perversely) as a sign of my own maturation—I had been forced to look inside myself and had found only a great emptiness there. Would this trip to Kenya finally fill that emptiness?" (301–302). The text seems to backpedal on itself, separating two of its major motifs that had been inextricably united. Obama suggests here that his "racial obsessions" are distinct from his search for his father. While the first two sections of the book present Obama's racial insecurities as a consequence of his absent father, here Obama implies that coming to terms with his identity as a black American does little to ameliorate his profound sense of paternal loss.

The dual endings offered in "Chicago" and "Kenya" affirm the twin trajectories of Obama's maturation. He must both find a community and find his father. These two searches are intimately tied to issues of race as Obama initially endows his absent father with romantic expectations of blackness and in finding a community, he returns again and again to various black father figures. However, while Obama comes to supplant his father in the "Kenya" section, his place in the Chicago community gestures toward other ways of establishing blackness. Paramount to this development is his declaration of faith and his involvement in Trinity United Church. Obama presents the church as representative of the black community as a whole. While we may read this as a convenient literary symbol, the connection Obama establishes here has had profound consequences. In the spring of 2008, he resigned from Trinity following the scandal surrounding his former pastor, Reverend Jeremiah Wright. This decisive action along with his speech on race, "A More Perfect Union," positioned Obama as a race-transcendent candidate, not beholden to the very community he strived so long to embrace. However, in the final years of his presidency, Obama reestablished the racial ties that define *Dreams from My Father*. His response to the overwhelming number of shootings of unarmed black men during his second term as well as the 2015 massacre at the Emanuel African Methodist Episcopal Church in Charleston, South Carolina, affirm the identity he struggled to attain in his first book. Obama concluded his presidency by embracing a noble and nurturing form of blackness that is at the root of his struggle in *Dreams from My Father* and indicative of the possibilities of pan-African American community.

BLACKNESS AND THE DREAM THAT IS HIS FATHER

Obama is the son of Barack Obama Sr., the first African student to study at the University of Hawaii. Although he already had a wife in Kenya, Obama Sr. married Stanley Ann Dunham after the two met in a Russian class.[1] Following the birth of their only child, Obama Sr. won a scholarship to pursue a doctorate at Harvard University in 1962. Because the scholarship did not provide enough money to support his new wife and son, Obama Sr. went to Cambridge by himself, leaving his young family with his caring in-laws. The long separation led to divorce two years later, and Obama Sr., with only a master's in economics, returned to Africa, where he remained until his death in 1986. He communicated with his son through intermittent letters and made one monthlong visit to Hawaii to seek medical help when Obama was ten years old. This was the only sustained physical interaction the two ever had.

As a child, Obama understands his father to be an almost mythical figure who won the admiration and respect of seemingly everyone he encountered. Obama's mother, maternal grandparents, as well as family friends describe a brilliant, eloquent, though somewhat arrogant young man. Obama learns the basic outline of his father's life—a childhood spent herding goats, a scholarship first to study in Nairobi and then at the University of Hawaii, where he focused on econometrics and graduated in three years at the top of his class. Extremely popular, Obama Sr. organized the International Students Association and became its first president. The stories about Obama's father stretch credibility as they describe a remarkably self-assured man who was unafraid to confront racists head-on or spontaneously sing before a crowd. Obama recalls how "the path of my father's life occupied the same terrain as a book my mother once bought for me, a book called *Origins*, a collection of creation tales from around the world" (10). The young Obama is unable to distinguish between the story of the earth's creation and the story of his own. Both involve invisible sources, larger-than-life characters, and an inheritance he can barely comprehend.

As Obama reflects on the confluence of his father's story with that of various creation myths, he notes how these puzzling narratives generated an array of questions that were equally ponderous and impossible to answer. He describes how he was troubled by such issues as "Why did an omnipotent God let a snake cause such grief?" and "Why didn't my father return?" but explains that "at the age of five or six I was satisfied to leave these distant mysteries intact, each story self-contained and as true as the next, to be carried into peaceful dreams" (10). This satisfaction with mysteries turned into dreams carries over into Obama's adult life, fostering a dangerous mythology as well as a critical lack of communication between family members.

In recounting the stories he learned about his father, Obama notes that there are significant absences in the family history. These puzzling gaps cause him to approach his maternal grandparents' vivid tales with profound skepticism. Regarding his parents' wedding, he discovers that "how and when the marriage occurred remains a bit murky. . . . There's no record of a real wedding, a cake, a ring, a giving away of the bride. No families were in attendance; it's not even clear that people back in Kansas were fully informed" (22). These omissions undermine the satisfying image, proffered by his mother and grandparents, of a happy interracial family, heralding a new multicultural age. Obama suspects that the stories he learns are reflections less of his father than of the storytellers themselves. He faults his maternal grandfather for "his tendency to rewrite history to conform with the image he wished for himself" (21) rather than acknowledge the racism endemic to the nation at large during the time of his parents' marriage. With the discerning perspective of age, Obama concludes in the book's opening chapter,

> I suppose that's what all the stories of my father were really about. They said less about the man himself than about the changes that had taken place in the people around him, the halting process by which my grandparents' racial attitudes had changed. The stories gave voice to a spirit that would grip the nation for that fleeting period between Kennedy's election and the passage of the Voting Rights Act: the seeming triumph of universalism over parochialism and narrow-mindedness, a bright new world where differences of race or culture would instruct and amuse and perhaps even ennoble.

Obama recognizes that the triumphant stories of his father and his white family's welcoming response to him feed a self-justifying national narrative. He muses, "With his black son-in-law and his brown grandson, Gramps had entered the space age" (23). However, this is a retrospective construction, and thus the kind of righteous national self-consciousness and progressivism that these stories produce is suspect, too influenced by contemporary desire to be entirely credible.

This tendency to rewrite the past is especially evident in the stories told by Stanley Dunham, Obama's maternal grandfather. Obama describes Dunham as ever earnest and enthusiastic, a twentieth-century pioneer who found a final frontier in Hawaii and the globalized world embodied by his grandson. However, for Obama, Dunham's energy and vision are inseparable from his whiteness: "His was an American character, one typical of men of his generation, men who embraced the notion of freedom and individualism and the open road without always knowing its price, and whose enthusiasms could as easily lead to the cowardice of McCarthyism as to the heroics of World War II. Men who were both dangerous and promising precisely because of their fundamental innocence; men prone, in the end, to disappointment" (16). Obama establishes a sharp contrast between the innocence of his grandfather and his own more worldly and critical perspective. Even as a child he lacks such a "fundamental innocence," though he seeks to preserve it in his white elders. For example, while in Indonesia, Obama quickly learns to censor his letters to his grandparents: "The world was violent . . . unpredictable and often cruel. My grandparents knew nothing about such a world, I decided; there was no point in disturbing them with questions they couldn't answer" (38). No doubt his grandparents were very aware of the cruelties of the world, but Obama's urge to shield them from his experiences suggests an inability to articulate and discuss struggles that cannot be easily remedied. He instinctively caters to his white family's preference for outsized myths over uncomfortable realities and upends the hierarchical relationship between son and grandfather. Here Obama has the more mature and expansive understanding of the world, while his grandparents are like children needing protection, safety, and even ignorance.

Obama recalls how his grandfather liked to introduce him to tourists as the "great-grandson of King Kamehameha, Hawaii's first monarch," promising the young Obama "that your picture's in a thousand scrapbooks . . . from Idaho to Maine" (25). Rather than explain how he is related to his dark-skinned grandson, Dunham escapes into humor and fantasy. Though his comment is innocuous, it feeds a mythic sensibility that denies the divisive dynamics of race. This incident exposes the foundation of what Obama identifies as his grandfather's most essential quality, his innocence—a well-intentioned desire to be part of the multicultural future that necessarily incorporates a past far removed from his own racial experience. This quality is especially evident in how Dunham understands his relationship to the experiences of African Americans. Obama explains that according to his grandfather, the family's move westward was precipitated by the racism he and his wife witnessed in Texas.

> And yet I don't entirely dismiss Gramps's recollection of events as a convenient bit of puffery, another act of white revisionism. I can't precisely because I know how strongly Gramps believed in his fictions, how badly he wanted them to be true, even if he didn't always know how to make them so. After Texas I suspect that black people became a part of these fictions of his, the narrative that worked its way through his dreams. The condition of the black race, their pain, their wounds, would in his mind become merged with his own: the absent father and the hint of scandal, a mother who had gone away, the cruelty of other children, the realization that he was no fair-haired boy—that he looked like a "wop." Racism was part of that past, his instincts told him, part of convention and respectability and status, the smirks and whispers and gossip that had kept him on the outside looking in. (21)

Although Obama begins this passage by stating that his grandfather's version of the past is not "another act of white revisionism," Dunham's insistence that he and his wife left Texas "because of their discomfort with such racism" (20) smacks of a desire to parade one's progressive high-mindedness. Obama grants his grandfather the sincerity of his retelling, but such sincerity is still mired in entrenched social dynamics that make blackness and racial victimization malleable, even exploitable categories. Dunham's "instincts" may be earnestly empathetic, but they ignore the specificity of racial oppression, trivializing difference by making whiteness a vessel for any experience of marginalization and struggle.

Obama also observes such qualities in his mother who arrives in Indonesia with "her innocence carried right along with her American passport" (41). Like her father, Ann Dunham glamorizes African American history. However, she does not make the mistake of appropriating stories of oppression and resistance as her own. Rather, in an attempt to supplement her son's Indonesian education, she insists on daily English lessons that include learning about important African American historical figures. This well-intentioned endeavor leaves Obama with outsized expectations of what it means to be black: "Every black man was Thurgood Marshall or Sidney Poitier; every black woman Fannie Lou Hamer or Lena Horne. To be black was to be the beneficiary of a great inheritance, a special destiny, glorious burdens that only we were strong enough to bear" (51). Obama's mother conflates her son's racial identity with the history of African Americans as if his black skin alone unites him to an entire community and culture. While this approach anticipates the possibility of pan-African American identity, it fails to acknowledge the gaps and differences that mark Obama's unique experience of race. Moreover, this conflation between African and African American identity neglects any education of Kenyan history and culture.

Despite his mother's misguided if inspiring vision of racialized legacies, Obama is not black like Thurgood Marshall or Fannie Lou Hamer. As Coates emphasizes, our former president is black in part as a result of choice and individual initiative. Reflecting on Obama's description in *Dreams from My Father* of how he used basketball as a gateway to black culture, Coates marvels at our president's conclusion: "I decided to become part of that world," writing, "This is one of the most incredible sentences ever written in the long, decorated history of black memoir, if only because very few black people have ever enjoyed enough power to write it." The shock of this sentence is the choice embedded in Obama's relationship to race. He decided to become part of this world. It was not cast on him; it was not an inescapable birthright. This formulation implies that he could have become something else, perhaps "a raceless cosmopolitan" as Coates suggests, or at the very least an American for whom race is incidental rather than elemental. Though Obama could never escape the color of his skin, he could have, like Ifemelu of *Americanah* or Julius of *Open City*, made his home in other countries or identified himself by his cultural tastes and intellectual proclivities rather than by an abiding commitment to struggling communities. He could have been an Afropolitan rather than an Afro-American. This embrace of blackness is at the heart of Obama's racial identity, an embrace actively fostered by his white family.

While Obama dutifully absorbs his mother's romantic version of African American history and subjectivity, he discovers on his own other, more troubling responses to being black. He begins the second chapter of *Dreams from My Father* with a description of finding an article in *Life* magazine about a black man who underwent a failed chemical treatment to turn his skin white. Obama's first response is to wonder if his "mother [knew] about this," and though he has a "desperate urge . . . to demand some explanation of assurance," he finds that he "had no voice for my newfound fear" (30). Just as he shields his grandparents from the frightening images of poverty and pain he witnesses in Indonesia, Obama does not tell his mother about the unsettling *Life* article. With his "uneven, ghostly hue" (30), the man is proof that his mother's account of African American life is a reflection of her innocence for it fails to include narratives of despair and self-destruction. Newly attuned to how "the black man on *Mission Impossible* spent all his time underground" and "there was nobody like me in the Sears, Roebuck Christmas catalog," Obama concludes, "I still trusted my mother's love—but I now faced the prospect that her account of the world, and my father's place in it, was somehow incomplete" (52). With this recognition, Obama implicitly defines himself against the innocence of his white family members. While they celebrate the triumphs and promise of the black struggle for civil rights, he is intimately aware of the quiet bias that feeds racial self-hatred and the desire to escape into whiteness. The optimistic innocence of his grandfather and mother simply cannot define his worldview. He instead describes himself as American but not innocent, ever aware of the abjection assigned to blackness and the loneliness of his particular situation.

Although Obama is skeptical of the stories his maternal family tells him about his father, he must admit that he too is guilty of treating his father as "a useful fiction, one that haunts me no less than it haunted my family" (25–26). This preference for the imagined over the real begins with Obama's first and only prolonged encounter with his father. During the month that Obama Sr. spends in Hawaii receiving medical treatment, the young Obama struggles to reconcile the man he knows from stories with the strict, somewhat frail father who orders his son to study rather than watch television and presents him with a series of handcrafted wooden toys. Obama quickly tires of his father's presence: "After a week of my father in the flesh, I had decided that I preferred his more distant image, an image I could alter on a whim—or ignore when convenient. If my father hadn't exactly disappointed me, he remained something unknown, something volatile and vaguely threatening" (63). As a child, Obama favors the myth over the man, the fiction over the truth. This preference underscores the generic instability of the text as a whole. Just as Obama is more comfortable with the romanticized image of his father, jettisoning the rather imperious man he meets as a boy, he crafts a story speckled with ready symbols and deliberate omissions. His comments on his father's stay aptly apply to the blend of fantasy and fact that amount to his "honest account" of his life. Like his maternal grandparents, Obama conjures not the real Obama Sr. in his book but a "distant image" that satisfies the narrative demands of his text—that is, a resolution to his acute racial anxiety.

Like his relatives, Obama is guilty of manipulating his father's image as a "useful fiction" (25) or as he also describes his father's appearance in family stories, an "attractive prop" that allows him to tell a satisfying story about himself. Although Obama recognizes how the real Obama Sr. is lost in these distortions and retrospective desires ("There was only one problem: my father was missing" [26]), even as an adult he continues to traffic in these dubious projections. The "something unknown, something volatile and vaguely threatening" is tamed by the fictions and literary constructs he produces for both himself and his readers. In *Dreams from My Father,* the "attractive prop" that Obama Sr. becomes for Obama is grounded in an elusive racial essence. Obama Sr. becomes the repository for his son's racial anxiety in part because the latter lacks black male role models to help him understand his racial identity. He explains, "I was trying to raise myself to be a black man in America, and beyond the given of my appearance, no one around me seemed to know exactly what that meant" (76). Obama finds some solace and guidance playing basketball with "a handful of black men" who "would teach me an attitude that didn't just have to do with the sport. That respect came from what you did and not who your daddy was" (79). This approach to identity is especially attractive to Obama because it values individual initiative over biology, action over blood.

The black men Obama encounters while an adolescent living with his maternal grandparents in Hawaii include his high school classmate Ray and the poet Frank.[2] Both offer models of black masculinity that do not easily cohere with Obama's experiences and in particular with his love and affection for his white family members. Recently transferred from LA, Ray is one of a handful of other black students at their elite private high school. Though Obama is often skeptical of Ray's exaggerated stories of women and celebrities, the two talk freely about how they are treated differently by students and teachers. Unlike Ray, Obama cannot dismiss "white folks" as inevitably racist: "Sometimes I would find myself talking to Ray about *white folks* this or *white folks* that, and I would suddenly remember my mother's smile, and the words that I spoke would seem awkward and false" (81). When Obama suggests, "Maybe we could afford to give the bad-assed nigger pose a rest," Ray shakes his head and replies, "A pose, huh? Speak for your own self." Wary of Ray's "trump card" since Obama must admit that he "was different, after all, potentially suspect," he "quickly retreat[ed] to safer ground" (82). His camaraderie with Ray ultimately exposes his most basic insecurities as he can never match his friend's seemingly more authentic experience. When Obama starts discussing Malcolm X with a follower of the Nation of Islam they meet playing basketball, Ray dismisses the exchange, noting, "I don't need no books to tell me how to be black" (87). Compared to Ray, Obama is ever an imposter, a black man who must always prove and perform his blackness.

Like Ray, Frank also offers a vexed model of black masculinity. He tells Obama that though he has been friends with the latter's grandfather for years, Frank can never sleep comfortably at a white person's house: "*Never*: Doesn't matter how tired I get, I still have to watch myself. I have to be vigilant, for my own survival" (90). Frank's comments affirm for Obama that he "was utterly alone" (91) because while his grandparents cannot relate to his experience of blackness, neither can the black men he knows understand his love for his white relatives. Before heading off to college, Obama visits Frank, who warns him that the "real price of admission" is "leaving your race at the door . . . leaving your people behind" (97). Frank seems to equate "race" with "family" here as both of these key aspects of the self are what he claims are left behind. But the family that Obama is leaving is his white family, and thus Frank's later assertion that in college "they'll train you so good, you'll start believing what they tell you about equal opportunity and the American way and all that shit" rings if not false, at least misapplied to Obama's actual circumstance. "The American way" has been a cornerstone of the values instilled by the Dunhams. If Obama is in danger of being "trained" rather than "educated," as Frank warns, this is a training that has long started at home.

Given this absence of adequate role models, Obama turns to his father for support. However, because Obama Sr. remains a vague figure who sends short, sometimes cryptic letters, Obama seizes on an image of his own creation, one fundamentally linked to blackness. Reflecting on this deeply racialized construction that has profoundly guided his life, Obama writes,

> It was into my father's image, the black man, son of Africa, that I'd packed all the attributes I sought in myself, the attributes of Martin and Malcolm, Du Bois and Mandela. And if later I saw that the black men I knew—Frank or Ray or Will or Rafiq—fell short of such lofty standards; if I had learned to respect these men for the struggles they went through, recognizing them as my own—my father's voice had nevertheless remained untainted, inspiring, rebuking, granting or withholding approval. You do not work hard enough, Barry. You must help in your people's struggle. Wake up, black man! (220)

For Obama, his father equates with blackness, which in turn signifies greatness and a passionate commitment to social justice. Because he is only an image, his father offers an unassailable model of racialized virtue that no living person can adequately emulate—except Obama himself. This formulation of blackness is consonant with his mother's history lessons that glorified the work of civil rights activists and artists. The absence of Obama's father signals not an absence of racial identity for Obama but a responsibility to live up to an exalted racial legacy, one rooted in the vision of an idealistic young white woman. Obama seems especially attuned to the ironies of this construction as he notes that according to his mother the burdens of black people were ones "we were to carry with style. More than once, my mother would point out: 'Harry Belafonte is the best-looking man on the planet'" (51). Despite this tongue-in-cheek comment, it is clear that this romantic image of blackness has deeply impacted Obama's sense of self as well as his obligation to others.

With such grandiose examples in mind, Obama embarks on a career in community organizing soon after graduating from college. He is motivated by twin desires: to live up to the image of his father he has constructed and to find a community of people who share his identity and values. Chicago's South Side offers him the opportunity to take part in the kind of activism that has helped shape and unify the black community in America. "In the sit-ins, the marches, the jailhouse songs, I saw the African-American community becoming more than just the place where you'd been born or the house where you'd been raised. Through organizing, through shared sacrifice, membership had been earned. And because membership was earned—because this community I imagined was still in the making, built on the promise that the larger American community, black, white, and brown, could somehow redefine itself—I believed that it might, over time, admit the uniqueness of my own life" (135). Obama here conceptualizes race or "membership" in the African American community as something to be "earned." It is a matter not of skin color but of commitment and action or, to return to the wisdom of the basketball court, it's "what you did and not who your daddy was." Knowing that "it was too late to ever truly claim Africa as my home," Obama moves to Chicago to earn his place in the black community. As with his outsized image of his father, Obama's conception of the African American community depends on hard work and individual achievement. Our president's precocious record of success and service appears to be deeply embedded in his racial anxiety and need to prove or "earn" his blackness. However, Obama's concluding hope that the African American community "might, over time, admit the uniqueness of my own life" speaks to dual desires. Most obviously, he wants to be admitted into this world, to belong to a history and people he has long studied and admired. But the word "admit" also suggests his hope that this community will admit or acknowledge how he is already a part of their legacy. For this community to "admit the uniqueness of my own life" is to affirm how his blackness need not be earned at all because experiences like his have always been foundational to African American subjectivity.

"THE KING IS OVERTHROWN"

Obama maintains his grand ambitions and idealized image of his father until his older half sister, Auma, comes from Kenya to visit him in Chicago. Obama describes how in the first days of her visit, they tacitly avoid speaking of their father, explaining, "It was as if our conversation stopped whenever we threatened to skirt his memory. It was only that night . . . that we both sensed we couldn't go any further until we opened up the subject" (212). Auma proceeds to describe a man far removed from the paternal image Obama has carried with him since childhood. She refers to Obama Sr. as "the Old Man," a term that Obama describes as "right to me, somehow, at once familiar and distant, an elemental force that isn't fully understood" (208). This identification elides how Obama shares his first name with his father, establishing a clear distance that is especially critical as Auma's story unfolds. She tells how because Obama Sr. spoke out against the increasing tribalism in the Kenyan government, he was blacklisted from ministry positions and relegated to a minor job in the Water Department. His career frustrations caused him to seek solace in alcohol and he became abusive, prompting the departure of his third wife. Obama Sr. was unable to provide a home for his children and could not pay their school fees.

Although life improved somewhat in his final years, Auma's description of these failures and frustrations unsettle Obama's most basic conception of his father. "The brilliant scholar, the generous friend, the upstanding leader—my father had been all those things . . . that image had suddenly vanished. Replaced by . . . what? A bitter drunk? An abusive husband? A defeated, lonely bureaucrat? To think that all my life I had been wrestling with nothing more than a ghost! For a moment I felt giddy. . . . The king is overthrown, I thought" (220). Obama is overwhelmed by his newfound liberation, proclaiming that his father was now "dead" because "he could no longer tell me how to live." Released from the pressure of his father's success and commanding image, Obama can now pursue his own course because, as he explains, "Whatever I do, it seems, I won't do much worse than he did" (221). For the first time, Obama expresses the deep insecurity and fear of failure that has driven his career ambitions. However, despite this sudden freedom, Obama also recognizes that he still does not know his father. Auma's story presents a wholly new image, but it remains hollow, devoid of an understanding of how Obama Sr.'s youthful vigor collapsed, of what motivated him to leave and then return to Kenya. Reflecting on his only encounter with his father—the month in Hawaii when he was ten—Obama blames their lack of intimacy on shared, but silent, fears of inadequacy: "He hadn't been able to tell me his true feelings then, any more than I had been able to express my ten-year-old desires. We had been frozen by the sight of the other, unable to escape the suspicion that under examination our true selves would be found wanting. Now fifteen years later, I looked into Auma's sleeping face and saw the price we had paid for that silence" (221). Assuming that Obama Sr. also feared that his "true se[lf] would be found wanting," Obama forces a commonality between them. From this perspective, it is not his son's youth that prevented Obama Sr. from sharing his most intimate thoughts with Obama, but his fear of inadequacy, the same fear of inadequacy that has troubled Obama throughout his childhood and early adulthood. The merger between father and son here is inexact—Obama was hardly of an age to express himself much less understand his father's life choices at the time of their meeting. However, the sense of shared insecurity serves Obama's greater purpose of highlighting the ways in which he adopts and transforms his father's legacy, thereby achieving his own paternal wisdom.

Auma's trip to Chicago represents the fulfillment of a previously canceled trip to New York when Obama was finishing his undergraduate studies at Columbia. However, Auma had to cancel that prior trip because of the sudden death of their sibling, David, a boy Obama never meets. As he recalls her canceled trip with the retrospective knowledge of what he learns in her visit a few years later, Obama wonders if his life would have been changed by no longer having an idealized conception of his father to motivate him: "Or maybe, if David hadn't died when he did, and Auma had come to New York as originally planned, and I had learned from her then what I would only learn later, about Kenya, and about our father . . . well, maybe it would have relieved certain pressures that had built up inside me, showing me a different community, allowing my ambitions to travel a narrower, more personal course, so that in the end I might have taken my friend Ike's advice and given myself over to stocks and bonds and the pull of respectability" (138). Looking back at his benighted self, Obama realizes that the image of his father was a fiction that he not only sustained but used to guide his life. The real Obama Sr. was in fact a failed bureaucrat; however, had Obama known this truth, he might not have driven himself into a life defined by community, service, and eventually politics. This admission is startling for contemporary readers aware that Obama is a two-term president as it suggests that the original impetus for Obama's commitment to justice and social change resides in the false image he had of his father. Obama's political career originates in these fabrications and his anxiety to live up to a fantasy version of this man.

Obama's construction of an especially demanding image of his father reflects the very nature of memoir as a uniquely flexible genre that mixes fact with desire, memory with reconstruction. And yet the formidable if false conception of Obama Sr. is what has motivated our forty-fourth president to such impressive heights. Here, fantasy literally blends into a reality that many believed to be an impossible achievement in their own lifetime: the election of a black man to the highest political office in the land. Obama's life history and the causes of his professional aspirations suggest that the very instabilities of truth, the blurring between fact and fabrication, are necessary to reach one's greatest potential. In this way, genre instability becomes not a clever narrative technique but constitutive of truly visionary political ambition.

A LEGACY OF ABANDONED BOYS

Obama's awareness that even with Auma's story he still does not know his father leads him to travel to Kenya to visit his large extended family and speak with the relatives who knew Obama Sr. personally. The most complete description of his father is told by Granny, one of his grandfather's wives, who partly raised Obama Sr. In the book's final chapter, Obama transcribes the history of his grandfather Onyango and his father Obama Sr. as told by Granny. She provides a full description of both men's lives, detailing their childhoods, marriages, and careers. Unlike the scattered stories that Obama has thus far collected about his forefathers, Granny's narrative account contextualizes the character and motivations of both men. It also represents a radical departure from the conventions of traditional memoir writing as Obama effectively concedes narrative control to Granny. Shifting from a patrilineal narration to a matrilineal one, Obama undermines his father's power over his own life story. In so doing, he further amplifies the text's generic instability to emphasize his father's increasingly diminished influence.

Reflecting on Granny's stories, Obama writes that he "was left with only a series of mental images" (427). The first image is that of his grandfather who as a young boy chased after the mysterious white men, staying with them for many months. He at last returns to his father, wearing odd European clothes:

> I see my grandfather, standing before his father's hut, a wiry, grim-faced boy, almost ridiculous in his oversized trousers and his buttonless shirt. I watch his father turn away from him and hear his brothers laugh. I feel the heat pour down his brow, the knots forming in his limbs, the sudden jump in his heart. And as his figure turns and starts back down the road of red earth, I know that for him the path of his life is now altered irreversibly, completely.
>
> He will have to reinvent himself in this arid, solitary place. Through force of will, he will create a life out of the scraps of an unknown world, and the memories of a world rendered obsolete. (427)

This image of his grandfather is then replaced by one of his father. Obama Sr.'s mother, Akumu, left her husband and her children when her son was only nine years old. "He's hungry, tired, clinging to his sister's hand, searching for the mother he's lost. The hunger is too much for him, the exhaustion too great; until finally the slender line that holds him to his mother snaps, sending her image to float down, down into emptiness. The boy starts to cry; he shakes off his sister's hand. He wants to go home, he shouts, back to his father's house. He will find a new mother. He will lose himself in games and learn the power of his mind" (428).

The two moments that Obama highlights from his grandfather and father's life histories are remarkably similar. Both boys experienced a deep separation from one of their parents—Onyango becomes permanently estranged from his father following his months with the white men, and Obama Sr. never truly reconciles with his mother. Although neither is actually orphaned, Obama emphasizes their separation from a key parental figure and the subsequent need of both men to compensate for that loss. Obama understands his father's later departure to the United States as emanating from the realization that "he, too, will have to invent himself," just as Onyango left Kenya to serve as a cook to the British. By juxtaposing parental separation with movement outside the homeland, Obama unites the isolation of his forefathers with his own journey. Like Onyango and Obama Sr., Obama is also abandoned by a parent, his father. And like the elder men, he too sets out into new territory to find and create an identity of his own.

The images that preoccupy Obama at the close of Granny's story indicate that the father he seeks is at last a reflection of himself. Jettisoning the lofty image he bore as a child as well as the frustrated alcoholic of Auma's memory, Obama discovers that the father he has searched for is the seeking, often uncertain man that Obama presents himself to be in this book. By establishing such clear parallels between Onyango, Obama Sr., and himself, Obama fashions a father in his own image; the elder men become the man he already is. And it is here that we must recall Obama's opening caution that "autobiography" is not the best description for this book as no autobiography concludes this neatly: the father that Obama has at last discovered is himself.

As he considers the images of his grandfather and father as both semiorphaned boys who re-create themselves through their interaction with Western culture, Obama identifies silence as the most pernicious aspect of the legacy he has inherited from them. He recognizes that though both men embarked on remarkably similar paths of reinvention, they did so largely unaware of such overlap. In the book's emotional climax, Obama understands that silence has isolated his forefathers from one another: "Oh. Father, I cried. There was no shame in your confusion. Just as there had been no shame in your father's before you. No shame in the fear, or in the fear of his father before him. There was only shame in the silence fear had produced. It was the silence that betrayed us. If it weren't for that silence, your grandfather might have told your father that he could never escape himself, or re-create himself alone. Your father might have taught those same lessons to you" (429). Obama links himself to his forefathers through the shared desire to become a man apart from his familial legacy. However, in doing so, he identifies this impulse toward reinvention as fundamentally flawed. Because of the abiding silence of his forefathers, Obama Sr. appears to have overemphasized his individual efforts while dismissing the possibilities of others. As Obama explains,

> The silence killed your faith. And for lack of faith you clung to both too much and too little of your past. Too much of its rigidness, its suspicions, its male cruelties. Too little of the laughter in Granny's voice, the pleasures of company while herding goats, the murmur of the market, the stories around the fire. The loyalty that could make up for a lack of airplanes or rifles. Words of encouragement. An embrace. A strong, true love. For all your gifts—the quick mind, the powers of concentration, the charm—you could never forge yourself into a whole man by leaving those things behind. (429)

Obama seems to suggest that because of his father's departure from Kenya as well as his silence, he never became "a whole man." The once mythical and seemingly infallible father is shown to be weak and isolated, a man without faith in his family much less humanity in general. However, we must again bear in mind that this representation of Obama Sr. still functions as an "attractive prop" for Obama's own narrative desires. The Obama Sr. presented here is not "a whole man" precisely so that his son may become one.

Though Obama merges the image of his father as a child with his own confusing childhood, he clearly separates himself from the man his father became. Obama will not be isolated by silence or deceived by material objects of Western progress. He instead stands as the inheritor of his forefathers' legacy and as the keeper of their mistakes. By creating a narrative of his paternal family, Obama breaks the damaging silence that kept the Obama men apart from one another. His narrative thus stands as a means of uniting them in a way that they were unable to do alone. In this way, Obama establishes continuity from father to son, recognizing patterns and insight that were invisible to his forefathers. This powerful perspective as well as the implication that his father did not become "a whole man" places Obama in a new position of fatherhood. It is possible to understand Obama as his own father in this crucial scene. However, as he rises from the graves of his forefathers, Obama is met by his young half brother Bernard and the servant boy Godfrey. Both boys are presented as fatherless, and Obama ends the book with an image of them walking into the valley together. Though it is easy to read Obama as the sole, commanding father figure in this closing scene, significantly, it is Bernard who has sought out the reflective Obama and Bernard who welcomes Godfrey on their walk home. Obama seems to gesture here toward the possibility of a younger generation guiding the elder, just as he might have guided his now deceased forefathers.

Obama conceives of familial continuity primarily in masculinist terms. He laments of Obama Sr., "Your father might have taught those same lessons to you. And you, the son, might have taught your father that this new world beckoning all of you involved more than just railroads and indoor toilets and irrigation ditches and gramophones, lifeless instruments that could be absorbed into the old ways" (429). However, the key stories of Obama's forefathers come from Granny; she ultimately offers the lessons and history that Obama craves. This gender inversion is not explored in *Dreams from My Father*, though in the preface, written in 2004 just as Obama was becoming a prominent political figure, the young senator admits a certain regret about the ultimate focus of his book. Referring to Ann Dunham, he writes, "I think sometimes that had I known she would not survive her illness, I might have written a different book—less a meditation on the absent parent, more a celebration of the one who was the single constant in my life" (xii). Obama makes this realization only after his mother's early death from breast cancer. With her passing, he discovers the depth of her absence, an absence impossible to fill with satisfying fictions.

In the epilogue to *Dreams from My Father*, Obama describes his final weeks in Kenya and briefly references his studies at Harvard Law School. However, the focus of this concluding chapter is his marriage to Michelle Robinson, "a daughter of the South Side" (439). Obama describes the wedding in novelistic detail, lingering on Auma's puffy eyes and his sister Maya's regal figure. He pays special attention to his eldest brother Roy, renamed Abongo, who has discovered new discipline and purpose through his conversion to Islam. Obama writes, "Abongo's new lifestyle has left him lean and clear-eyed, and at the wedding, he looked so dignified in his black African gown with white trim and matching cap that some of our guests mistook him for my father" (441). Like a father, Abongo assuages Obama's prenuptial nerves and assures him that he need not spend any more time primping in front of the mirror. However, even as Obama links Abongo to his father, the very next paragraph critiques Abongo's dogmatic ways: "His conversion has given him solid ground to stand on, a pride in his place in the world. From that base I see his confidence building; he begins to venture out and ask harder questions; he starts to slough off the formulas and slogans and decides what works best for him. He can't help himself in this process, for his heart is too generous and full of good humor, his attitude toward people too gentle and forgiving, to find simple solutions to the puzzle of being a black man" (441–442).

The condescending tone of this passage suggests that while Abongo continues to struggle with his identity and specifically his racial identity, Obama has found some resolution "to the puzzle of being a black man." He has asked the hard questions and found within himself satisfying answers. The rich description of his wedding is at odds with the absence of details surrounding the marriage of his parents. The vague allusions but affirming narrative of interracial harmony between Obama Sr. and Dunham is replaced by a realistic account of his wedding, which brought together his Kenyan and American relatives with his new family of in-laws. The answers to Obama's own racial identity puzzle lie here as he becomes both African and American, both father and son, and at last distances himself from the paternal lineage that frames so much of his first book.

OUR PASTOR IN CHIEF

As mentioned previously, *Dreams from My Father* effectively has two endings: the conclusion offered at the end of "Kenya" and the final scene of "Chicago." These dual endings speak to the divided strands of Obama's black identity. A part of his black heritage resides in Kenya amid the stories of his father, and the other thrives in the city that will soon be the home of his presidential library. Obama's relationship to Chicago and its black residents initially reflects the intensity of his desire for a racial home. When he first moves to the Windy City, he attempts to make it his own, indulging in the very kind of imagined connections that once inspired his maternal grandfather:

> And as I drove, I remembered. I remembered the whistle of the Illinois Central, bearing the weight of thousands who had come up from the South so many years before; the black men and women and children, dirty from the soot of the railcars, clutching their makeshift luggage, all making their way to Canaan Land. I imagined Frank in a baggy suit and wide labels, standing in front of the old Regal Theatre, waiting to see Duke or Ella emerge from a gig. The mailman was Richard Wright, delivering mail before his first book sold; the little girl with the glasses and pigtails was Regina, skipping rope. I made a chain between my life and the faces I saw, borrowing other people's memories. In this way I tried to take possession of the city, make it my own. Yet another sort of magic. (145–146)

Obama of course has no memory of the Great Migration, and his visions of Frank or Regina, a woman he meets in college, are no more than willful fabrications. Obama admits to appropriating "other people's memories," even drawing on his readings of Richard Wright to unite his experiences with the world he hopes to claim as his own. This is indeed a form of magic as Obama conjures a connection to a place he visited only once as a child. There is no real memory here, only the overwhelming desire to create one.

Although Obama's approach to Chicago bears echoes of Stanley Dunham's attempt to claim a part of African American history for himself, unlike his grandfather, Obama is resolutely committed to the hard, often thankless work of community organizing. While Dunham reimagined his experiences with racism to fashion a narrative of righteous condemnation and transcendence, Obama immerses himself in the frustrating battle for better schools, housing, and job opportunities. His successes are few, but even if the job training center and housing renovations never materialize, Obama develops strong ties to various community members, becoming a trusted figure in local politics. This transformation is not built on magic but rather reflects a determined effort to make life better for the black people he encounters.

After a few years, Obama decides to go to law school in order to better serve the people he comes to love and admire. While he questions if he will be seen as a sell-out for leaving his position, others celebrate his decision: "That was one of the lessons I'd learned these past two and a half years, wasn't it?—that most black folks weren't like the father of my dreams, the man in my mother's stories, full of high-blown ideals and quick to pass judgment. They were more like my stepfather, Lolo, practical people who knew life was too hard to judge each other's choices, too messy to live according to abstract ideals. . . . As far as they were concerned, my color had always been a sufficient criterion for community membership, enough of a cross to bear" (278). Obama proposes an entirely different conception of blackness here, one not generated by fantasies of his father or the glories of the African American past but rooted in the community itself. Rather than an identity that must be "earned," he suggests that his color always affirmed his claim to this world. However, as he continues his reflections, he admits that color does not equate with the kind of commitment and service he has long sought. His black skin may have been sufficient to make him part of this community, but he still strives for more. He demands not just "simple acceptance" because "you could be black and still not give a damn about what happened in Altgeld or Roseland" (278). He continues, "But to be right with yourself, to do right by others, to lend meaning to a community's suffering and take part in its healing—that required something more. . . . It required faith" (278–279). This startling conclusion places faith at the center of Obama's search for identity. To become a "black American" is to claim his part in a community of faith.

Obama concludes the middle portion of *Dreams from My Father* with his discovery of faith at the Trinity United Church of Christ, led at the time by Reverend Jeremiah Wright. Though best known for a handful of fiery video clips that were incessantly replayed during the 2008 presidential election, Reverend Wright appears in Obama's first book as a wise, caring pastor who offers the most satisfying model of black masculinity for the young Obama. Where Obama Sr. is described as an absent ancestor, Reverend Wright is vitally present. A celebrated scholar and a passionate pastor, Wright combines "anger and the humor of the streets" with "book learning and the occasional twenty-five-cent word." This ability to synthesize disparate elements immediately captures Obama's attention: "it became clear in that very first meeting that, despite the reverend's frequent disclaimer, it was this capacious talent of his—this ability to hold together, if not reconcile, the conflicting strains of black experience—upon which Trinity's success had ultimately been built" (282). This is precisely what Obama has long sought—a community leader who unites the wide variety of ways to be black in the United States. Listening to Reverend Wright's sermon, titled "The Audacity of Hope" (and the title of Obama's second book, a series of essays outlining his policy positions, published months before he announced his presidential candidacy), Obama finds the faith, the "something more" that will allow him "to be right with yourself." Obama ends the Chicago section of his book with Wright's sermon, suggesting that his search for belonging and community ends in Trinity Church.

This happy conclusion is of course belied by the controversy ignited in early 2008 when clips of various speeches given by Reverend Wright were broadcast over and over again on news outlets and the internet. "No, no, no, not God Bless America. God damn America," Reverend Wright is seen declaiming, and "America's chickens are coming home to roost," he pronounces following the attacks on 9/11. In these passionate outbursts, completely decontextualized from the longer, more complex sermons Reverend Wright preached in both instances, Obama's pastor, the man who married him and baptized his children, is seen as an incendiary apostate. He appeared to fulfill the worst white fears of violent black anger, fueling militant visions of an America ever divided by racial hatred. To maintain the viability of his presidential bid, Obama had no choice but to distance himself from his former pastor, and in his most famous speech, "A More Perfect Union," delivered at Constitution Center in Philadelphia, he denounced Reverend Wright's comments. In May 2008, he resigned his membership from the church.

Obama's separation from Reverend Wright marked a decisive moment in his political career, solidifying the anodyne racial image Obama sought to cultivate on the campaign trail. Throughout the run-up to the 2008 election, Obama was dogged by questions of race and authenticity. Was he a secret Muslim? Was he a Kenyan national? How might he pursue a specifically black agenda if elected to the Oval Office? Before his March 2008 speech on race, Obama opted for a kind of race-transcendent approach. He consistently alluded to race tangentially rather than directly, mastering what Gwen Ifill described as the delicate task of "putting whites at ease without alienating blacks" (189–190). In his first major national speech, the keynote address at the 2004 Democratic Convention, Obama spoke of the divide between red and blue states, not between white and black America. A coded racial message could be read in his rhetoric, but by making such sentiments secondary to his call for a unified America, Obama appealed to a multiracial electorate eager for a new approach to race relations. Though he certainly spoke to black audiences with a different cadence and style, he avoided specific mention of race and refused to comment on racially charged comments directed at him. When his own future vice president, then senator Joe Biden, called him "clean and articulate," Obama brushed off the comment rather than engage with the long racial history at play in such a remark. But the clips of Reverend Wright could not be so easily ignored. These were not comments that could be dismissed with a generous grin or overlooked as the antiquated customs of a previous generation. Obama would have to redefine his relationship to the man who, as described in *Dreams from My Father*, led him to the heart of the black community.

Obama wisely did not make Reverend Wright the centerpiece of "A More Perfect Union" though he did mention him specifically. He reiterated his strong disagreement with Wright's comments but also quoted from the passage in *Dreams from my Father* that describes his first service at Trinity. Obama then concluded,

> Like other predominantly black churches across the country, Trinity embodies the black community in its entirety—the doctor and the welfare mom, the model student and the former gang-banger. . . . The church contains in full the kindness and cruelty, the fierce intelligence and the shocking ignorance, the struggles and successes, the love and yes, the bitterness and bias that make up the black experience in America. And this helps explain, perhaps, my relationship with Reverend Wright. As imperfect as he may be, he has been like family to me. He strengthened my faith, officiated my wedding, and baptized my children. Not once in my conversations with him have I heard him talk about any ethnic group in derogatory terms, or treat whites with whom he interacted with anything but courtesy and respect. He contains within him the contradictions—the good and the bad—of the community that he has served diligently for so many years.
>
> I can no more disown him than I can disown the black community. I can no more disown him than I can my white grandmother—a woman who helped raise me, a woman who sacrificed again and again for me, a woman who loves me as much as she loves anything in this world, but a woman who once confessed her fear of black men who passed by her on the street, and who on more than one occasion has uttered racial or ethnic stereotypes that made me cringe.

Obama establishes a number of important connections here. First, he clarifies his understanding of Trinity as representative of the black community as a whole. This conflation is consistent with his description of the discovery of his faith at the end of the Chicago section in *Dreams from My Father*. To be a part of Trinity is to recognize his place as a black American and to see no divide between his unique experience and the history of African Americans more broadly. His faith and identification with Trinity are thus inextricable from his racial identity. Obama then describes Reverend Wright as a family member who has always modeled respectful behavior to people of all backgrounds. While he does not condone Wright's comments, he refuses to disown him. To do so would be equivalent to denying a member of his white family. His relatives, both black and white, have acted on racial sentiments he does not share, but in his vision of family, there is space for difference and even disagreement. His church, his community, and his family are all defined by an inclusive form of diversity.

"A More Perfect Union" represents Obama's most detailed discussion of race in the United States. Though it was crafted as a way to move on to other issues—to perfect the union that is the nation—a month later Reverend Wright made a series of media appearances that led Obama to resign from Trinity Church. A new series of inflammatory comments were set loose amid questions about Obama's patriotism, religious faith, and personal judgment. He had little choice but to sever his relationship with the church. Obama framed his resignation as a way to preserve Trinity as a place free of politics and to provide greater peace to its members, many of whom had been accosted by journalists and photographers following the start of the Wright scandal. Obama's resignation at last succeeded in putting an end to the Wright controversy, accomplishing what his speech first aimed to achieve. Wright ceased to be a ubiquitous presence in news headlines because the key connection between Obama and his former pastor had at last been cut.

A week later, Hillary Clinton dropped out of the presidential race, conceding the Democratic nomination to Obama. The confluence of these two events is striking, though Clinton's decision likely had more to do with her waning delegate count than with Obama's resignation from Trinity. Instead, the timing of these events highlights how at the very moment Obama became the first black presidential nominee of a major political party, he left the community that he previously identified as the heart of his African American life. Obama did not, of course, stop being black when he resigned from Trinity, but he did signal to the American public that he was willing to sacrifice an important part of his past and his very identity in order to present himself as a viable presidential candidate. By distancing himself from Reverend Wright and the black church as a whole, Obama removed himself from a key aspect of his African American life. It bears noting that after leaving Trinity, Obama and his family never adopted a home church in Washington, DC, and instead attended services with a variety of congregations in the area. Although many of these have been African American churches, Hamil R. Harris of the *Washington Post* reports, "Pastors and members of the churches he has attended have resigned themselves to the fact that Obama might visit but most likely won't join." This tacit recognition on the part of black congregations reflects an understanding of the limits of racial identification. As our first black president, Obama can be only so black. A black man could be elected to the Oval Office, but the black church remains outside the ultimate site of political power.

Obama's cautious stance on issues of race, as some critics have argued, began to change in the final years of his presidency. Writing in the *New York Times* in August 2015, Michael Eric Dyson proclaimed, "We finally have the president we thought we elected: one who talks directly and forcefully about race and human rights." Dyson's comments followed the first anniversary of the death of Michael Brown in Ferguson, Missouri, and the rise of the #BlackLivesMatter movement, events that propelled the nation as a whole into a fresh reexamination of the racial divides that continue to define the country. However, Obama's more forceful approach is not solely the result of a nation newly reminded of its persistent inequalities and the specific dangers black men face every day. With his tenure drawing to a close, Obama was at last free to speak candidly and act resolutely on a host of concerns specific to the black community. In his final years in the Oval Office, he demanded greater enforcement of legal bans on residential discrimination, launched "My Brother's Keeper," a new effort focused on empowering boys and young men of color, and called for police body cameras as a way to hold law enforcement officials accountable for civilian deaths. These initiatives would have exacted a much higher political price had they been proposed earlier on in his presidency. But with the 2016 election well on its way, Obama took advantage of his final years to focus on the very concerns that defined his work as a community organizer in Chicago: poverty, fair housing, job opportunities, and educational advancement for disenfranchised African American communities.

Dyson's characterization of Obama as "the president we thought we elected" suggests a return to previous forms as if the political calculations and media spin that had long defined his presidential image could at last fall away to reveal the true Obama: a man who has always been deeply and uniquely committed to the well-being of African Americans, a man who is not shrewdly race transcendent but adamantly black. That Obama emerged most forcefully in the eulogy he delivered for the Reverend Clementa Pinckney, one of nine people shot at the Emanuel African Methodist Episcopal Church in Charleston, South Carolina, on June 17, 2015. This speech will be best remembered for Obama singing a few lines of the popular hymn, "Amazing Grace." It is a moment unparalleled in the history of presidential oration. Obama begins with his eyes cast down and his voice, usually so clear and confident, slows with a trace of hesitation. He looks not out at the audience but to his far right as if searching for backup, and as he sees the men and women behind him rise, his head lifts, his voice steadies, and he leads the crowd. "I once was lost but now am found; was blind but now I see."

Earlier in his speech Obama uses the refrain "we've been blind" to bolster a series of policy points: "For too long, we were blind to the pain that the Confederate flag stirred in too many of our citizens . . . we've been blind to the way past injustices continue to shape the present . . . we've been blind to the unique mayhem that gun violence inflicts upon this nation." This use of anaphora frames a political speech as a consequence of grace, for it is grace that allows us to see. His reference to the hymn transforms the death of the AME congregants into an opportunity for social transformation. But while we can safely assume that Obama was never blind to the pain caused by the Confederate flag or the mayhem of gun violence, there is a profound revelation at work in this speech. The grace that Obama speaks of does not vest him with new sight; instead, we are made to see. And what is plainly visible is the Obama who found his faith in Chicago's Trinity United, who understood the black church to represent the black community and who defined his purpose and identity by the "audacity to hope." Though he never refers to Reverend Wright in his eulogy, his former pastor wields a profound if invisible influence on the speech. Obama here becomes our pastor in chief, and if grace will lead us home, then Obama at last finds his home in the black church, offering it as the heart of the nation's grief.

CONCLUSION

Blackness Now

This project was conceived and written under Obama's presidency. As a national symbol and a writer with a powerful story, he embodies many of the qualities I identify with pan-African American literature. His first book reflects a mode of blackness that is unshackled from the hierarchical frame of the ancestor as it merges conscious choice with African heritage. Obama demonstrates how blackness is best understood as a wide spectrum that recognizes history as a cherished commitment as well as the multiple consciousness embedded in dark skin. Commentators and historians have already started to assess what this age of Obama has been, and while most of those reflections will evaluate his social and political contributions, there is an important literary legacy here as well. Obama has already aligned himself with writers like Malcolm X and James Baldwin, but I would like to propose that something more than probing self-reflection and incisive social critique undergirds these comparisons. Obama affirms a model of blackness for the twenty-first century that is inextricably linked to political engagement. While this is by no means a novel formulation, it illuminates contemporary cultural shifts and the urgent conditions that define our fraught historical moment. Obama's model of public service recalls the injunctions of W. E. B. Du Bois, the activism of Ida B. Wells, and the promise of Martin Luther King Jr. He contributes to a broader legacy of African American writing, identity, and vision that reaches for a better world while also recognizing the particularities of twenty-first-century challenges.

In invoking Obama as a model of blackness tied to political engagement, I do not mean to suggest that all black Americans align with the Democratic platform or must adhere to a socially liberal agenda; rather, our former president's conception of blackness returns us to his years as a community organizer in Chicago where he dedicated himself to improving public housing conditions and developing employment opportunities for the poor. As critics have long noted and at times bemoaned, Obama is not a radical but a reformer. He is a pragmatist whose search for consensus honors the community he calls home. Obama's emphasis on community reminds us that cultural and political movements are not launched by lone individuals. This is especially true of Obama, who despite being the foremost black politician in all of American history, remains distant from the most significant political uprising of our time: the Black Lives Matter movement. In 2016, Obama invited a number of activists affiliated with Black Lives Matter groups, but they refused to attend. Aislinn Pulley, a community organizer in Chicago, explained in an online statement that she "could not, with any integrity, participate in such a sham that would only serve to legitimize the false narrative that the government is working to end police brutality and the institutional racism that fuels it."[1] Despite the deep schism between a group that opposes the deification of a single leader or handful of leaders and a man whose reputation is quickly burnishing into mythology, both Black Lives Matter and Obama remain fiercely devoted to supporting the black community. This shared commitment and the political activism it engenders are foundational to the flourishing of pan-African American literature.

Among its many reverberations, the 2016 presidential election demonstrates the necessity of energizing that community in all its diversity and struggle. Writing for the *New Yorker* weeks after Donald J. Trump shocked the world with his victory in the electoral college, Chimamanda Ngozi Adichie issued a clarion call to arms based in the urgent need for starkly clear language and vigorous political engagement:

> Now is the time to resist the slightest extension in the boundaries of what is right and just. Now is the time to speak up and to wear as a badge of honor the opprobrium of bigots. Now is the time to confront the weak core at the heart of America's addiction to optimism; it allows too little room for resilience, and too much for fragility. . . . Now is the time to refuse the blurring of memory. Each mention of "gridlock" under Obama must be wrought in truth: that "gridlock" was a deliberate and systematic refusal of the Republican Congress to work with him. Now is the time to call things what they actually are, because language can illuminate truth as much as it can obfuscate it.

Adichie's fierce essay is far removed from the lazy detachment of her protagonist Ifemelu. Where Ifemelu escaped the injustices of race by returning to Nigeria, Adichie stands firm in calling out the bigotry of our forty-fifth president and the racism that impeded so much of Obama's vision for the country. This is the critique not of an outsider but of someone deeply concerned with the survival and triumph of the United States as a global beacon of freedom and hope. While

Ifemelu scorned her transformation into blackness, Adichie claims here a fervent commitment to America rooted in a sharp awareness of race. She implicitly joins Obama in rallying for a country that she describes as having "always been aspirational to me" or, as he has phrased the trajectory of his life's work, toward "a more perfect union."

However, well before the results of November 8, 2016, black America had reached a point of crisis. Obama appeared powerless to prevent a headline that became so familiar as to fall into cliché. Unarmed black man shot to death by police. Details change. Sometimes the man is not a man but a boy like twelve-year-old Tamir Rice or a young woman like Rekia Boyd. Sometimes the implement of death is not a gun but a chokehold, as in the case of Eric Garner. Every tragedy is unique, every circumstance unjust in its own particular way, but the headline repeats. The city changes, proof only that this isn't a southern thing or an urban thing; it is all American. Ferguson, Missouri; Saint Paul, Minnesota; North Charleston, South Carolina; Los Angeles, California; Tulsa, Oklahoma; Baton Rouge, Louisiana; Charlotte, North Carolina. Unarmed black man fatally shot by an officer. Again and again and again.

Despite all the eloquence and intricacy of the novels studied here, this simple story has become the dominant black narrative of our time. A black man targeted by police, sometimes with credible cause, sometimes with none at all, dies. It matters not if the victim traces ancestors back to the slave South or to modern-day Nigeria or Haiti. Such distinctions mean nothing to frightened, trigger-ready officers or to citizens of all kinds trying to make it home.

Black writers of the wide American diaspora have been forced to grapple with what blackness means under such conditions of violence and vigilance. In the aftermath of the shooting at the Emanuel African Methodist Episcopal Church in Charleston, South Carolina, that left nine dead, Claudia Rankine concluded, "The condition of black life is one of mourning" (145). Of course, the condition of black life in the United States can never be divorced from diaspora or the journey across the Atlantic, but there is something far more immediate here than the nature of that migration, be it centuries or only years old. For Rankine, blackness is about living with the inevitability of grief and the necessity of transforming mourning into political action. Rankine credits Mamie Till Mobley's insistence that her son's brutalized body be displayed in an open coffin as inaugurating "a new kind of logic." She explains, "By insisting we look with her upon the dead, she reframed mourning as a method of acknowledgment that helped energize the civil rights movement of the 1950s and '60s" (148). For Rankine, the transformative potential of blackness comes not by aligning with African Americans who trace their roots to antebellum slavery or with others whose families reside in the Caribbean or those who have homes in Lagos and New York. Rather, the radical power of blackness comes by aligning with the dead: with Emmett Till as well as Philando Castile, with the girls killed in the 16th Street Baptist Church bombing as well as the names beneath tomorrow's headline.

Rankine's comments point to the urgency at the heart of black life in twenty-first-century America. African American or American African? Afropolitan or purveyors of poverty porn? These are academic debates that little matter when a black man or woman is pulled over for a broken taillight or is suspected of brandishing a weapon that ultimately proves to be no more than a bottle of pills, a toy, a wallet, a book. Is the only blackness that matters now the one written indelibly on the skin, the one that transforms a father or a daughter, a son or a mother into a clear and present danger? Obama suggested as much when he spoke about the death of Trayvon Martin at a press briefing in March 2013. With palpable grief lining his face, our then president intoned, "My main message is to the parents of Trayvon Martin. You know, if I had a son, he'd look like Trayvon. And I think they are right to expect that all of us as Americans are going to take this with the seriousness it deserves." By linking Martin to the son he might have had, the president presented blackness not as a matter of shared ancestral history but as a condition of visibility and threat. Though his father hailed from Kenya, not Florida, Obama suggests that black skin ultimately unites he and the slain boy in a common fraternity and experience of oppression. Once again paternity for Obama signals the codification of race as he becomes an absent father for Martin. This imagined relationship sutures Obama to a black community that defies narrow historical boundaries. In this formulation, slavery is not the root of blackness. Instead blackness is born through the daily realities and indignities of being black in America. To have dark skin is to be subject to the violent suspicion of neighbors, to be targeted and followed, and thus to live in a perpetual state of danger. It is to live at the threshold of death. Slavery set the terms of what blackness and, most importantly for this context, what black masculinity mean in the American imagination, but these distortions signify on all black bodies, regardless of when or how they arrived on these violent shores.

Rankine's conception highlights one of the central paradoxes of black life in America. To live in a state of mourning and threat is to live without the safety of a home. And yet the dead make this hallowed land that cannot be abandoned; the dead demand a home be made here. To align with the dead is to stand on the bloody ground of history. Reflecting on the people killed by police, Teju Cole wonders, "If it is true, as our ancestors always suspected, that the dead continue to exert some influence on the places where they lived and died."[2] Julius of *Open City* fears to grapple with the dead of New York, both the Africans of the slave burial ground and the other specters of violence that make the city a rememory of the distant and recent past. Cole reminds us that to know the facts of such atrocity is to recognize "how it marks us, the streets on which we move, the places in which we live."[3] Blackness in this country is inseparable from acknowledging and confronting the dead.

Edwidge Danticat frames the matter differently but with a similar awareness of the pervasive vulnerability of black bodies. In an essay for Jesmyn Ward's collection *The Fire This Time: A New Generation Speaks about Race* (2016), Danticat cites a piece published in the *Washington Post* by immigration attorney and law professor Raha Jorjani that compares the experience of African Americans to that of refugees.

> Suppose a client walked into my office and told me that police officers in his country had choked a man to death over a petty crime. Suppose he said police fatally shot another man in the back as he ran away. That they arrested a woman during a traffic stop and placed her in jail, where she died three days later. That a 12-year-old boy in his country was shot and killed by the police as he played in the park.
>
> Suppose he told me that all of those victims were from the same ethnic community—a community whose members fear being harmed, tortured or killed by police or prison guards. And that this is true in cities and towns across his nation. At that point, as an immigration lawyer, I'd tell him he had a strong claim for asylum protection under U.S. law. (206)

Danticat notes that the term "refugee" has been applied to African Americans at different points in history, such as during the Great Migration or in the aftermath of Hurricane Katrina. But these discrete events reflect a more pervasive reality captured in Danticat's recollection of her upbringing in Brooklyn. "We, immigrant blacks and African Americans alike, were treated by those who housed us, and were in charge of schooling us, as though we were members of a group in transit. The message we always heard from those who were meant to protect us: that we should either die or go somewhere else. This is the experience of a refugee" (207). Danticat distinguishes between immigrant blacks and African Americans only to observe that larger social forces ignore such variations. Immigrant and native born, together they are outsiders in this world, people who do not belong.

For Danticat, the familiar enraging headline poses particular concern for her children: "Each time a black person is killed in a manner that's clearly racially motivated, either by a police officer or a vigilante civilian, I ask myself if the time has come for me to talk to my daughters about Abner Louima and the long list of dead that have come since" (211). The "talk" is not simply about instructing her children in how to comport themselves in front of police officers. For Danticat, it is an introduction to the violence suffered by family friend Abner Louima and to the dead. To live here is to know the dead. This is not a matter of historical enlightenment. It is a matter of survival.

Reflecting on the continued death of innocent black men and women in an essay focused primarily on James Baldwin, Cole concludes, "The news of the day (old news, but raw as a fresh wound) is that black American life is disposable from the point of view of policing, sentencing, economic policy, and countless terrifying forms of disregard. There is a vivid performance of innocence, but there's no actual innocence left. The moral ledger remains so far in the negative that we can't even get started on the question of reparations" (16). Cole's use of the term "reparations" reverberates with the title of Ta-Nehisi Coates's acclaimed 2014 essay "The Case for Reparations." Reparations are often invoked in reference to the colossal sin of slavery, but Coates focuses on living African Americans who have been victimized by housing discrimination and red-lining. Though Cole suggests the impossibility if not the necessity of reparations, his emphasis on the disposability of black lives again makes the dead the foundation of belonging. The dead affirm his claim to justice, to life, to presence in this country.

When does a Nigerian or a Haitian or a Jamaican become an American? When does an African become an African American? Obama and Adichie suggest that political engagement is the foundation of both racial and national community. Rankine, Danticat, and Cole posit that to live here is to reckon with the dead, the dispossessed and the disposable, and to embrace them as your own. Both models compose the struggle that Coates bequeaths to his son in *Between the World and Me*, a struggle that is at once wearying and beautiful. Pan-African American literature charts a journey toward that struggle, and while not all of the protagonists discussed here ultimately embrace the challenge and community that defines American blackness, all of the texts do by deliberately signifyin(g) on key African American literary tropes. The talking book, rememory, invisibility, the ancestor, absent fathers: these are themes emblematic of black struggle in the United States. By disentangling blackness from the experience of antebellum slavery, pan-African American literature transforms our understanding of how race operates and evolves. Blackness not only is about a historical legacy but encompasses the daily work of confronting and resisting injustice.

This might make for a tidy though vaguely abstract conclusion if the stakes were not so high, if last week's and next month's headlines didn't announce the death of yet more black men and women gunned down for being black. For Rankine, mourning is not simply about sadness and grief; it has become the engine of a movement. She celebrates the Black Lives Matter campaign for its staunch commitment to justice as it "continues the mourning, and refuses the forgetting in front of all of us" (151). The African American literary tradition has long been marked by its inextricable relationship to political change. The abolition of slavery is inconceivable without the voices of Frederick Douglass and Sojourner Truth, just as James Baldwin and Lorraine Hansberry brought eloquence, insight, and narrative force to the civil rights movement. Where Black Power once fueled the Black Arts Movement, so pan-African American literature finds its political cognate in the Black Lives Matter movement.

Initially started as a hashtag following the acquittal of George Zimmerman, the man who shot and killed Trayvon Martin, the Black Lives Matter campaign has expanded to include worldwide demonstrations from Canada to Ghana. The movements' queer founders, Patrisse Cullors, Alicia Garza, and Opal Tometi, reflect the broad range of black life in the United States. Though raised as a Jehovah's Witness in Los Angeles, Cullors practices Ifa, a religious tradition of Nigeria, and is the founder of Dignity and Power Now, an organization dedicated to prison reform. Garza, the daughter and granddaughter of domestic workers, is the special project director at the National Domestic Workers Alliance, while Tometi, the daughter of undocumented Nigerian immigrants, directs the Black Alliance for Just Immigration. The diversity of the founders and their deeply personal political commitments affirm how black identity has come to incorporate multiple experiences distinct from the legacy of slavery. Concerns about immigration are just as crucial to this new civil rights movement as the widening carceral state and persistent disparities in educational and professional opportunities. In fact, parsing distinctions between African Americans and African immigrants becomes not only irrelevant but counterproductive given the pressing political concerns that unite black Americans of all backgrounds.

The hashtag has quickly transformed into a rallying cry that articulates what Tometi calls "our new ideology."[4] This is a campaign both marked by its inclusivity of a diverse black experience yet also deeply committed to preserving the singularity of its call. Unlike what Garza calls "the narrow nationalism that can be prevalent within some Black communities, which merely call on Black people to love Black, live Black and buy Black, keeping straight cis Black men in the front of the movement," Black Lives Matter "affirms the lives of Black queer and trans folks, disabled folks, Black-undocumented folks, folks with records, women and all Black lives along the gender spectrum." Black Lives Matter thus opposes not only antiblack racism but liberation movements that have marginalized certain members of the black community. With its decentralized structure and absence of formal hierarchy, it celebrates the vast spectrum contained within blackness.

The Black Lives Matter movement returns us to one of the central qualities of the diasporic subject, what Paul Tiyambe Zeleza terms "multiple consciousness." Where Du Bois once understood black subjectivity through double consciousness, we must now recognize the complexity that adheres to every black subject. All of the pan-African American novels examined here demonstrate an awareness of multiple consciousness. Every discussion of race in *Americanah* or *Open*

City or *All Our Names* involves intricate dynamics of class, gender, nationality, and citizenship. As the founders of the Black Lives Matter campaign remind us, there is no unitary black subject but a series of simultaneously overlapping and diverging experiences. Pan-African American literature makes clear the intersectionality that has always been central to black life.

We know now that there is no discussion of race without gender or class or sexuality or other forms of social privilege. Black Lives Matter and pan-African American literature make explicit one more form of identity foundational to blackness: the dead. In "Death in the Browser Tab," Cole, who like Rankine has argued for the importance of the Black Lives Matter movement, describes his experience watching the video of Walter Scott's death multiple times. Cole travels to North Charleston and finds the parking lot where Scott was pulled over. He traces the route of the chase to the spot where Scott fell. He notes the small memorial left there along with drooping flowers hanging from a chain-link fence. Later he reflects, "The videographic afterimage of any real event is peculiar. When the event is a homicide, that afterimage can cross over into the uncanny: the sudden, unjust, and irrevocable end of the long story of what one person was, who he loved, all she hoped, all he achieved, all she didn't, become available for viewing and reviewing" (205). Scott becomes a figure of the uncanny for Cole just as the black dead in *Open City* haunt Julius. The possibilities of who Scott was and wasn't establish a site for Cole's own projections. Scott becomes a reflection of the writer, the uncanny double he watches and chases but cannot find.

Cole closes his essay by describing his third encounter with the video. "Finally, I start to watch footage of Walter Scott's last moments. It's the third time, and it makes me uneasy and unhappy. The video begins with the man holding the camera racing toward the fence. A few seconds later, Walter Scott breaks away from Michael Slager. Slager plants his feet and raises his gun. There is still time. He shoots once, then thrice in quick succession. Scott continues to run. There is still time. This is when I stop the video and exit the browser" (206).

Scott remains for Cole running. The dead man is alive. Pan-African American literature does not seek the impossible task of resurrecting the dead. The dead are to be mourned and remembered. And through that process they become the foundation of belonging, of home.

ACKNOWLEDGMENTS

It has taken me five books to realize that all of my work is about the same thing: home. How to make a home, the language of home, what race means in that home, when the other place becomes your place. It seems like no coincidence then that this is the first book I have written in what I hope will be my home for a very long time—Bloomington, Indiana. Thus I begin by thanking my colleagues in the IU English Department who welcomed me with such warmth and generosity. I am especially grateful for the support of Paul Gutjahr, Shane Vogel, and Scott Herring; the feedback of Purnima Bose; and the model of Susan D. Gubar. Profound thanks as well to Gordon Hutner, whose support and vision for the special issue of *ALH* on twenty-first-century African American literature was instrumental in shaping my thoughts on contemporary black writing. He has become the best teacher of my career. A nod to Dinah Holtzman for seeding the title of this book. And finally, most deeply, thanks to my mother, Sara Antonia Li, who continues to make all things possible.

I have long known what home is, but it has taken my whole life to actually arrive at one. When I first visited Bloomington, it felt immediately recognizable. It was casual and friendly like the Minneapolis of my youth. And also primarily white, which, after a childhood in the Midwest and a career in higher education, feels familiar, if not always comfortable. Here the handyman spends longer telling me about his grandkids than he does fixing the washing machine. Here a teenage boy welcomes me under his umbrella in a sudden downpour and together we walk all the way to my front door. I delight in these small kindnesses even as I know that they are not so readily offered to others in my town, to women wearing headscarves, to men with dark skin, to certain children in hoodies. I'm beyond fortunate to have had the opportunity to choose Bloomington as my home, and if I've learned anything from writing this book, it's that the injustices of a place are not a reason to leave but precisely why we must stay.

NOTES

INTRODUCTION

1. Morrison explains that the first word immigrants to the United States learn is "okay." Bonnie Angelo, "The Pain of Being Black: An Interview with Toni Morrison," in *Conversations with Toni Morrison*, ed. Danille Taylor-Guthrie (Jackson: University Press of Mississippi, 1994), 255.

2. In the wake of the 2016 election, Morrison returned to these ideas in an essay for the *New Yorker*, writing, "Unlike any nation in Europe, the United States holds whiteness as the unifying force. Here, for many people, the definition of 'Americanness' is color." Morrison's claims are supported by the work of sociologists Cordero-Guzman, Smith, and Grosfoguel, who demonstrate that immigrants to the United States learn that "only whites are fit for citizenship, for full membership in the polity and society, so make sure that when your group's ethnicity and race are defined, they fall on the 'white ethnic' and not the 'native minority' side of the color line" (quoted in Christina M. Greer, *Black Ethnics: Race Immigration, and the Pursuit of the American Dream* [New York: Oxford University Press, 2013], 23).

3. See Felicia R. Lee, "New Wave of African Writers with an Internationalist Bent," *New York Times*, 29 June 2014, http://www.nytimes.com/2014/06/30/arts/new-wave-of-african-writers-with-an-internationalist-bent.html?smid=pl-share&_r=2.

4. The multiple forms of consciousness described by Zeleza are affirmed by Taiye Selasi's description of her own experiences in the United States: "It was a sort of triplicate alienation. I was alienated from other brown people by color, by culture, by residence, by language" (Taiye Selasi, "'From That Stranded Place' [2015]. Interview with Aaron Bady," *Transition* 117 [2015]: 159).

5. Quoted in Rachel L. Swards, "'African-American' Becomes a Term for Debate," *New York Times*, 29 August 2004, https://www.nytimes.com/2004/08/29/us/african-american-becomes-a-term-for-debate.html.

6. In *Black Ethnics*, Greer argues that "black ethnics," that is blacks from Africa or the Caribbean, "are perceived as an elevated minority group, not a model minority like Asian Americans . . . but an elevation above their black American counterparts, the widely accepted 'last-place' racial group" (13). Nearly half of all African immigrants to the United States have a bachelor's degree, and in 2000 the median income for Nigerian immigrant families exceeded that of black Americans by more than 50 percent.

7. Humphries writes, "In the case of immigrant Africans as black transnationals, the way they respond to the U.S. racial order is conditioned by whether race is a fundamental organizing principle of socioeconomic relations in their home countries and by their level of exposure to racial structuring (Waters; Jones-Correa; Glick Shiller and Fouron). For this reason, race may not be a delineating factor for many Africans unless they have had extended contact with or experienced direct subjugation by Europeans, as in South Africa" (Jill M. Humphries, "Resisting 'Race': Organizing African Transnational Identities in the United States," in *The New African Diaspora*, ed. Isidore Okpewho and Nkiru Nzegwu [Bloomington: Indiana University Press, 2009], 275).

8. Chimamanda Ngozi Adichie, interview by Anderson Tepper (Goodreads, 2013), http://www.goodreads.com/interviews/show/857.Chimamanda_Ngozi_Adichie.
9. A 2004 *New York Times* article titled "Top Colleges Take More Blacks, but Which Ones?" describes Gates and Guinier as particularly troubled by the paucity of African Americans at Harvard. "What concerned the two professors, they said, was that in the high-stakes world of admissions to the most selective colleges—and with it, entry into the country's inner circles of power, wealth and influence—African-American students whose families have been in America for generations were being left behind." Sara Rimer and Karen W. Arenson, "Top Colleges Take More Blacks, but Which Ones?," *New York Times*, 24 June 2004, https://www.nytimes.com/2004/06/24/us/top-colleges-take-more-blacks-but-which-ones.html.
10. Cecil Brown's *Dude, Where's My Black Studies Department? The Disappearance of Black Americans from Our Universities* (Berkeley, Calif.: North Atlantic Books, 2007) offers a more aggressive if at times offensively hyperbolic perspective on the dangers posed to black studies and African American students by the influx of various black immigrants.
11. Although black immigrants from the Caribbean currently exceed their African counterparts (in 2009 there were 1.7 million black Caribbeans in the United States and 1.1 million from Africa), if trends continue, by 2020 Africa will be the major source of the U.S. black immigrant population.
12. See Swards's "'African-American' Becomes a Term for Debate."
13. In the introduction to *The New African Diaspora*, Isidore Okpewho cites an unpublished paper by Ali Mazrui delivered at Binghamton, New York, in April 1996. In "The African Diaspora: African Origins and New World Self-Fashioning," Mazrui offers the term "American African" to refer to new-diaspora Africans living in the United States (13–14).
14. Consistent with this usage, throughout this study I employ the term "African American" to refer to descendants of enslaved Africans brought to the United States.
15. Distinguishing between the "old" model of diaspora offered by Paul Gilroy's influential *The Black Atlantic* (1993) and a "new" post–civil rights diaspora involving voluntary migration, Chude-Sokei argues that the literature of the Newly Black Americans "finds itself in a context overdetermined by multiple demands of affiliation and by the tensions between rival claims of trauma and memory, all within the crowded and obfuscating skin of racial classification" (Louis Chude-Sokei, "The Newly Black Americans," *Transition* 113 [2014]: 52–71, 54).
16. Although many of the most prominent of these writers are Nigerian, no single country predominates as the source of African immigrants. See Randy Capps, Kristen McCabe, and Michael Fix, "New Streams: Black African Migration to the United States," in *Young Children of Black Immigrants in America: Changing Flows, Changing Faces*, ed. Randy Capps and Michael Fix (Washington, D.C.: Migration Policy Institute, 2012), 45–73.
17. Noting the passing of pan-Africanism as a viable means of uniting the people of the continent, Achille Mbembe describes the movement as having become "institutionalized and ossified" with a tendency of invoking nativist conceptions (Achille Mbembe, "The Subject of the World," in *Facing Up to the Past: Perspectives on the Commemoration of Slavery from Africa, the Americas, and Europe*, ed. Gert Oostindie [Kingston: Ian Randle, 2001], 26). Similarly, Toyin Falola and Kwame Essien present an "academic post-mortem" of pan-Africanism in *Pan-Africanism and the Politics of African Citizenship and Identity* (New York: Routledge, 2013).
18. The writers described here include both African immigrants and the descendants of African immigrants. For example, Teju Cole was born in Kalamazoo, Michigan, to Nigerian parents but moved to Lagos shortly after his birth. He returned to the United States to attend college, graduating from Kalamazoo College and studying at the University of Michigan and Columbia University. Though American by birth, Cole identifies strongly with Nigeria.

19. See Koser's "New African Diasporas: An Introduction," in *New African Diasporas*, ed. Khalid Koser (New York: Routledge, 2003), 1–16.

20. See Gates's *The Signifying Monkey: A Theory of African-American Literary Criticism* (New York: Oxford University Press, 1988).

21. The most prominent novels by authors of the new African American diaspora were published very soon after the publication of *The Norton Anthology of African American Literature*. This chronology might suggest that there simply hasn't been enough time to demonstrate the value of these works. However, both Cole and Adichie were well-established writers prior to the acclaim received for *Open City* (New York: Random House, 2011) and *Americanah* (New York: Knopf, 2013). Cole's *Every Day Is for the Thief* (New York: Random House, 2015) was first published in 2007, and Adichie authored two previous novels in addition to the short story collection *The Thing around Your Neck* (New York: Anchor, 2010), which includes stories set in the United States. Mengestu's much celebrated *The Beautiful Things That Heaven Bears* (New York: Riverhead Books, 2007) as well as many novels by Chris Abani, including *GraceLand* (New York: Picador, 2004) and *The Virgin of Flames* (New York: Penguin, 2007), might easily have been included in the 2014 edition of *The Norton Anthology of African American Literature*.

22. In the introduction to *Dreams from My Father: A Story of Race and Inheritance* (New York: Three Rivers Press, 1995), Obama writes, "What has found its way onto these pages is a record of a personal, interior journey—a boy's search for his father, and through that search a workable meaning for his life as a black American" (xvi).

23. Similarly, Saidiya Hartman writes in *Lose Your Mother: A Journey along the Atlantic Slave Route* (New York: Macmillan, 2008), "The language of race developed in the modern period and in the context of the slave trade" (5).

24. Later in the novel, she changes the title of the blog to *Raceteenth or Various Observations about American Blacks (Those Formerly Known as Negroes) by a Non-American Black*.

25. Adichie has admitted that she based much of Ifemelu on herself, and in interviews she affirms this perspective on how race governs social relations in the United States, while in Nigeria it is far less significant. See Adichie, interview by Anderson Tepper.

26. Another model of racialized identity consistent with the diversity affirmed by the Mecca comes from recent developments in critical mixed race studies. In the first issue of the *Journal of Critical Mixed Race Studies*, G. Reginald Daniel, Laura Kina, Wei Ming Dariotis, and Camilla Fojas identify egalitarian pluralism as a multiracial identity formation that recognizes the "equality of difference" ("Emerging Paradigms in Critical Mixed Race Studies," *Journal of Critical Mixed Race Studies* 1:1 [2014]: 10).

27. Locke called Harlem the Mecca of the New Negro in 1925, while more recently, Atlanta and Washington, DC, have been hailed as black Meccas because of their support for black economic and political advancement. A 2011 *New York Times* article by Kim Severson, titled "Stars Flock to Atlanta, Reshaping a Center of Black Culture" (25 November 2011, http://www.nytimes.com/2011/11/26/us/atlanta-emerges-as-a-center-of-black-entertainment.html?_r=0), describes the influx of affluent blacks to the area and the impact of an entertainment tax credit. The city is referred to as having "always been a black mecca." In "Black Meccas or Urban Graveyards" (*Clutch*, November 2011, http://www.clutchmagonline.com/2011/11/black-meccas-or-urban-graveyard), Kymberly Sheckleford describes both Washington, DC, and Atlanta as "newly minted" black Meccas.

28. Although not directly referenced in Coates's description of his interview with Dr. Jones, the 2013 film *12 Years a Slave*, based on the 1851 slave narrative by Solomon Northup, may have been an influence in her description of her son's death.

29. Coates makes this argument most compellingly in two recent essays published in the *Atlantic*, "The Case for Reparations" (June 2014, http://www.theatlantic.com/magazine/archive/2014/06/the-case-for-reparations/361631/) and "The Black Family in the Age of Mass Incarceration" (July–August 2015, http://www.theatlantic.com/magazine/archive/2015/10/the-black-family-in-the-age-of-mass-incarceration/403246/).

30. *Americanah* is being made into a film starring Lupita Nyong'o and David Oyelowo, while *Open City* was named a best book on more than twenty year-end lists, an astonishing accomplishment for a debut novel.

31. Ekotto and Harrow also identify "a gulf between those who can travel and those who cannot, a gulf that has become both greater than ever before and yet also more permeable" (Frieda Ekotto and Kenneth W. Harrow, eds., *Rethinking African Cultural Production* [Bloomington: Indiana University Press, 2015], 2).

CHAPTER 1—SIGNIFYIN(G) ON THE SLAVE NARRATIVE

1. Dinaw Mengestu, "Children of War," *New Statesman*, 17 June 2007.

2. Teju Cole, "The White-Savior Industrial Complex," *Atlantic*, 21 March 2012.

3. Beah has been accused of fabricating much of his experiences. His editor and agent at Farrar, Straus and Giroux strongly deny the allegations. See Gabriel Sherman, "The Fog of Memoir: The Feud over the Truthfulness of Ishmael Beah's *A Long Way Gone*," *Slate*, 6 March 2008.

4. Dave Eggers, "It Was Just Boys Walking," *Guardian*, 26 May 2007.

5. Bob Thompson, "A Heartbreaking Work of Fiction," *Washington Post*, 28 November 2006.

6. Lee Siegel, "The Niceness Racket," *New Republic*, 27 April 2006.

7. Siegel provides a close reading of the scene in which rebels harass his family and attack his father: "No less than three similes cushion the reader from the blow inflicted on the father and its effect on his young son. And they are not particularly fresh similes, either. The rhythm of the sentences is lovely; the subjunctive is absolutely correct. But the rhythm gives the ugly thing a prettifying framework, and the inappropriately formal subjunctive makes the violence even more remote."

8. Following Twitchell, I refer to Valentino as the narrator of *What Is the What* and to Deng as the real-life person.

9. Eggers, "Just Boys Walking."

CHAPTER 2—UNCANNY REMEMORIES IN TEJU COLE'S *OPEN CITY*

1. Bhabha elaborates on the uncanny aspects of the migrant experience by noting, "Repeatability, in my terms, is always the repetition in the very act of enunciation, something other, a difference that is a little bit uncanny" (131). A doubling of experience involving points of departure and arrival is at the heart of the identities established through migration.

2. Colloquium with Teju Cole, April 2015, Indiana University.

3. Colloquium with Teju Cole.

CHAPTER 3—THE IMPOSSIBILITY OF INVISIBILITY IN THE NOVELS OF DINAW MENGESTU

1. *The Beautiful Things That Heaven Bears* was published under the title *Children of the Revolution* in the United Kingdom in 2007.

CHAPTER 5—BECOMING HIS OWN FATHER

1. Dunham went by Ann and hated her first name, which reflected her father's desire for a son.
2. Although identified only by his first name, Frank in *Dreams from My Father* refers to the poet and journalist Frank Marshall Davis.

CONCLUSION—BLACKNESS NOW

1. Aislinn Pulley, "Black Struggle Is Not a Sound Bite: Why I Refused to Meet with President Obama," *Truthout*, 18 February 2016, http://www.truth-out.org/opinion/item/34889-black-struggle-is-not-a-sound-bite-why-i-refused-to-meet-with-president-obama.
2. *Intercept*, "Officer Involved," n.d., https://theintercept.co/officer-involved/.
3. *Intercept*, "Officer Involved."
4. Diane Lederman, "Founders of #BlackLivesMatter Have Long History of Working for Social Change," *MassLive*, 30 March 2015, http://www.masslive.com/news/index.ssf/2015/03/founders_of_blacklivesmatter_h.html.

WORKS CITED

Abani, Chris. *GraceLand.* New York: Picador, 2004.

———. *The Secret History of Las Vegas.* New York: Penguin, 2014.

———. *The Virgin of Flames.* New York: Penguin, 2007.

Adichie, Chimamanda Ngozi. *Americanah.* New York: Knopf, 2013.

———. Interview by Anderson Tepper. Goodreads, 2013. http://www.goodreads.com/interviews/show/857.Chimamanda_Ngozi_Adichie.

———. "Now Is the Time to Talk about What We Are Actually Talking About." *New Yorker,* 2 December 2016. http://www.newyorker.com/culture/cultural-comment/now-is-the-time-to-talk-about-what-we-are-actually-talking-about.

———. *The Thing around Your Neck.* New York: Anchor, 2010.

Ahmed, Sara. "Declarations of Whiteness: The Non-performativity of Anti-racism." *Borderlands* 3:2 (2004). http://www.borderlands.net.au/vol3no2_2004/ahmed_declarations.htm.

Amsden, David. "Truly Heartbreaking." *New York Magazine,* 30 October 2006. http://nymag.com/arts/books/reviews/23147/.

Angelo, Bonnie. "The Pain of Being Black." *Time,* 22 May 1989, 120–122.

———. "The Pain of Being Black: An Interview with Toni Morrison." In *Conversations with Toni Morrison,* edited by Danille Taylor-Guthrie, 255. Jackson: University Press of Mississippi, 1994.

Appiah, Kwame Anthony. *In My Father's House: Africa in the Philosophy of Culture.* New York: Oxford University Press, 1993.

Beah, Ishmael. *A Long Way Gone: Memoirs of a Boy Soldier.* New York: Farrar, Straus and Giroux, 2007.

Bernstein, Robin. *Racial Innocence: Performing American Childhood from Slavery to Civil Rights.* New York: New York University Press, 2011.

Bhabha, Homi K. *The Location of Culture.* New York: Routledge, 1994.

Brown, Cecil. *Dude, Where's My Black Studies Department? The Disappearance of Black Americans from Our Universities.* Berkeley, Calif.: North Atlantic Books, 2007.

Bulawayo, NoViolet. *We Need New Names.* New York: Reagan Arthur Books, 2013.

Bwesigye, Brian. "Is Afropolitanism Africa's New Single Story?" *Aster(ix) Journal,* 22 November 2013. http://asterixjournal.com/afropolitanism-africas-new-single-story-reading-helon-habilas-review-need-new-names-brian-bwesigye/.

Capps, Randy, and Michael Fix, eds. *Young Children of Black Immigrants: Changing Flows, Changing Faces.* Washington, D.C.: Migration Policy Institute, 2012.

Caruth, Cathy. "Introduction." In *Trauma: Explorations in Memory,* edited by Cathy Caruth, 3–12. Baltimore: Johns Hopkins University Press, 1995.

Chude-Sokei, Louis. "The Newly Black Americans." *Transition* 113 (2014): 52–71.

Clark, Msia Kibona. "Questions of Identity among African Immigrants in America." In Okpewho and Nzegwu, *New African Diaspora,* 255–270.

Coates, Ta-Nehisi. *Between the World and Me.* New York: Spiegel & Grau, 2015.

———. "The Black Family in the Age of Mass Incarceration." *Atlantic*, July–August 2015. http://www.theatlantic.com/magazine/archive/2015/10/the-black-family-in-the-age-of-mass-incarceration/403246/.

———. "The Case for Reparations." *Atlantic*, June 2014. http://www.theatlantic.com/magazine/archive/2014/06/the-case-for-reparations/361631/.

———. "My President Was Black." *Atlantic*, January–February 2017. https://www.theatlantic.com/magazine/archive/2017/01/my-president-was-black/508793/.

Cole, Teju. "Death in the Browser Tab." *New York Times Magazine*, May 21, 2015. https://www.nytimes.com/2015/05/24/magazine/death-in-the-browser-tab.html.

———. *Every Day Is for the Thief*. New York: Random House, 2015.

———. *Known and Strange Things: Essays*. New York: Random House, 2016.

———. *Open City*. New York: Random House, 2011.

———. "The White-Savior Industrial Complex." *Atlantic*, 21 March 2012. http://www.theatlantic.com/international/archive/2012/03/the-white-savior-industrial-complex/254843/.

Dabiri, Emma. "Why I'm Not an Afropolitan." *Africa Is a Country*, 21 January 2014. http://africasacountry.com/2014/01/why-im-not-an-afropolitan/.

Daniel, G. Reginald, Laura Kina, Wei Ming Dariotis, and Camilla Fojas. "Emerging Paradigms in Critical Mixed Race Studies." *Journal of Critical Mixed Race Studies* 1:1 (2014): 6–65.

Danticat, Edwidge. "Message to My Daughters." In Ward, *Fire This Time*, 205–215.

de Certeau, Michel. *The Practice of Everyday Life*. 1984. Translated by Steven Rendall. Berkeley: University of California Press, 2011.

Dimock, Wai Chee, and Lawrence Buell, eds. *Shades of the Planet: American Literature as World Literature*. Princeton: Princeton University Press, 2007.

Dostoevsky, Fyodor. *The Brothers Karamazov*. 1880. Translated by Richard Pevear and Larissa Volokhonsky. New York: Farrar, Straus and Giroux, 1990.

Douglass, Frederick. *Narrative of the Life of Frederick Douglass, an American Slave, Written by Himself*. Rev. ed. Edited by William L. Andrews and William S. McFeely. New York: Norton, 1996.

Du Bois, W. E. B. *The Souls of Black Folk*. 1903. New York: Dover, 1994.

Dyson, Michael Eric. "President Obama's Racial Renaissance." *New York Times*, 1 August 2015. http://www.nytimes.com/2015/08/02/opinion/sunday/president-obamas-racial-renaissance.html?_r=0.

Ede, Amatoritsero. "The Politics of Afropolitanism." *Journal of African Cultural Studies* 28:1 (2016): 88–100.

Eggers, Dave. *A Heartbreaking Work of Staggering Genius*. New York: Simon & Schuster, 2000.

———. "Ishmael Beah." *Vanity Fair*, July 2007.

———. "It Was Just Boys Walking." *Guardian*, 26 May 2007. http://www.valentinoachakdeng.org/essay.php.

———. *What Is the What: The Autobiography of Valentino Achak Deng. A Novel*. New York: Vintage, 2006.

Ekotto, Frieda, and Kenneth W. Harrow, eds. *Rethinking African Cultural Production*. Bloomington: Indiana University Press, 2015.

Ellison, Ralph. *Invisible Man*. New York: Vintage, 1952.

———. *Shadow and Act*. New York: Vintage, 1995.

Eze, Chielozona. "Rethinking African Culture and Identity: The Afropolitan Model." *Journal of African Cultural Studies* 26:2 (2014): 234–247.

———. "We, Afropolitans." *Journal of African Cultural Studies* 28:1 (2016): 114–119.

Falola, Toyin, and Kwame Essien, eds. *Pan-Africanism and the Politics of African Citizenship and Identity*. New York: Routledge, 2013.

Farred, Grant. "America's Africa: Barack Obama and the Aporia of Race." *Safundi* 8:1 (January 2007): 103–108.

Freud, Sigmund, David McLintock, and Hugh Haughton. *The Uncanny*. New York: Penguin, 2003.

Gates, Henry Louis, Jr. *The Signifying Monkey: A Theory of African-American Literary Criticism*. New York: Oxford University Press, 1988.

Gates, Henry Louis, Jr., and Nelly McKay. "Introduction: Talking Books." In *The Norton Anthology of African American Literature*, 2nd ed., edited by Henry Louis Gates Jr. and Nelly McKay, xxxvii–xlvii. New York: Norton, 2003.

Gates, Henry Louis, Jr., and Valerie Smith. "Introduction: Talking Books." In *The Norton Anthology of African American Literature*, 3rd ed., edited by Henry Louis Gates Jr. and Valerie Smith, xxxv–xllvii. New York: Norton, 2014.

Gilroy, Paul. *The Black Atlantic: Modernity and Double Consciousness*. Cambridge, Mass.: Harvard University Press, 1994.

Goyal, Yogita. "African Atrocity, American Humanity: Slavery and Its Transnational Afterlives." *Research in African Literatures* 45:3 (Fall 2014): 48–71.

Greer, Christina M. *Black Ethnics: Race Immigration, and the Pursuit of the American Dream*. New York: Oxford University Press, 2013.

Gyasi, Yaa. *Homegoing: A Novel*. New York: Knopf, 2016.

———. "I'm Ghanian-American. Am I Black?" *New York Times*, 18 June 2016. http://www.nytimes.com/2016/06/19/opinion/sunday/im-ghanaian-american-am-i-black.html?_r=0.

Habila, Helon. *Oil on Water*. New York: Norton, 2010.

———. "*We Need New Names* by NoViolet Bulawayo: Review." *Guardian*, 20 June 2013. http://www.theguardian.com/books/2013/jun/20/need-new-names-bulawayo-review.

Harris, Cheryl I. "Whiteness as Property." *Harvard Law Review* 106:8 (1993): 1709–1791.

Harris, Hamil R. "Obama Worships in D.C. before MLK Day, but Has Never Chosen One Church." *Washington Post*, 15 January 2012. https://www.washingtonpost.com/local/obama-worships-in-dc-before-mlk-day-but-first-family-has-never-chosen-one-church/2012/01/15/gIQA2KWq1P_story.html.

Hartman, Saidiya V. *Lose Your Mother: A Journey along the Atlantic Slave Route*. New York: Macmillan, 2008.

———. *Scenes of Subjection: Terror, Slavery, and Self-Making in Nineteenth-Century America*. New York: Oxford University Press, 1997.

Hill, John Henry. "Five Years and One Month Secreted." In *Slave Narratives of the Underground Railroad*, edited by Christine Rudisel and Bob Blaisdell, 106–115. Mineola, N.Y.: Dover, 2014.

Houston, Pam. "Pam Houston Talks with Toni Morrison." In *Toni Morrison: Conversations*, edited by Carolyn C. Denard, 228–259. Jackson: University Press of Mississippi, 2008.

Huddart, David. *Homi K. Bhabha*. New York: Routledge, 2006.

Humphries, Jill M. "Resisting 'Race': Organizing African Transnational Identities in the United States." In Okpewho and Nzegwu, *New African Diaspora*, 271–302.

Ifill, Gwen. *The Breakthrough: Politics and Race in the Age of Obama*. New York: Doubleday, 2009.

Intercept. "Officer Involved." N.d. https://theintercept.co/officer-involved/.

Iweala, Uzodinma. *Beasts of No Nation: A Novel*. New York: HarperCollins, 2005.

Jacobs, Harriet A. *Incidents in the Life of a Slave Girl*. Cambridge, Mass.: Harvard University Press, 1987.

Jal, Emmanuel. *War Child: A Child Soldier's Story*. New York: St. Martin's, 2010.

Julien, Eileen. "The Critical Present: Where Is 'African Literature?'" In *Rethinking African Cultural Production*, edited by Frieda Ekotto and Kenneth W. Harrow, 17–28. Bloomington: Indiana University Press, 2015.

Kondadu-Agyemang, Kwado, Baffour K. Tayki, and John A. Arthur, eds. *The African Diaspora in North America: Trends, Community Building and Adaptation*. Lanham, Md.: Lexington Books, 2006.

Koser, Khalid. "New African Diasporas: An Introduction." In *New African Diasporas*, edited by Khalid Koser, 1–16. New York: Routledge, 2003.

Kristeva, Julia. *Strangers to Ourselves*. Translated by L. S. Roudiez. London: Harvester Wheatsheaf, 1994.

Lederman, Diane. "Founders of #BlackLivesMatter Have Long History of Working for Social Change." *MassLive*, 30 March 2015. http://www.masslive.com/news/index.ssf/2015/03/founders_of_blacklivesmatter_h.html.

Lee, Felicia R. "New Wave of African Writers with an Internationalist Bent." *New York Times*, 29 June 2014. http://www.nytimes.com/2014/06/30/arts/new-wave-of-african-writers-with-an-internationalist-bent.html?smid=pl-share&_r=2.

Lipsitz, George. "The Possessive Investment in Whiteness: Racialized Social Democracy and the 'White' Problem in American Studies." *American Quarterly* 47:5 (September 1995): 369–387.

Locke, Alain, ed. *The New Negro: Visions of the Harlem Renaissance*. 1925. New York: Touchstone, 1997.

Mbembe, Achille. "The Subject of the World." In *Facing Up to the Past: Perspectives on the Commemoration of Slavery from Africa, the Americas, and Europe*, edited by Gert Oostindie, 21–28. Kingston: Ian Randle, 2001.

McQueen, Steve, dir. *12 Years a Slave*. Regency Enterprises, 2013.

McWhorter, John. "Why I'm Black, Not African American." *Los Angeles Times*, 8 September 2004. http://articles.latimes.com/2004/sep/08/news/oe-mcwhorter8.

Mengestu, Dinaw. *All Our Names*. New York: Knopf, 2014.

———. *The Beautiful Things That Heaven Bears*. New York: Riverhead Books, 2007.

———. "Children of War." *New Statesman*, 14 June 2007. http://www.newstatesman.com/books/2007/06/africa-war-burma-beah-sudan.

———. *How to Read the Air*. New York: Riverhead Books, 2010.

Morgenstern, Naomi. "Mother's Milk and Sister's Blood: Trauma and the Neoslave Narrative." *Differences* 8:2 (Summer 1996): 101–126.

Morrison, Toni. *Beloved*. New York: Plume, 1987.

———. "Making America White Again." *New Yorker*, 21 November 2016. http://www.newyorker.com/magazine/2016/11/21/making-america-white-again.

———. "On the Back of Blacks." 1993. In *What Moves at the Margin: Selected Nonfiction*, edited by Carolyn C. Denard, 145–148. Jackson: University Press of Mississippi, 2008.

———. *Playing in the Dark: Whiteness and the Literary Imagination*. New York: Vintage, 1992.

———. "Rootedness: The Ancestor as Foundation." In *What Moves at the Margin: Selected Nonfiction*, edited by Carolyn C. Denard, 56–64. Jackson: University Press of Mississippi, 2008.

Musila, Grace A. "Part-Time Africans, Europolitans and 'Africa Lite.'" *Journal of African Cultural Studies* 28:1 (2016): 109–113.

Ngugi, Mukoma Wa. "The Black Man's Nod." *Callaloo* 36:1 (Winter 2013): 86–88.
Northup, Solomon. *12 Years a Slave: Illustrated: Narrative of Solomon Northup, a Citizen of New-York, Kidnapped in Washington City in 1841, and Rescued in 1853 from a Cotton Plantation in Avoyelles Parish, in the Mississippi Valley of Louisiana.* Updated ed. Marksville, La.: Avoyelles, 2013.
Obama, Barack. *Dreams from My Father: A Story of Race and Inheritance.* New York: Three Rivers Press, 1995.
———. "A More Perfect Union." In *The Speech: Race and Barack Obama's "A More Perfect Union,"* edited by T. Denean Sharpley-Whiting, 237–251. New York: Bloomsbury, 2009.
———. "Remarks by the President in Eulogy for the Honorable Reverend Clementa Pinckney." 26 June 2015. https://www.whitehouse.gov/the-press-office/2015/06/26/remarks-president-eulogy-honorable-reverend-clementa-pinckney.
Oguine, Ike. *A Squatter's Tale.* Portsmouth, N.H.: Heinemann, 2000.
Okparanta, Chinelo. *Under the Udala Trees.* New York: First Mariner Books, 2015.
Okpewho, Isidore. "Introduction: Can We Go Home Again?" In Okpewho and Nzegwu, *New African Diaspora,* 3–30.
Okpewho, Isidore, and Nkiru Nzegwu, eds. *The New African Diaspora.* Bloomington: Indiana University Press, 2009.
Peek, Michelle. "Humanitarian Narrative and Posthumanist Critique: Dave Eggers's *What Is the What.*" *Biography* 35:1 (Winter 2012): 115–136.
Pierre, Jemima. *The Predicament of Blackness: Postcolonial Ghana and the Politics of Race.* Chicago: University of Chicago Press, 2013.
Powers, Samantha. "Bystanders to Genocide." *Atlantic,* September 2001. http://www.theatlantic.com/magazine/archive/2001/09/bystanders-to-genocide/304571/.
Prose, Francine. "The Lost Boy." *New York Times Book Review,* 24 December 2006. http://www.nytimes.com/2006/12/24/books/review/Prose.t.html?_r=0.
Pulley, Aislinn. "Black Struggle Is Not a Sound Bite: Why I Refused to Meet with President Obama." *Truthout,* 18 February 2016. http://www.truth-out.org/opinion/item/34889-black-struggle-is-not-a-sound-bite-why-i-refused-to-meet-with-president-obama.
Rankine, Claudia. "The Condition of Black Life Is One of Mourning." In Ward, *Fire This Time,* 145–156.
Rimer, Sara, and Karen W. Arenson. "Top Colleges Take More Blacks, but Which Ones?" *New York Times,* 24 June 2004. https://www.nytimes.com/2004/06/24/us/top-colleges-take-more-blacks-but-which-ones.html.
Rooks, Noliwe M. *White Money/Black Power: The Surprising History of African American Studies and the Crisis of Race in Higher Education.* Boston: Beacon, 2006.
Rose, Jacqueline. *The Case of Peter Pan, or The Impossibility of Children's Fiction.* Philadelphia: University of Pennsylvania Press, 1984.
Rudisel, Christine, and Bob Blaisdell, eds. *Slave Narratives of the Underground Railroad.* Mineola, N.Y.: Dover, 2014.
Santana, Stephanie Bosch. "Exorcising Afropolitanism: Binyavanga Wainaina Explains Why 'I Am a Pan-Africanist, Not an Afropolitan' at ASAUK 2012." *Africa in Words,* 8 February 2013.
Schultheis, Alexandra. "African Child Soldiers and Humanitarian Consumption." *Peace Review* 20:1 (2008): 31–40.
Selasi, Taiye. "African Literature Doesn't Exist." *Savannah Review,* no. 2 (November 2013): 53–66.
———. "Bye-Bye Babar." *The LIP,* 3 March 2005. http://thelip.robertsharp.co.uk/?p=76.

———. "'From That Stranded Place' (2015). Interview with Aaron Bady." *Transition* 117 (2015): 148–165.

Severson, Kim. "Stars Flock to Atlanta, Reshaping a Center of Black Culture." *New York Times*, 25 November 2011. http://www.nytimes.com/2011/11/26/us/atlanta-emerges-as-a-center-of-black-entertainment.html?_r=0.

Shaw-Taylor, Yoku, and Steven A. Tuch, eds. *The Other African Americans: Contemporary African and Caribbean Families in the United States*. Lanham, Md.: Rowman & Littlefield, 2007.

Sheckleford, Kymberly. "Black Meccas or Urban Graveyards." *Clutch*, November 2011. http://www.clutchmagonline.com/2011/11/black-meccas-or-urban-graveyard.

Shepperson, George. "Pan-Africanism and 'Pan-Africanism': Some Historical Notes." *Phylon* 23:4 (1962): 346–358.

Sherman, Gabriel. "The Fog of Memoir: The Feud over the Truthfulness of Ishmael Beah's *A Long Way Gone*." *Slate*, 6 March 2008.

Siegel, Lee. "The Niceness Racket." *New Republic*, 23 April 2007. https://newrepublic.com/article/62544/the-niceness-racket.

Smith, Sidonie. "Narrated Lives and the Contemporary Regime of Human Rights: Mobilizing Stories, Campaigns, Ethnicities." In *Transcultural Localisms: Responding to Ethnicity in a Globalized World*, edited by Yiorgos Kalogeras, Eleftheria Arapoglou, and Linda Manney, 143–164. Heidelberg: C. Winter, 2007.

Swards, Rachel L. "'African-American' Becomes a Term for Debate." *New York Times*, 29 August 2004. https://www.nytimes.com/2004/08/29/us/african-american-becomes-a-term-for-debate.html.

Thompson, Bob. "A Heartbreaking Work of Fiction: In a New Novel, Dave Eggers Tells Sudanese Victim's True Story." *Washington Post*, 28 November 2006. http://www.washingtonpost.com/wpdyn/content/article/2006/11/27/AR2006112701573_pf.html.

Twitchell, Elizabeth. "Dave Eggers's *What Is the What*: Fictionalizing Trauma in the Era of Misery Lit." *American Literature* 83:3 (2011): 621–648.

Wagner, Bryan. *Disturbing the Peace: Black Culture and the Police Power after Slavery*. Cambridge, Mass.: Harvard University Press, 2009.

Wainaina, Binyavanga. "How to Write about Africa." *Granta* 92 (2005). https://granta.com/how-to-write-about-africa/.

Ward, Jesmyn, ed. *The Fire This Time: A New Generation Speaks about Race*. New York: Scribner, 2016.

Wright, Michelle M. *Becoming Black: Creating Identity in the African Diaspora*. Durham, N.C.: Duke University Press, 2004.

———. "Can I Call You Black? The Limits of Authentic Heteronormativity in African Diasporic Discourse." *African and Black Diaspora* 6:1 (2013): 3–16.

Zeleza, Paul Tiyambe. "Diaspora Dialogues: Engagements between Africa and Its Diasporas." In Okpewho and Nzegwu, *New African Diaspora*, 31–60.

INDEX

ABOUT THE AUTHOR

STEPHANIE LI holds the Susan D. Gubar Chair in Literature at Indiana University, Bloomington. She is the author of four previous books, including *Something Akin to Freedom: The Choice of Bondage in Narratives by African American Women*, *Signifying without Specifying: Racial Discourse in the Age of Obama*, and *Playing in the White: Black Writers, White Subjects.*